Strange Wives

The Paradox of Biblical Intermarriage

By
Stanley Ned Rosenbaum, PhD
With
Rabbi Allen Secher

Edited by Mary Heléne Pottker
Rosenbaum

Cover Design and Book Layout by Custom-book-tique.com

Cover image: "Ruth," bas relief sculpture (c) 2006 by Rivkah
Walton; all rights reserved. Used by permission of the artist,
www.studio-rw.com. Rivkah M. Walton, MFA

rosenbaumresources.com

This book is an 85,000-word love letter to my Catholic wife who,
paradoxically, made it possible.

Stanley Ned Rosenbaum

CONTENTS

Foreword

Who else but Ned Rosenbaum could come up with such sterling (tongue in cheek) chapter titles as, "Guess Who's Coming to Purim," "Who Was Mrs. Moses," "Samson and What's Her Name," "Beware of Greeks Bearing Whatever"? Who else but Ned Rosenbaum would worry about "Was God Ever Intermarried"? Who else but Ned Rosenbaum would name this exploration of Biblical intermarriage *Strange Wives?*

Calling him a character shortchanges him. Bright, considerate, brilliant, intense, clever, funny, curious, with a burningly wry sense of humor. His passions were profound: for his wife Mary, his children, his students, and most of all The Cubs, for whom he was the world's chief sufferer. Bowling followed close behind. And there was his overarching passion for Judaism, both in his personal practice and in his professional life, as possibly the only Jewish recipient of a PhD in Near Eastern and Judaic Studies from Brandeis to have been married to a non-Jew.

His marriage to a Catholic woman was never referred to as intermarriage, but rather a mixed marriage. I quote from their book, *Celebrating Our Differences:* "I don't understand this woman. Her grandparents were champion bowlers; her uncle played AAA ball before the Second World War; and a cousin had a basketball scholarship. She can't differentiate between Bo Jackson and Mahalia Jackson. No doubt about it sports fans, ours is a mixed marriage."

Mary once wrote a letter in which she described Ned as "a man strong enough to weep." To which he responded, "Naturally when I read it, I cried. I also cry at weddings, funerals, when the American flag goes by, and during commercials featuring babies. There's no shame in letting it all hang out." That sensitivity was his essence.

11

But, to those we must add his wit. To be with Ned was to feel charmed, embraced, welcomed, and challenged to stretch your intellectual curiosity.

Add brilliance and scholarship to his passions, which you will witness on the pages that follow. And witness his two other scholarly works: *Amos of Israel; A New Interpretation* and *Understanding Biblical Israel: A Reexamination of the Origins of Monotheism.* As much as Ned loved teaching, his students shared the love and, in turn, adored him. Well beyond retirement, Ned continued to spread bon mots; at the memorial service held at Dickinson College, where he taught Judaic Studies for most of his career, a former student said, "Not a week goes by that I don't think of something he taught me"—after forty years!

I first met Ned and Mary in the early nineties, when we gathered with Joan Hawxhurst to form the Dovetail Institute, an international support group for interfaith couples. For twenty years, Dovetail provided the third leg to an often wobbly mixed-marriage stool, due in no small part to the wondrous efforts of the Rosenbaums. Many a couple was able to weather the storm under the Rosenbaums' umbrella.

A few years ago, while sharing another agonizing Cubs loss, I made a suggestion to Ned that, since we had been providing counsel to couples and parents for years, we show them that intermarriage was not a new phenomenon. Our Biblical ancestors wrestled or rejoiced with the situation. Very often it was not a problem at all, but rather a celebrated fact. Ned agreed that a book was the natural outgrowth of our efforts, and thus began our scholarship. We rarely had the chance to sit together, Ned being in Kentucky and me in Montana. Viva the Internet. We researched, wrote, and edited each other's work, with Ned providing the yeoman's effort. Eventually Mary added her superb editing skills.

Why all this praise in a preface? Ned died a short time ago in a tragic auto accident. It was left to Mary and me to complete *Strange Wives*. I introduced him to you in this preface so that you can recognize his voice on every page. Picture a Jewish Mr. Chips at the lectern, creating a brilliant world of understanding and sunshine.

I grieve for you, my brother. You were most dear to me.
Your love was wonderful to me.
How the mighty have fallen
II Samuel 1:26

Allen Secher

Introduction

Our title is taken from Ezra 10:11: "Separate yourselves from the peoples of the land and from your strange (Heb. רבמוז) wives."

Since the 1960s, the issue of Jewish intermarriage has been reliably estimated as growing from less than ten percent to over fifty percent, and the number seems to be growing. Recently, however, the subject has become the focus of much scholarly attention. Jewish opposition to intermarriage is well known. Yet more than a million couples in the United States alone stand under the intermarried chupah.

To those couples we pose the following question:

Abraham, Moses, Ruth, David, Samson, Joseph, Esther, Solomon.

What do they all have in common?
They were intermarried.

Jewish tradition always assumed that in biblical times intermarriage was rare and aberrant until after the fall of the Temple in 586 b.c.e., that women marrying "Israelite " men automatically converted (Ruth), and that Israelite men generally did not marry non-Israelite women. Those few who did (Esau) ceased to be Israelite. How Jewish tradition decides who is Jewish and who isn't is a complicated and, at times, self-serving business.

Using the tools provided by modern scholarship to examine Hebrew Scripture, we find that Israel was partly founded by significant intermarriage of the various tribes and groups that formed it in the pre-monarchic period. It may come as a surprise to those who accept the tradition that "all Israel" are descendants of one man's family, but early Israelites were a very heterogeneous

15

group. Their early willingness to reach across tribal and ethnic boundaries was a source of strength, which Jews later forgot or chose not to remember.

However, we are reminded of the Book of Esther which, though fictional, proposed that the entire Jewish community in Persia in the fifth and fourth centuries b.c.e. was saved by the action of its intermarried heroine. Nonetheless, we intend to lay out only what the Bible itself has to say that bears on the subject of intermarriage before Ezra and Esther. A dispassionate look at Hebrew Scripture indicates that biblical Israel itself was formed by the aggregation of various peoples, peoples who intermarried. This situation is already apparent when we examine the stories of the Patriarchs and Matriarchs. Even if not historically true, these stories still reflect what must have been real situations in the times of the writers, if these can be determined.

So an early account in Numbers 25 reports that Israel "acquired" 32,000 Moabite (or Midianite) virgins who, presumably, worked their way into the Israelite genetic fabric, as did unnumbered women later captured in war. Jewish tradition seems to assume that all such women, á la the righteous Ruth, "converted." But religious conversion was not a recognized category of human behavior until Talmudic times, some 800 or more years after the period in which Ruth is set. In any case, there was no fixed religion that could have been labeled "Judaism" in Ruth's period (Judges) for her to convert to.

Hebrew Scripture contains much evidence that shows most women in Israel, and not only women, were far from monotheistic for centuries after their settlement on the land. Moreover, as we hope to show here, women had maintained their own religion, a religion of and for women, but one that their husbands were generally in sympathy with until the destruction of the Jerusalem Temple in 586 b.c.e.

The paradox of Jewish history that this book uncovers is that "the people who dwell apart" began their history as anything but.

Despite the professions of the authors, one a rabbi and the other a Ph. D. in Judaic Studies, we do not assume that any of the characters mentioned in the Bible before the time of David are historical. That, however, is of little consequence. We are not claiming that all of the Bible's stories are fiction. But, historical or not, the stories about these characters reflect the customs and mores of the writers' societies.

Our earliest biblical forbearers presumably lived somewhere near the end of the Bronze Age. It was a time when the ancient near eastern societies were rife with polytheism and, as all societies tend to be, both ethnocentric and endogamous. They usually sought marriage partners from among their own people as Abraham did for Isaac and Jacob did for himself.

What we pose in the following pages is this: while prohibitions against some intermarriage may be found in Torah, evidence elsewhere in Scripture suggests that these prohibitions were put in later, as much as five hundred years after Moses's time, by people who had by then developed their own reasons for wanting it so.

Chapter I. Biblical Intermarriage: Understanding the Problems

1. Biblical Intermarriage: Since When?

The guiding myth1 of Israel's descent from the sons of Jacob, Israel himself, and their residence in the land named after him has obscured the reality that lies behind it. Sylvia Fishman, in her recent study on modern intermarriage, *Double or Nothing: Jewish Families and Mixed Marriage,*[2] typifies this by unquestioningly accepting Shaye Cohen's observation that "Biblical Israel was living on its own land and had no need for a general prohibition of intermarriage with all outsiders."[3]

This is a dramatic oversimplification that we will address in Chapter IX. For now, note that not only was Israel's "own land" also the home of many other peoples, but Israel itself began life as a loose-knit coalition of many different groups.

Jewish tradition has taken steps to minimize or even conceal the extent of intermarriage, partly because it no longer remembers how heterogeneous early Israelites were. But it is also the case that the history of Jewish-Christian relations in Europe for most of the past thousand years has been one of such animosity and separation that this situation has been back-read into Israel's history even unto the earliest periods.

From the height of the Inquisition, more and more European Jews were compelled to live in ghettos, greatly restricting their contact with non-Jews and, of course, any opportunity to intermarry. If the separation was often physically enforced by Christians, it was certainly useful to Jews who wished nothing more from their Christian neighbors than to be left alone.

19

The ghetto experience—and even more, the ghetto mentality—outlived the physical ghettos and, more than anything else, colored the Jewish view of previous Jewish history. The re-introduction of ghettos by the Nazis was a "booster shot" the community didn't need.

In the eighteenth century, the more Enlightened European governments saw that integrating Jews into their respective societies would be of vastly more benefit to them, the gentiles, than isolating their Jews, despite the "risks" this might pose. The French took the lead in this; at Paris in 1806, a "Sanhedrin"—really a group of carefully selected Jewish community representatives—was asked a series of questions designed to show that French Jews could and should be integrated into French society. The third of these questions was, "Can a Jewess marry a Christian, and a Jew a Christian woman? Or does the law allow the Jews to intermarry only among themselves?"[4]

It was a set-up. But if the French authorities knew what the responses would be in advance, there is little doubt the average Frenchman did not. Most Westerners today, Christian or Jewish, would also be surprised, so widespread is the notion that all intermarriage is and always has been against Jewish law.[5]

But wishing to join French society as much as Napoleon's government wished them to, the Jewish leaders carefully distinguished between religious intermarriage, which they could not condone, and civil marriage, which they could accept.[6]

However, to begin a study of intermarriage here is to arrive at a symphony performance that is already in its final movement. The history of intermarriage among those people we now call Jews and their biblical ancestors might be conveniently though roughly divided as follows:

1. Pre-Israelite 1500 - 1000 b.c.e.[7]
2. Israelite/Biblical 1000 - 200 b.c.e.
3. Rabbinic 200 b.c.e - 400 c.e.
4. Post-Talmudic 400 -1215 c.e.
5. Christian Triumphalist 1215 - 1800 c.e.
6. Modern 1800 c.e. -

That is to say, the modern period begins about 1800; specifying 1806 would not be amiss, but in any case it is roughly contemporary with the French Revolution. This book deals primarily with the first three periods, though we will have occasional observations about more modern developments.

Traditional histories of the Jews or Judaism usually beg an important question. They assume that "Israelites" or at least "Jews" are an identifiable, homogeneous and separate people from Abraham's time to the time when gentile governments first started making laws restricting Jewish intercourse with majority' populations.[8]

Consequently, these histories do not see intermarriage as any sort of problem until the time of Ezra, sometime in the fourth pre-Christian century. Even as comprehensive a study as H. H. Ben Sasson's *A History of the Jewish People* [9] does not identify the problem of intermarriage earlier than Ezra's time (fifth century b.c.e.). They are right, but for the wrong reason. There was intermarriage, more in fact than tradition remembers, it just wasn't seen as much of a problem. And besides, the more history piled up, the more Jews had other, more important things to write about.

Even before the institution of ghettos in the fifteenth century, Jewish histories were usually little more than "lachrymose" (the term is Yosef Hayim Yerushalmi's) chronicles of all the evils that gentiles had visited upon Jews. Modern Jewish histories are, no doubt, darkened further by the confinement of eastern Jews to a

Pale of Settlement in Imperial Russia, the place from which so many American Jews' ancestors came, and most of all by the extermination of a third of Europe's Jewish population between 1933 and 1945 at the hands of Nazis and their too-willing collaborators. If Jewish histories have been lachrymose, there's been a lot to cry about.

Historically, Jews have often been accused of misanthropy, but perhaps "healthy paranoia" might be nearer the mark. A history that includes centuries of exile from one's homeland and millennia of persecution must necessarily induce into any sensitive person the idea that someone is out to get you. Conversely, our post-World War II romantic image of biblical Israel, made popular by movies based on the Bible and reinforced by generations of under-informed Sunday school teachers, merely compounds the problem.

The contemporary situation of an embattled Israel, struggling these past fifty-five years for survival amongst more than twenty hostile Muslim states—even building fences at certain points to discourage the entrance of Palestinians from infiltrating—reinforces the notion that not only has Israel always been "a people who dwell apart," but also that, from biblical Israelites to modern Israelis, most will say they much prefer it this way.

Retrojecting modern or contemporary conditions into one's past history is no new thing, but such back-readings must never be uncritically accepted. A closer view suggests that the Bible knows better.

Before Ezra's time, the Bible's regulations of marriage concerned such issues as one man marrying two sisters or marrying both a woman and her daughter. These were ultimately prohibited, as was the marriage of two people who shared the same father but had different mothers. Here, however, we have the possibility that the two mothers might have had differing religions: think of Solomon and his seven hundred wives, or David and his ten.

As we observed above, what moderns think of as intermarriage was not initially seen as much of a problem. Only Samson's parents and Esau's mother, Rebekah, make any fuss about it in principle, and we don't know whether their stories are contemporary with the events they describe or were written much later, when Israel's agenda had changed. (See Deut. 7:3 and 23:9.)

If by intermarriage[10] we mean the marriage of two people with differing religious beliefs and practices, that goes back well into Patriarchal times: that is, the time of Abram, Sarai, their children and grandchildren. At this point in time, somewhere around 1500 b.c.e. all societies were so rife with polytheism that they had not constructed the rigid boundaries separating peoples and their faiths that we know today; that is what Ezra tried to do.... a thousand and more years later.

We will at some point need to distinguish intermarriage in which one partner converts from what we presently call interfaith marriage, but such distinctions were pretty much unknown through most of biblical times. Why?

For one thing, without some notion of a matrilineal principle—that is, the idea that a child's religion should follow that of its mother (which came much later in Jewish history) a wife's religion, any religion followed by women, did not matter enough to need to be, as it was finally, suppressed. Consequently, the Bible is surprisingly full of accounts of intercourse with outsiders, sometimes with people that its later collectors/writers no longer realized were foreigners: for example, the Benjaminites.

Intercourse, sexual and otherwise, includes all relations of Jewish men with the rest of the world. As to sexual relations, the account of Aaron's grandson Pinchas skewering an Israelite in the act of copulation with a Moabite (or was she Midianite?) woman might seem to put a damper on that sort of thing.[11] In fact, it did not.

Later stories of Samson, Joshua, David and Solomon, to name a few, all feature relations with gentile women. This may have been frowned upon, but it was in no way prohibited. Knowing this, the Talmud's treatment of the biblical prohibition of intermarriage with Ammonites and Moabites (peoples living East of the Jordan) offers the clever suggestion that the prohibition against marrying them did not apply to their womenfolk!

We are fortunate, though, that the rabbis chose thus to split hairs and not simply expunge or otherwise irrevocably change what they knew or thought to be Israel's history. Some changes were made, but in many cases we can read the underlying history as one reads pencil-marks that have been incompletely erased.

This is no surprise. For centuries the Judeo-Christian tradition has been in the hands of Jewish (and Christian) men. This gives them an Israelo-centric and male-centered viewpoint. Their histories are those of kings, the wars of kings and the theologies of male priesthoods. (If males were parthenogenic, there might be no mention of women at all.) Recent feminist writings in biblical studies offer a counter-gambit as feminists seek to extol the importance of biblical and post-biblical women as over against men within the Israelite context. Tirzah Firestone writes, "I began writing this book in a state of anger at the ways that women and the feminine path have been devalued or omitted from Jewish history."[12]

This works well enough for the post-biblical figures with whom Firestone deals, but in the case of Hebrew Scripture, the non-Jewishness of so many of the Bible's key female figures does not seem to concern feminist writers. Of Yael and Rahab, Tikvah Frymer-Kensky writes, "confronted by history and destiny, each woman abandons whatever claims the Canaanites might have to her loyalties, deceives the Canaanite men, and acts for God and Israel."[13]

24

A less starry-eyed look at the texts, however, produces compelling evidence that women had their own religious agenda and that they continued with it long after the introduction of monotheism.

Feminists, whether rabbis or scholars, seem unconsciously to accept the traditional notion that women, whether foreign or domestic, submerged themselves in the menfolks' religion but that, when they did not, it was a deviation on their part. Thus, when Phyllis Bird writes of "queens and queen-mothers who introduced foreign cults and objects,"[14] the reader does not understand that these were not innovations, but rather the normal expressions of the female religion that they had brought with them to their marriages.

More recent scholarship—for example, the works of Christine Hayes and Shaye J. D. Cohen—shows that, indeed, the idea that Israelite/Jewish law has always forbidden intermarriage is simply incorrect. As Cohen puts it, "The Talmudim are aware that the prohibition of intermarriage is a product of second-temple times."[15] This being so, the door is now open for a serious study of intermarriage in the time before Ezra.

2. Sorting the Sources: Preliminary Notes on How (Not) to Read Scripture

Something Happened - Ken Kesey

There are points of agreement between the Bible's retelling of Israel's history from, say, the time of David, and what we are able to glean from foreign sources, but whether this gives confidence in the biblical view of things is very much in dispute. The further we delve back into history, the less historical reliability Scripture has. We need to keep in mind that the Bible, let alone traditional commentaries on it—the Talmud and Midrashim—were not put in written form until centuries after the events they comment upon, so that whatever truth lay behind the stories might simply have been forgotten.

For another thing, later biblical tradents often augmented the texts they were transmitting in order to forward their own, contemporary concerns. That this or that text concerning intermarriage is found in the Torah (the first five books) in no way indicates that it was a concern of Moses. Scripture has its own agenda, and this includes deliberately denigrating Saul and his Benjaminite kin while extolling David and his son Solomon.

Despite this, some modern writers on the Bible often seem incapable of doing more than telling the Bible's own story in modern words, in some cases mistaking for history texts that are clearly not meant as history. Neither philosophy (Job) nor prophecy (Hosea) dressed in the clothes of history should be mistaken for history itself.

To elaborate: the prophet Hosea (mid-eighth century b.c.e.) is famous for his marriage to the prostitute Gomer, or so one would think from a superficial reading of his book. Traditional rabbis, exercised by this union, proposed that Gomer "went straight" after the marriage, but for this Scripture provides no real evidence. It is more likely that Hosea's story is rather a criticism of the *three* Israelite kingdoms of his day, symbolized by the three children attributed to the marriage.

Was his an intermarriage? Well, there is a Gomer mentioned in Gen. 10:2 as a descendant of Japheth and, as we'll see in Chapter X, Japheth seems to symbolize a Greek element in the earliest, pre-Israelite mix, but latter-day Gomer's ethnicity is of no concern to the writer of Scripture so we cannot tell. The commentaries, even Scripture itself, did not have the recovery of historical truth as their chief or highest goal. Nonetheless, one may read rabbinic commentaries with an eye toward seeing what sorts of unions were acceptable to them, if not also to earlier generations.

The historical existence of any of the characters the Bible mentions before the kingship of David is itself a matter of some dispute. For the purposes of this book, however, the dispute is irrelevant. In fact, it could be argued that the less historical they are, the better. That is to say, fictional accounts would more clearly mirror situations that could only have been true within certain parameters, or else the audiences for which they were intended would fail to appreciate them. (The question that we might wish to decide, if we can, is when such and such a text was written.)

Samson is clearly not an historical figure and he is famously intermarried, twice in fact. So, fiction or no, he sheds light on the Israelite view of intermarriage in the time before Israelite law sought to prohibit it. Again, if named characters themselves are not historical, it is no proof that their actions do not reflect real social situations. The trick is to determine whether these conditions obtained at the times in which the various stories are set. However, if one reads Scripture carefully one cannot help but conclude that intermarriage was hardly an exceptional situation at any time in Israel's history up to and including Ezra's.

The more one tries to penetrate the mists of Israel's history, the hazier things become. The first scriptural suggestion of intermarriage, admittedly enigmatic, is found in Gen. 6:4:

> There were giants in the earth in those days; and also after that, when the sons of God came in unto the daughters of men, and they bare children to them, the same became mighty men which were of old, men of renown. (Authorized/King James Version)

Modern Jewish translations read "divine beings" for "sons of God"; the older commentators, for example Rabbi Solomon ben Isaac (Rashi, French, eleventh century c.e.), were not willing to concede even that much. He saw them as strictly human.

In any case, except for an allusion to them in Deuteronomy (2:10f., 21), these beings promptly disappear from the history. This prompts us to ask, why are they here at all? The most straightforward answer would be that these verses express a knowledge of and a desire to explain the super-tall people they knew from certain countries in Africa and whose progeny today populate America's National Basketball Association.

Other, more esoteric, explanations aren't lacking—Rashi also reads it as a condemnation of polygamy—but from our point of view, these brief mentions are interesting for what they lack: namely, any flat-out condemnation of intermarriage. And that is the more surprising if Gen. 6:4 is inter-species. Of course, these two isolated verses say nothing of common folks' practices or of marriage to unconverted women or men. For this information we must mine Scripture very carefully indeed, and so we shall.

For example, the prostitute Rahab, who hid Joshua's spies during their reconnoitering of Jericho, is said to have converted, married him and borne children whose descendants included Jeremiah the prophet and Huldah, his prophetess contemporary; the New Testament extends her descendants to include Jesus! Would stories like these be concocted if intermarriage were always clearly and completely out of bounds?

Incorporation of gentiles well after the fact—a bit like the Mormon practice of baptizing the dead of other faiths—was one strategy for diminishing the import of intermarriage; denial was another. Thus Asenath, the obviously Egyptian wife of Joseph, was claimed as an Israelite, the daughter of Dinah, Joseph's half-sister.[16] We may read the denial of this union as an intermarriage as some proof that it did, in fact, occur. Later authorities attempted to conceal the truth because it did not fit with the Jewish-isolationist agenda they felt compelled to adopt. (In this they were no different than any nationalist group's reading of its own history.)

We should say here that Scripture does not represent some later Jewish conspiracy to hide the truth. To borrow a title from Ken Kesey, "Something happened," but in many cases what that was will simply have been forgotten long before the final editors came to their task. As Christine Hayes demonstrates,[17] blanket prohibition of intermarriage is a product of rabbinic times.

3. A Bird's-eye View of Israel's Geography

"The land was ours before we were the land's." – Robert Frost

Our understanding of the peoples of biblical Israel, however, cannot be gotten in a void. We need to know something about their geography, history and pre-history both as they knew them and as we now know them. What shaped their lives and thoughts? How does this differ from the picture of the biblical mundane quotidian that we are now able to imagine?

First, Canaan/Israel is a real crossroads. Travelers on foot, donkey or camelback have to traverse it to get from Egypt to Mesopotamia; traders bringing goods between the Mediterranean and the Indian Ocean could and did portage their wares across the narrow neck of the Sinai Peninsula. The land routes were also followed by armies, a fact that led to the dramatic rerouting of Israel's history on more than one occasion.

Trade in the area goes back millennia before the people we are interested in entered the arena of history. In this regard, we note that the word "Canaanite" is used three times in Scripture with the meaning "trader," a fact that will be of interest to us later. A lot of different people passed through or lived in the New Jersey-sized piece of real estate we call Israel. Joshua 12:9 gives a list of thirty-one kings living in Israel at once. This is a number that's half as many more than that of New Jersey's counties, so the extent of their "kingdoms" would be considerably smaller.

It remains difficult to determine how many of the peoples who coalesced to form Israel originated in the land of the same name, but some most certainly did.[18] The different human groups whose bones dot Israel's landscape from the time well before any kingdoms arose cannot be identified by "nationality," but their physical features represent many different groups. Archaeologists consequently concentrate on trying to determine whether different settlements show markedly different cultures.

According to the biblical account, the original Israelites were migrants who settled among "Canaanites" and "Amorites," but the latter is a geographical expression—it means "westerner"—while the former seems to derive from an Akkadian word meaning "blue cloth." So the term "Canaan" is akin to calling some part of a country its "breadbasket." (We might theorize that Jews were into *shmattes*—"the rag trade"—before there were Jews!) The Bible (Gen. 9:25-27) regards Canaan as father of a nation, but no one living between the Jordan River and the Mediterranean would have called him/herself Canaanite as a tribal/ethnic marker. Moreover, as we shall see, some of those living there prior to the advent of Israel allied themselves with the newly minted Israelites, making distinctions among them even harder to maintain.

Once in Canaan, Israelites did not always remain. Uncertain agricultural conditions complicated by lack of rain occasionally drove some of them to seek sustenance in Egypt, a land not dependent on rainfall for successful agriculture. This should alert us to the reality that early Israelites lived among other peoples outside of Israel as well as in. Did they mix with them, and if so, how much?

To answer these questions is one purpose of the present work.

Israel, unlike other ancient near Eastern kingdoms such as were found in Egypt and Mesopotamia, did not think of itself has having been around since the dawn of time. In Genesis' own Table of Nations (Chapter 10), Israel does not enter the scene until some ten generations after Shem the son of Noah; that's twenty generations after Adam. Only the most conservative of religious people would accept the above named as historical, but there may be and probably are historical truths buried in these stories. If we can only get to them. There are certainly insights into the nature of Israelite society, at least at the time the accounts were finally put together, and perhaps earlier.

Modern scholarship does not accept the literal truth of Genesis's first eleven chapters, but these are still useful in providing an early picture of how Israel thought of itself. As Fernand Braudel says, "There is no society, however primitive, that does not bear the 'scars of events,' nor any society in which history has sunk completely without a trace."[19]

Israel's pre-history is marked by two cataclysmic events of the sort that would certainly qualify for inclusion as "scars." They are the devastating incursion of the Aegean into the Black Sea about 7,500 years ago and the explosion of the volcanic island Thera (Santorini) ca. 1550 b.c.e. The latter happened fully within historic times and seems to have been recorded by the Egyptians of Ahmosis. We detail these events in Chapter V, but it is worth taking a moment to summarize them here.

In *Noah's Flood*, William Ryan and Walter Pittman[20] present dramatic evidence for the creation of the Black Sea as we now know it. It seems that prior to 5500 b.c.e., the Black Sea was a small, fresh-water lake created by the Don, Dniester and Volga rivers. The Mediterranean, a salt-water ocean, was some four hundred feet higher, but separated from the Black Sea by a small spit of land. Melting glaciers from the last Ice Age caused the world's ocean levels to rise until, eventually, aided by a large storm out of the southwest, the land spit was broached.

The ensuing waterfall, the authors say, caused the level of the Black Sea to rise by about one foot a day for an entire year, until an area the size of Iowa, some 60,000 square miles, was submerged. The volume of water was 1,000 times greater than Niagara Falls and its noise was heard all the way across to the Crimea—soon to become the Crimean Peninsula.

Now imagine the effect of this on those people living on the shores of the lake, at least on those who were far enough away to have survived. This is, as the authors say, Noah's flood, or at least the event that generated the Noah flood story. Similar stories of a worldwide flood throughout the Ancient Near East were carried far and wide in the northern hemisphere by the survivors and passed on to their descendants. No doubt the tale grew somewhat in the telling, but the actual event was of unprecedented magnitude, at least for that part of the world which is home to our biblical ancestors and their neighbors.

Santorini, a volcanic island about sixty-three miles north of Crete, exploded either in 1628 or in 1550 b.c.e.: that is to say, fully within the time of recorded history; Egyptian records seem to favor the lower date. We get some idea of its physical effects from the explosion of Krakatau (now called Krakatoa) on August 27, 1883.[21] Krakatau's eruption is estimated to have been only one-third the magnitude of Santorini's, yet the sonic boom it generated reverberated around the world seven times. The explosion of Santorini must have produced far greater effects.

Huge tsunamis, darkness at noon and for a long time thereafter, red sunsets caused by the persistence of particulate matter in the air: these are remembered in a somewhat garbled manner in the "plagues" of the Exodus story, even though the explosion was likely not contemporary with the exit of Moses-led Israelites. What interests us here is the movement of peoples displaced by the immense tidal wave that washed the shores of the eastern Mediterranean. This, too, seems to be remembered in the Bible. Later we will see why this seems to apply especially to the tribe of Dan.

This does not, by itself, prove that these disparate elements mixed in any significant way, but it certainly sets up the possibility that they did. After all, they would have had several centuries in which to get acquainted.

Even according to the highest chronology, that used by conservative scholars, the barest beginnings of Israel—what was for a long time referred to as the Patriarchal period—would have come a thousand years after civilizations had started elsewhere in the Ancient Near East. These included the Hittites, who flourished in southeastern Anatolia. Meanwhile Egypt and Sumer emerged at either end of the Fertile Crescent, that large, boomerang-shaped territory presently occupied by Iraq, Syria, Lebanon, Israel and Egypt. Minoan and Mycenaean civilizations, while not quite this old, certainly pre-date anything that could be called Israel.

The chronology we employ puts Israel's barest beginnings near the end of the Bronze Ages, a period of more than two thousand years ending about 1200 b.c.e. More specifically, the time of Israel's founders was probably somewhere around 1500 b.c.e., but Israel did not become a nation even in contemporary terms for another 500 years. What took so long?

While Sunday school teachers taught us that Israelites were still one big, if unhappy, family, the truth is closer to the situation of Afghanistan, Iraq or the former Yugoslavia. In other words, biblical Israel was a country that might have been described as a dotted line drawn around an area that included a lot of different ethnic groups. At no time during the period before the monarchy did all the tribes of Israel join together to fight a common enemy, while Israel's lack of homogeneity is attested by the break-up of the kingdom after less than a hundred years of rule, first by Saul, and then by David and Solomon.

The upland valleys of central Israel conduce to settlement by people who, once settled, wouldn't want to wander far from where they lived. Similarly, Israelites would be disinclined to stray far from where their ancestors were buried. Not for nothing has

Judaism, followed by Christianity and Islam, identified THE place, presently in Hebron, where all the Patriarchs and Matriarchs save Rachel are interred. Had Abraham wished to do more than acquire land for a family burial ground in Canaan, to build his own state, it would have been a parlous business—especially for as small a group of retainers (Gen. 14 credits him with a household of 318) as he had.

If the Bible knows anything like the Latin maxim *cuius regio euius religio,* "who owns the territory has the religion," it doesn't show it here. The man from whom Abraham bought the plot in which to bury Sarah was one Ephron the Hittite. (Hatti was a powerful kingdom in southeastern Anatolia.) Rather than joining the Hittites, Abraham steadfastly sticks to his newfound faith. Of course, that wouldn't always be the case with his descendants, as we shall see.

4. How to Understand Biblical History

"...for one brief, shining moment..." – Camelot

As we indicated above, the period during which Israel was a united kingdom was quite brief: less than a century. Compared to the centuries of Mesopotamian and Egyptian dynasties, it was indeed a brief moment; how brightly it shone is a matter of some debate. As Johannes Pedersen observed nearly a century ago, "The fact that monarchy has left no impression on the preserved laws, shows how little it has been assimilated to Israelitic popular life."[22] The issue is compounded by the way we read biblical history, so we ought to address this question first.

The last biblical events are traditionally supposed to have happened in the time of Ezra and Nehemiah—with whom we will shortly begin. Scholars would extend that date toward us by as much as three centuries,[23] but in either case biblical history ended more than 2,000 years ago. We must therefore be aware of the "angle" from which we read it.

Just as we are taught in physics to avoid parallax error—that is, looking at something too much from one side—reading history, especially religious history, from one side invites us to accept the bias of its writers, in this case Judean survivors of Israel's two (or more) kingdoms. Reading ancient history (and remember that much of the Bible's history was "ancient" to the people who wrote it down) also invites what we call the error of "historical compression." This happens when we look directly back through history so that events which actually took place decades or even centuries apart appear to follow each other closely.

The Bible lends itself to this sort of thing because already by the end of biblical times the authors were looking back at events some of which had occurred over a thousand years before their time. An example of this is the story of "the" Exodus, which is probably a composite of several "flights" from Egypt that took place over several centuries.[24]

Similarly, biblical writers were prone to retroject the beginnings of things with which they were familiar deeper into history than was actually the case. For example, the Bible credits the Patriarchs with using camels, but archaeologists tell us camels were not domesticated until much later. The Bible's early modern critics gleefully pointed to such discrepancies to discredit Scripture, but those phantom camels won't bear the weight the critics put on them. The truth is that after being familiar with these "ships of the desert" for over a thousand years, the Bible's collators probably did not remember when camels had first come into use.

There are Bible stories aplenty that tells us when some things began. These are called "etiological" stories. For example, clothing began with Adam and Eve, the eating of meat and drinking of wine with Noah and so forth. But the advent of camel domestication would hardly rate a notice.

Other stories, the so-called "miracles," need to be treated in a different way. Modern readers of the Bible should put aside a prejudice that says, in effect, if the Bible's miracles are unbelievable, then nothing that it says can be taken at face value. There is often some kernel of historical truth from which these stories have grown. Remember, the writers of biblical stories lived in a pre-scientific age.

Conversely, modern traditional readers, Jews and Christians, need to move away from the Bible's position that Israel always was a uniform group of people presenting a unified, cohesive, even clannish face to the outside world. To do otherwise is to retroject into biblical history the situation to which Napoleon's rabbis were responding; that is, they assumed that the ghettoization of Jews, voluntary or involuntary—as it was in Europe from 1515[25]— was, more or less, a permanent feature of Jewish history.

What is needed is to, as it were, look down on the history from above so that we can both see the order in which things happened and appreciate the distance between events. Another advantage of a "satellite's eye view" of history is it helps us recognize that Israel was a small player on a great world stage. (That Israel has remained center stage for so long is a mystery that the present work does not address.)

We hope here to introduce such a perspective.

5. The Bible's Marriage-go-round

Following the Talmud, the French Jews argued that the biblical prohibitions against intermarriage to Moabites and Ammonites only applied to foreign men, and to Egyptians for only three generations after the Exodus and to a short list of proscribed nations found in various places in Scripture. But it was all quite academic. Residents of nineteenth century Egypt were hardly the Egyptians of Pharaoh, and as for the others, all of them had ceased to exist.

Looked at more closely, the Torah's prohibitions against intermarriage differ one from another—and what is most interesting to us is that they do not seem to have been very effective. (See Hosea 2:16f.) This may very well be because the early pronouncements were not originally intended to ban all intermarriage. In truth, legislation from the Christian side, from the Council of Elvira (306 c.e.) and the laws of Constantius in 339 c.e. to Hitler's Nuremburg Laws, have been both more persistent and more effective.

Certainly in royal circles there was no heed paid to any bans. The much-celebrated David, who supplanted his father-in-law, Saul, married many foreign women and was himself succeeded by the son born to him by Bathsheba, who had been the wife of another Hittite, one Uriah; the life of her son Solomon, who became mother of the following king, Rehoboam, was Ammonite. We put it this way to indicate what we will expand upon later, namely, that some of the marriages entered into by these early royals were what we would today call intermarriages. The question is: would they?

One thing that immediately stands out is the extent of intermarriage in royal families. Solomon's "seven hundred wives and three hundred concubines," may be an exaggeration—at least it is to be hoped—but his marriage to foreign women cannot be denied. It was, after all, no different than the practice of other Ancient Near Eastern regimes. But Solomon's harem, whatever its size, tends to distract us from similar unions made by other kings of Israel, North and South.

Ancient Near Eastern peoples had a variety of overlapping gods, and there is a growing body of opinion[26] that Israel and Judah had them, too, despite the Bible's attempts at denial. Intermarriage in the Bible, then, would not be so much a matter of people who had different gods marrying, because that would not have mattered much, but rather marriage between two people who came from significantly different points on the Canaanite cultural continuum.

Royal intermarriages were designed to cement tribal or at least family relationships, but they did not always work out well in practice. David was often on the run from Saul and had to take refuge beyond Saul's jurisdiction, among Ammonites or Philistines. History repeated itself when David again had to flee from his own son Absalom and take refuge with an Ammonite ally.

We might note here that, technically, the word "Jew" is hardly appropriate before the year 586 b.c.e, the year of the destruction of Solomon's Temple in Jerusalem. "Jew" derives from "Judean," and that from "Judah": the southern part of the kingdom which Solomon's father had done so much to put together. Even the word "Israelite" is something of an anachronism. It is the burden of the first part of this book that between 1500 and 1000 b.c.e., the nascent Israelite community was composed of a number of different ethnicities not all of which could be called Semitic. On this reading, ethnic or tribal intermarriage—for example, that between Benjamin and the rest of "Israel"—would have been fairly common.

To say this with any confidence, however, requires that we take some time to examine the parameters of marriage in biblical times. This is a difficult prospect because, while there are a surprising number of stories about strong women in Scripture—Sarah, Miriam, Deborah, Tamar (I), Ruth, Esther—several of whom are intermarried, there is little evidence concerning the everyday relationships formed between men and women of different families.[27]

Some things may be inferred from stories and from laws concerning women, bride prices, and so forth and some, perhaps, from documents that reveal marriage customs of neighboring peoples. Given the paucity of hard evidence, we are compelled to marshal what is there and see whether any sound suggestions might be based upon it.

The scope of our investigation includes relationships that we would scarcely call marital, such as concubinage and women taken as war prisoners who are then married into their conquerors' families. Even if converted, they would scarcely have made ardent synagogue goers.

It is an irony of history that modern descendants of the Northerners, now called Samaritans, though they consider themselves Jews, are not considered Jews by the state of Israel, so that a marriage between an Israeli and a Samaritan is considered a mixed marriage. This discrimination goes back to Ezra.

In the last part of our work, we examine two things; Jewish responses, both rabbinic and secular, to the problems posed by living in a diaspora where persecution was not uncommon and discrimination was a fact of life. We find that Jewish responses, such as Philo's reaction[28] to persecutions in Alexandria or the rabbinic declaration of gentile "impurity," are just that, reactions to exclusion by the dominant majority.

Finally, we address the question of whether Israel's God was ever "intermarried." The question is meant seriously because there is reason to think that for a time there were elements in Israel who concluded that God, even if unmarried before, necessarily succeeded to the consort(s) of the other god(s) whom he had vanquished.

Notes to Chapter I

1. In saying this, the authors in no way wish to delegitimize ancient or modern Israel. In fact, we feel that what actually happened there towards the end of the Bronze Age—the emergence of the people we now know as Jewish—is, if anything, more exciting than the Bible's account of it.

2. Sylvia Barack Fishman, *Double or Nothing? Jewish Families and Mixed Marriage* (Hanover NH and London: Brandeis U. P., U P of New England, 2004), 134.

3. Shaye J. D. Cohen, *The Beginnings of Jewishness: Boundaries, Varieties, Uncertainties* (Berkeley: University of California Press, 1999), 261.

4. *Transactions of the Parisian Sanhedrin,* May 30, 1806. London: C. Taylor, 1807.

5. The 2001 JPS commentary, *Etz Hayim,* done for the Conservative Rabbinical Assembly, comments on Gen. 24:3: "Jewish law requires that Jews marry Jews." (131) This deliberately back-reads into biblical history something that modern denominations wish to see there, but this misimpression has been with us for a long time. The late first/early second century Roman historian Tacitus *(Histories* 5:2) flatly declares that Jews abstain from marrying gentiles, but he is speaking in and probably about the period after Rome had destroyed the Second Temple.

6. This may seem like hair-splitting, but it has a solid foundation. "The [Talmudic] rabbis deny a universal Pentateuchal prohibition against intermarriage." Christine E. Hayes, *Gentile Impurities and Jewish Identities: Intermarriage and Conversion from the Bible to the Talmud* (NY: Oxford University Press, 2002), 145. Such a distinction might help settle the problem of how to classify homosexual households.

7. We use a later date for the so-called "Patriarchal period" than those traditionalists whose reliance upon biblical chronology causes them to posit Abraham as a nineteenth century b.c.e. figure.

8. This began already in the fourth century with the Council of Elvira and the decree of the emperor Constantine. See Jacob R. Marcus, *The Jew in the Medieval World* (NY: Atheneum, 1969 [1938]), 4f. The law of Constantine applied to "Jews, Samaritans and Heaven-Worshippers." Marcus terms the last named group "a sect closely allied to Judaism." We think it denotes those gentiles who had attached themselves to Judaism without formal conversion.

9. Haim Hillel Ben Sasson, ed., *A History of the Jewish People* (Cambridge, MA: Harvard University Press, 1976). With contributions from six leading scholars, it was the standard for its generation. However, Jewishness, per se, begins about halfway through that history.

10. The use of this word is a literary convenience wished upon us by the centuries in which the veracity of all the Bible contains was assumed. There is no proof that the people in question existed, let alone when they lived, but for this study that is not a matter of any consequence.

11. *Midrash Rabbah* on Num. 25:6-9. *Avodah Zarah 36b* (Brooklyn: Soncino, 1951) 176ff provides the death penalty if the copulation takes place in public. This implies that the act in question was not case of simple intercourse, but a public act. If so, it must have had religious implications as well; that this discussion is found in *Avodah Zarah* ("strange/foreign worship" and therefore forbidden to Jews) proves it.

12. Tirzah Firestone, *The Receiving* (San Francisco: HarperOne, 2002), 5.

13. Tikvah Frymer-Kensky, *Reading the Women of the Bible* (New York: Schocken, 2002), xxi and 56. She also speaks of "The

biblical metaphor of Israel as a woman..." and "Just as these women, not politically powerful themselves, are privileged to know the will of God, so too Israel, small and marginal between [rather, among] the great empires of the world, is nevertheless the bearer of God's word."15/9.

14. P. Bird "The Place of Women in the Israelite Cultus," in Patrick Miller et al, *Ancient Israelite Religion*, Philadelphia: Fortress, 1987, 404.

15. Cohen, The Beginnings of Jewishness, 246.

16. Louis Ginzberg, *Legends of the Jews* (Philadelphia; Jewish Publication Society, 1954), I: 77.

16. Jonathan N. Tubb, *Canaanites* (Norman: Univ. of Oklahoma Press, 1998).

17. In Gentile Impurities and Jewish Identities: Intermarriage and Conversion from the Bible to the Talmud (New York: Oxford University Press, 2002).

18. One thinks of the Phoenicians and their monopoly on royal purple, but they came much later. Perhaps theirs was only a new wrinkle in the old cloth trade?

19. Fernand Braudel, "Histoire et science sociales: la longue duree," *Annales, Economies, Societe, Civilizations* 13 (1958) 36-37, quoted in Rosenbaum, *Understanding Biblical Israel,* (Macon GA: Mercer UP, 2002), 33.

20. William Ryan and Walter Pittman, *Noah's Flood* (NY: Simon and Schuster, 1998).

21. Simon Winchester, *Krakatoa* (NY: HarperCollins, 2003).

22. Johannes Pedersen, *Israel: Its Life and Culture,* London: Oxford University Press, 1926, I:23

23. Even though we will quote different translations, by "Bible" we mean the Torah/Prophets/Writings as edited and finally arranged by Jews at the end of the first Christian century.

24. See Moses/Exodus/Joshua, Chapter 7 in Rosenbaum, *Understanding.*

25. Venice sequestered its Jews on the island of Nuovo Geto ("New Iron Foundry") giving us the word "ghetto."

26. Diana V. Edelman, ed., *The Triumph of Elohim; From Yahwisms to Judaisms* (Grand Rapids MI: Wm. Eerdmans, 1996).

27. Daniel Jeremy Silver writes, "According to prevailing custom, the wife came into her husband's clan but did not have to adopt her husband's faith." *A History of Judaism, I: From Abraham to Maimonides* (NY: Basic Books, 1974), 65.

28. Philo. As cited by Cohen, *Beginnings,* 74-75.

Chapter II. Put Away Your Strange Wives: Ezra and Nehemiah

Like a diamond, the Jewish people crystallized as a result of extreme outside pressure. – RaGBaG[1]

1. A Jew-o-centric Universe?

Alone among all the peoples of the Ancient Near East, Jews have survived until this present day. Indeed, the names of many ancient peoples would not be known had they not been included in the Hebrews'[2] Scripture. Others were unknown even to our biblical ancestors. Some of both the known and the unknown have been given flesh by archaeological excavations, but only in the past century or so.

Writing in Baghdad a thousand years before the advent of modern archaeology, the Jewish philosopher Saadia Gaon[3] maintains that the most valuable part of a thing is always at its center: the pupil in the eye, the seed in the fruit, the earth in the solar system, and the Jews on the planet whose center is Jerusalem. Yet despite Saadia's "proof," for most of its history Israel's position in the world—even that small corner of the world that they knew— was quite modest.

The country at its largest extent was hardly bigger than New Jersey, in an area of some 4,000,000 square miles. To put it another way: the Persian Empire, of which Judah was a part in Ezra's time, was divided into satrapies (provinces)—one hundred twenty-seven of them. Judah was only one of four that the Persians called "Across the [Jordan] River."

One would not know this from reading Hebrew Scripture. Some modern critics may complain[4] that the Bible knows nothing of the Egypt in which the Patriarchs allegedly lived for four centuries or of the titanic struggles among Egypt, Hatti and Mitanni for control of the very land upon which Israel lived. The criticism would be lost on the collectors of Scripture, for whom these kingdoms were distant memories, if that, and even more upon their spiritual descendants.

Given the circumstances, it is hardly to be wondered at that Jews have long lived in a Jew-o-centric—or, to use a more conventional term, ethnocentric—universe. How not? Most nations do likewise, and as the only recognizable survivor among such mighty neighbors as the Assyrians, the Babylonians, the Persians, the Greeks of Alexander, the Romans of the Caesars and the mighty and long-lived Egypt of the Pharaohs, Jews may be excused for concluding that they were and remain the apple of their God's eye.

As such, Jews have long conceived of themselves as always being apart from and over against their neighbors, a position that has been enhanced by the isolation forced on them over the past 1,700 years, first by Christians and then by Muslims. (Obviously, the Holocaust in Europe and the situation of modern Israel since 1948 has only sharpened this perspective.)

True, the notion of being a people who dwell apart has aided Jewish survival under the most difficult of circumstances, but it also often induced a narrowing of their field of vision when Jews wrote their history. For example, Jews responded to the destruction of Jerusalem (586 b.c.e.) and their consequent Diaspora not by abandoning the God who seemed to have abandoned them, but by concluding it was part of God's plan for them to convert the gentiles. All of them. (Though we hasten to add that Judaism never made becoming Jewish a prerequisite for salvation.)

When we seek to investigate problems in Jewish history—for example, the extent to which Jews or their Hebrew ancestors intermingled with gentiles and why—we must not confine ourselves to the accounts in Hebrew Scripture. We must also use whatever sources are available to assess properly Israel's place among the nations at any given point.

Fortunately, there is an ever-increasing amount of outside material available. And we need all we can get to balance the often one-sided and polemic accounts in the Bible. We begin by examining the books of Ezra and Nehemiah—possibly written by the same person[5]—because they deal with the relations of Judeans, Israel's Southern survivors, with peoples they considered foreign. These include residents of what had once been their own Northern Kingdom.

The subject that interests us most is that most intimate of human relations, marriage, but here, too, we cannot allow ourselves to focus too narrowly. That is, we cannot just accept Scripture's word for who was foreign and who not, nor neglect the long history of close relationships among peoples, including Israel's two kingdoms, that characterizes its earlier history. However, we begin by examining the two biblical figures most often identified as opponents of intermarriage.

2. Ezra the Revolutionary

Prohibition presupposes previous practice. – RaGBaG

Ezra was born in Babylon in the fifth pre-Christian century. Officially, he held the offices of priest and scribe in the Diaspora community there, though what exactly he did, his book doesn't tell us. It hardly matters. For Jewish tradition, Ezra is a kind of patron saint.

He holds a place second only to Moses, whose brother, Aaron, he lists as an ancestor though they are separated by fourteen generations. Just as Moses is credited with almost single-handedly getting recalcitrant Israelites to accept the Torah, Ezra is credited with stemming the tide of dissolution that threatened to overtake Judah eight hundred years later—that is, a century or so after the Jerusalem Temple's destruction.

As presented to us, his problem was that extensive intermarriage between Judeans and their neighbors threatened the community's Jewish[6] integrity. This was no new problem. More precisely, it wasn't new, but was only now seen as a problem where it had not been so before. Why just now? We shall see.

First, however, we note that intermarriage was commonplace among Israelites all the way back to Abraham, himself at least twice intermarried! During that early time, many people attached themselves to Israel in one way or another. One outstanding example of this is given in Numbers 31:32, which reports that 32,000 Midianite virgins were taken into Israel as booty.[7] We'll discuss this further below, but if the children of such women became fully enfranchised Jews, what does this say about their position—if not their mothers'—in the community? They must have been, like victims of the Borg of *Star Trek*, assimilated....

So Ezra was swimming against a tide of intermingling/ intermarriage that had been running for a thousand years. And after Ezra? The revolutionary nature of his action may be inferred when we note that, however successful Ezra's measures were in his own time—and we're not sure they were—they certainly did not become the view of "mainstream" Israel after his time.

It is part of the genius of Jewish tradition, however, that it can reach back into history for Scriptural support of positions that only came to be normative hundreds of years later. Beginning in the Hellenistic period (323 - 146 b.c.e.), opposition to intermarriage began in earnest. Targum Pseudo-Jonathan, which took shape in the early centuries of the Common Era, uses Lev. 18:23, clearly a prohibition of child sacrifice, as a prohibition against intermarriage! Ezra, no doubt, would have smiled. His strictures against intermarriage have been employed, willy-nilly, as a kind of portable ghetto to keep Jews safe within their own community walls for the past two thousand years: that is, since the inclusion of the books of Ezra and Nehemiah[8] in canonical Scripture.

What finally emerged after centuries of rabbinic and modern elaboration on the theme was something that appears to the untrained eye as a single, unified stance against intermarriage alongside the denial that intermarriage was much in evidence before Ezra's heroic actions. This view falsifies history in both directions. First, as per our epigraph, prohibition presupposes previous practice—in this case, rather a long history of previous practice. On the other hand, only by a long stretch of the imagination can Ezra's situation and those of Diaspora or modern Jews be seen as equivalent.

There are biblical texts that argue against or appear to prohibit intermarriage. But they are a bit like those mining claims "salted'" with iron pyrites to give the appearance of a rich and earlier deposit. The best known of these, Deut. 7:3, probably was not written, or even thought of, until five hundred years after Moses's time. Changing the metaphor somewhat, we need to go back and find what "grain of sand" it was; that is, what initial irritation caused Ezra's "pearl" of opposition to intermarriage to begin growing.

The question is complex. Did Ezra wish only to purify the priesthood? If so, did he differentiate between high priestly families and ordinary priests? Or, as some scholars think,[9] was he interested in prohibiting all future intermarriage of Judean men and women with gentiles? Did this include negating even the possibility of gentile conversion? If the latter, then his stance would certainly be unprecedented, at least according to a Jewish tradition that sees adherence by foreigners to Israelite religion as a possibility as far back as Abraham's time.

As interesting as such arguments might be for the scholars who make them,[10] we feel their enterprise does not take sufficient account of the actual situation Ezra faced. Neither his nor Nehemiah's book provides many details as to just exactly what he tried to do, and the success—or lack thereof—that their efforts achieved is debatable. We think Ezra saw his job as protecting the Jewish integrity of the Judean community from a "hostile takeover," not by foreign invaders or foreign religious practices, but by near neighboring peoples, some of whom could creditably claim to be Jewish; in Ezra's eyes, such claims were unwarranted.

We note here that Ezra's directive was not also directed at Jewish women—that is, he does not seem to acknowledge any problem of Jewish women marrying non-Jewish men. We know that this took place, too, though we don't know on what scale. Ezra's neglect is understandable: Jewish women in his time were probably still two hundred years away from having legal standing to initiate divorce, and that in very narrow circumstances.

STRANGE WIVES

In this chapter we will try to understand just what it was that Ezra wanted to accomplish. To do this successfully we have to be very careful to distinguish Ezra's situation from those of the communities and interpreters of the law who came after.

At this point, however, we need to step back and look at the regional/political situation in which Judah found itself and the history that produced it.

3. The Myth of Israelite Unity

Behold, how good and pleasant it is when brothers dwell in unity.
– Ps. 133:1 (RSV)

Most people, if they can tell you anything at all about biblical Israel, have been taught that it was a small nation constantly defending itself against such larger, aggressive neighbors as Egypt, Assyria and even Aram (Damascus). This is true enough, at various times. But let us remember that in the Ancient Near East, just as in the modern Middle East, virtually no country of any size is homogeneous.

The psalm's sentiment above is admirable, but it hardly describes biblical reality. Our traditions, both Jewish and Christian, do a poor job of exploring the divisions within Israel itself, but these were deep and, for the present purpose, more important.

As we shall see, most Israelites were brothers by mutual adoption and they very seldom lived peaceably together. But that seems to have been forgotten over the long centuries in which Israel fought to survive. As this chapter's epigraph indicates, the pressure of history, especially in the past two thousand years, has produced a Jewish people that sees itself as having existed over against various gentiles ever since God revealed himself to Abraham. Christianity, eager to assume the mantle of Judaism, readily accepted this view because it made the Church's triumphal succession easier to represent.

A closer look at Israel's history, however, shows that between the formation of Israelite kingship under Saul and Ezra's return to Jerusalem, Israel was not so much a nation as it was a "geographical expression," to borrow a phrase from Otto von Bismarck. Put another way, Israel was a united kingdom for only a

54

hundred of the six to seven hundred years we are speaking of; for some eighty-five percent of that time, it was not.

There was a scant century of superficial political unity under Saul, David and Solomon, but after that the country contained two and sometimes three kingdoms jockeying with each other for primacy in the region—something like Croats, Serbs and Bosnians in the years following the demise of Marshall Tito of Yugoslavia. The existence of three kingdoms is implicit in Hosea's metaphorical three "children of harlotry" and explicit in Hosea 5:5, where he uses Israel, Judah and Ephraim to indicate separate entities. (Hosea's time, ca. 740 b.c.e—*pace* Yehezkel Kaufmann—was one that saw the kind of rivalry Ezra worked so diligently to overcome. Tradition still clings to the idea that Hosea's story of his marriage to a harlot was literally true, and some scholars delete Judah from 5:5, not on very good grounds, we think.)

Bismarck was speaking of nineteenth century Italy, where at least the boundaries on three sides were determined by water. In Israel's case, only the Mediterranean usually stayed in one place; the other boundaries fluctuated wildly north, south and east. It should not be surprising, therefore, if we found proof of greater fragmentation within Israel than our tradition remembers.

> We do know from the Bible that the North became a separate kingdom, Israel, as over against Judah, the Southern Kingdom. Israel persisted—not without its own internal divisions—for some two hundred years after Solomon's death in 922 b.c.e. When the Northern tribes (seven, not ten of them) broke from the confederacy, their rallying cry had been "To your gods (*'elohim*), O Israel," and not, "to your tents" (*'ohelim*), as the text presently reads.[11] (More in Chapter VIII, Choosing Up Sides)

Later, pious editors did not wish to admit—or perhaps they no longer knew—how polytheistic early Israel was. But this is crucial. If Israel was polytheistic, then marriage among tribes was per force intermarriage as we would define it, even if they did not.

That early Israel was, in fact, multi-ethnic is apparent from many places in Scripture. The best example of this may be the strange aftermath of the war between "all Israel" and the tribe of Benjamin chronicled in Judges 19-21: namely, a prohibition against further intermarriage with this group. Why this strange punishment? The majority's response was ad hoc, situational, but it hints at Benjamin's essential foreignness, which we will discuss at greater length below.

Another example: after 722 b.c.e. the population of the North became so mixed with people imported by its Assyrian occupiers that later Judeans, who had arrogated to themselves the job of "keepers of the flame," saw these Samaritan Northerners as non-Jews. In Israel today marriages between Israelis and the dwindling number of Samaritans who inhabit the area around Afula in the North are considered intermarriages and cannot be performed in Israel proper. Before Ezra's time, however, there was no state rabbinate to interdict such unions.

We cannot say whether a unified Israel might have survived the attentions of its predatory neighbors, but the divided "House of David" could not stand. Less than one hundred fifty years later (586 b.c.e.), the North was overrun and thousands of its people were exiled to Babylon. For most of its history, then, Israel—whether one kingdom, two or several—could only maintain its autonomy by a judicious selection of alliances with the two or three of the "superpowers" that surrounded it. There was not, there could not be, a concept of neutrality because, as Jesus later put it, "He who is not for me is against me."

The world political situation changed drastically after 539 b.c.e, when Cyrus of Persia became the "first kid on his block to rule the world." That is, Persia was able successfully to conquer much of the Near East, including Egypt, thus making the whole region one empire, at least for a time.

Egypt, however, chafed under Persian dominance and revolted shortly before Ezra's time. The revolt was put down, but it demonstrated Persia's need for compliant allies in the region. Judah could be such an ally. Hence Ezra, with his desire for Judean purity, had something to trade with his Persian employers: permission to re-organize the province in return for its loyalty and stability. Ezra's "commission" from the Persian government (Ezra 7:1), added to his priestly credentials, must have given him powerful leverage with which to begin.

4. Ezra and the Politics of Divorce

Our study of biblical intermarriage initially concentrates on the careers of Ezra and his contemporary Nehemiah for two reasons. The first is their well-known appeal (Ezra, chs. 9-10; Neh. 9:2) for Judean men to divorce their "strange [=foreign] wives" and to refrain from further intermarriage involving either their sons or their daughters. (Scholars seem to think that the community returning from Babylonian Exile was free of the taint of intermarriage, but a careful reading of Ezra suggests otherwise.)

Under Ezra, the prohibition against (all?) intermarriage became institutionalized, at least for a while, though perhaps not all Israelites abided by it. Ezra 10:15 lists some hold-outs, according to the RSV, but NJPS offers a different translation, one that shows no opposition.

Simply from the above difference in translations one can see that this is a complex issue. For starters, it involves the status of children born to intermarried couples. Salo Baron interprets the word *mamzer,* which we loosely translate as "bastard," as coming from a phrase meaning "from a foreign people," indicating that children of intermarriage are ipso facto bastards. But his clever folk etymology is not correct. A child born to a Jew and a foreign woman would not be a *mamzer* even if the woman was already married (EJ ad loc *mamzer* and see Chapter XI), judging by the example of the 32,000 Midianite virgins in Numbers 31:32.[12]

Did Ezra mean to include all gentiles and both men and women in his strictures? What were the grounds upon which the prohibition was based? If Ezra had the same Torah that we do—including Numbers—we might conclude that he meant his prohibition to apply only to gentile men, as later tradition insists, yet it is the "foreign wives" that he fulminates against. Why?

Allegedly, Ezra feared that marriage to foreign women would (re-)introduce foreign religious practices into Israel, but this is too narrow a focus. It is true, as we'll see in Chapter VII, that women had what might be called their own religion, but this religion was well-nigh universal—that is, it cut across ethnic lines and always had done so. Also, almost all of Scripture is written from a male perspective, so we don't know how many Israelite women brought home "strange husbands" á la Esther, and what this might have done to family ecology in the Persian period.

Earlier periods provide only scraps of foreign-husband stories that would be pertinent to our subject: Jael, who married one Heber the Kenite, a clan of the usually despised and proscribed Amalekites; and Bathsheba, if she was Israelite, who was married to Uriah the Hittite. (If she was Hittite, then her marriage to David would be an intermarriage.

Jacob's daughter, Dinah, whom we will also discuss in Chapter IV, was taken by force, a kind of de facto marriage that was not unusual in the ancient world. Hers was the first biblically acknowledged intermarriage, at least between two humans, though it has become known as the "rape of Dinah" (Gen. 34)—providing her family and modern feminists with a rallying point, however anachronistic the latter's position is.

Briefly, when the prince of Shechem proposed marriage to the Israelite Dinah, with whom he had just had a sexual union, her family did not claim it was against their law. Canaanites who were willing to adopt Jewish practices such as circumcision, and to leave off such practices as sexual congress in the service of their own religion, could join Israel. Ezra would try to change that dramatically. By his time Dinah's story, if historical, would have happened a thousand years before. However, it is not at all certain the events described therein really happened. They may simply have been concocted to justify the Israelite takeover of the important city of Shechem.

There must have been much more inter-ethnic marriage on the common level, but of this the Bible provides no record except the general prohibition (Deut. 7:3) not to give Israelite daughters to foreign men or take foreign daughters for the sons of Israelites. Fortunately, we are not completely dependent upon Scripture for useful information.

As to the question of how widespread intermarriage was, every year seems to produce new information concerning our subject. The most recent find in Israel is that of the temple at Maqqedah (probably Khirbet el-Kom, fifteen miles west of Hebron) where several gods, including Israel's, seem to have been worshipped. Even more astonishing, the finds there seem to indicate the presence of a family in which a man and his son, from their names, represent differing religions.[13] Of course, that seems have occurred earlier as well, to judge by the names in King Saul's (ca. 1020 - 1000 b.c.e) family.

To return to Ezra, the first of his demands was no small thing. Divorced women had reduced value in the marriage market, a fact that they and their parents would have resented. It may be instructive to point out that when Herod Antipas divorced his Nabatean wife (ca. 33 c.e.) in order to marry his brother's ex-wife—something that Jewish law forbids—the first wife's father, a Nabatean king, declared war and soundly thrashed him.[14]

Not every divorced woman in Ezra's time had a king for a father, of course, but we might wonder what souring of relations would have followed these ideologically motivated divorces. And since marriage between families was often the mortar that cemented business dealings, the men who followed Ezra's directive might have done so at considerable cost to themselves.

Here we might point to the Murashu Tablets, a series of 730 business documents from a banking house in Persia nearly contemporary with Ezra. Judging by the names the archive contains, it would seem that Jews were by no means self-isolating, though the archive sheds no light on intermarriage in Persia.

Still, "prohibition presupposes previous practice." That is, Ezra and Nehemiah were apparently reacting to a real situation, one which they felt threatened the political and social integrity of Judean Judaism. How long had this been the case? How long had their compatriots been marrying "foreigners" and how widespread was the practice?

How long is difficult to determine, though we propose that the marriages made by the Patriarchs were, in fact, intermarriages.

The second reason for beginning here is that it was during this period, which most scholars put between 450 and 350 b.c.e., that we think much of Scripture was gathered, edited and organized. This is important because, although what later became the Hebrew Bible originated from many places within historic Israel, North and South, what emerged at the end of the canonization process some five hundred years later reflects the prejudices of the final editors, Judeans.[15]

From our vantage point nearly two thousand years later, we, the Jewish and Christian descendants of these Judeans, tend to see and applaud only the South's vilification of the North. The Northern Kingdom, according to its opponents, had deserted the Davidic monarchy and introduced the Baal cult and the use of bull-bovine images in the Yah cult. The Bible blames Jeroboam I, the breakaway king of the North after Solomon's death, with instituting golden calves "from Dan to Beersheva." Scripture manages somehow to overlook that it was none other than Ezra's esteemed ancestor, Aaron, who seems to have invented this image. After all, it was Aaron who oversaw the creation of the original golden calf.

We would be wrong to spend any time arguing the last point, because by doing so we would lose track of the other rivals and enemies, both foreign and domestic, faced by Ezra's returnees. These included the Samaritan remnants of the Northern Kingdom then powerful in Jerusalem and people living across the Jordan, principally the powerful Tobiah family. The ruins of their imposing hill fortress, Iraq al-'Amir—only a long day's walk from Jerusalem—still stands about eleven miles west of Amman.

In addition, there will have been at least some Benjaminites[16] still looking for the restoration of Saul's family or at least an independent state of their own, and Ashdodites, inhabitants of the thriving port city of Ashdod south of present day Tel Aviv, who had some sort of independent existence. That is to say, competition among various groups was not principally about religion except insofar as religion served the twin ends of economic power and political control.

Concerned as we are about the "economics of salvation," the place of material economics in everyday religion goes largely unnoticed. But in the long run, earthly economics are equally important. After all, who pays for the religious establishment? The answer is, ultimately, that the people bear a large part of the load, either directly through support of local priests and shrines,[17] or indirectly through the taxes that support royal religious establishments.

But the people's purse, as it were, is not bottomless, so support of multiple religious establishments becomes a zero-sum game. The more some get, the less there is for others. Seen in this light, Israel's increasingly exclusive monotheism—its insistence upon a single deity and ultimately on only one legitimate site for worship— is more than a theological challenge; it is a call for Israelites to deprive the various local and/or polytheistic shrines of their livelihood.

King Josiah (ruled 640 - 608 b.c.e.) was the first ruler seriously to challenge the local shrine system, and while the Bible credits him with great success, reading the prophetic "reports" of those who came after indicates that the battle did not abate. Economically, then, the stakes Ezra was playing for were very high. But if religion cannot be separated from economics, neither can it be separated from politics.

5. To the Samaritans: Thanks, but No Thanks

During the centuries between the fall of the Temple and Ezra's return, Samaritans and Jews from the eastern side of Jordan, along with their non-Jewish allies, had established themselves on both sides of the river. As the Judeans now tell it, Samaritans offered to assist in the effort to rebuild the Temple, the better to control whatever was going on in Jerusalem.

Ezra declined the Samaritan offer of help in the rebuilding of the city (4:1) because he was trying to re-establish Judean hegemony in its own territory. When their Trojan horse tactic failed, the Samaritans and their allies tried mightily to interfere with Ezra's work in Jerusalem, going so far as to denounce it to the Persian king.

Ezra's riposte was to amalgamate and deliberately change the prohibitions against intermarriage found in Deuteronomy and Exodus in order to exclude the groups that were rivals for power. Thus, he omits Hivites and Girgashites—found in the list of prohibited unions in Deut. 7:3 (Hivites are also included in Exodus 34:11)—and substitutes Egyptians, Ammonites and Moabites (but not Edomites from Deut. 23:8), giving him a "master list" greater than any single list he may have consulted.

It could be argued that he was simply combining the sources that he had, but in that case why omit Hivites and Girgashites? Did Ezra really have such a precise bureau-of-census file on all these peoples that he knew which still existed, which were worth accounting for and which not?

In answering these questions we should be mindful of Colin Renfrew's observation[18] that when we simply draw dotted lines around pieces of ancient geography and assign the enclosed inhabitants a name beginning with a capital letter as though all of them were connected in some significant manner, we are creating artificial nations.[19] There were never any self-identifying Amorites or Canaanites; the first is merely an Akkadian term meaning "westerners," and the second refers to peoples living between the Jordan River and the Mediterranean. It is doubtful that any of these people regularly used either term to describe themselves.

Clearly, Ezra took Deut. 23:2-9 to be a prohibition of intermarriage, though it is not at all certain this was its original intent. Later rabbis (*Yebamoth* 8.3) trying to read it that way, probably in light of Ezra, were forced to what Shaye Cohen calls the "desperate exegesis"[20] of concluding that the inclusion of Ammonites and Moabites applied only to their menfolk. We will discuss this matter further in Chapter IV. For now we need to emphasize that Ezra's main interest in erecting barriers between his Judeans and others was not sexual, social or religious: it was political.

Judah had often gotten into trouble seeking political alliances with or protection from Egypt. (See Isaiah 31, for example.) Ezra, as a Persian government appointee, would be sensitive to the necessity of avoiding close relations with Egypt, the long-time rival of Mesopotamian powers for influence in Israel. That he did not specifically include Samaritans among those slated for divorce seems puzzling at first. Later rabbinic authorities ruled that Samaritans were not Jews because their ancestors had converted out of fear—Kings reports that the foreigners settled in Samaria had sent for a Levite because of a local plague of lions—and not "for the sake of heaven." But we have no reason to think that this judgment was in force in Ezra's time.

Adding Samaritans to the list of proscribed nations would have easily been seen as spurious, of course, but it is more likely that Israelite-Samaritan marriages were so common at all levels that to dissolve them would have produced social as well as economic chaos. As it was, it took three months to work through the short list of families included in Ezra 10.

It is with Ammon and Moab that we should be initially concerned. Why did Ezra include them in his list of prohibited unions? Genesis 19, which provides a legal basis for the proscription of (all of) Ammon and Moab, is an elaborate and well-known story that acknowledges both groups as blood-relatives of Abraham through his nephew, Lot, hence relatives of his descendants as well. We'll have more to say about their earlier history and relations with Israelite groups in Chapter X. In Ezra's time, however, there was a more relevant reason to exclude them, or at least the Ammonites, from any membership in the Jewish community.

The fall of the Temple and the death of King Zedekiah in 586 b.c.e. had not been the last gasp of Judean autonomy. The Babylonian conquerors had found a prominent man, Gedaliah (ben Ahikam ben Shaphan), who agreed to govern Judah as a Babylonian agent. He was, however, assassinated only four years later in a plot apparently backed by one King Baalis of Ammon.[21] Whether Baalis opposed Gedaliah's pro-Babylonian policies, had his own puppet in mind or wanted to rule Judah himself, we don't know.

One hundred and fifty years later, motives wouldn't matter. Ezra found it convenient to exclude all Ammonites from the lists of those eligible to marry Jews, and for good reason. (Moabites may have been included because of their association with Ammon in Gen. 19 or for the Baal Peor incident. Note that the tradition expressed in Sifre, Deut. 252 is harder on Ammon than on Edom and Egypt.)

The Ammonite Tobiah, or one of the Tobiads, was married to a daughter of the returning priestly family of Shechaniah (Shabaniah). This gave Tobiah some needed leverage—needed because Ezra

2:60 indicates that Tobiah's family could not prove they were Israelite—among the Judeans, whom he no doubt wished to govern or to incorporate into his own Transjordanian kingdom. Herein hangs a tale if we can unravel it.

In the first thousand years of Israelite history, it was more likely for Jewish men than for Jewish women[22] to "marry out." Why? A significant number of men, we think, were already engaged in the international caravan trade in Patriarchal times. When we couple this with the practice of having wives at every terminus,[23] the likelihood of intermarriage during Israel's formative period increases dramatically. Also, as Ezra must have known, Deut. 21:10ff. contains instructions for the treatment of foreign captives whom Israelite men took as wives. This is the situation that he set about terminating.

Ezra 10:17 zeroes in on "the men who had brought home foreign women," (NJPS) among whom were some women who had borne children. The text then goes on for twenty-five verses listing names and ends abruptly with 10:44: "All these of priestly families who were found to have brought foreign women..." The fact that the text breaks off here without a real conclusion is some mark of its authenticity but it creates difficulties in understanding what it was Ezra sought to accomplish or whether he was able to accomplish it.[24]

It largely depends upon how one reads 9:1-2. We usually read:

The people of the land (1) and the priests (2) and the Levites (3) have not separated themselves from the peoples of the land...They have taken their daughters as wives for themselves...it is the officers and prefects who have taken the lead in this trespass. (NJPS)

Before Ezra's time, and perhaps later, the phrase "people of the land" denoted those belonging to the upper classes. We now tend to equate it with Greek *hoi polloi*, "the masses," because that's what it came to mean by Jesus' time. We suggest reading (9:1-2) thus:[25] "The *leading* people of the land, *that is*, the priests and the Levites..." If men of the leading classes had foreign wives, we might assume that intermarriage permeated Israelite society from top to bottom, and that that was Ezra's concern. On the other hand, upper classes tend to be more cosmopolitan, lower classes more conservative, so it is not at all certain how widespread intermarriage was.[26]

Alternatively, we might posit that he meant to create a three-tier "system" that was strictest on high priestly families, less strict with ordinary priests and fairly loose as regards everyday Israelites. Talmon suggests[27] that Ezra's community, the more than 40,000 returnees from Babylon, had maintained a greater cohesion in Exile then had those Jews left in Israel, hence, prohibiting intermarriage would only ratify what their practice had been. But does this square with the information that men from the exilic community had brought home foreign wives? And if Ezra were down-the-line opposed to all intermarriage, one wonders how much of the resident population would have supported him.

In fact, we don't know how integrated into Persian society the Jews had become in the six or so generations between 586 b.c.e and Ezra's return. There is, after all, the intriguing story of Esther, married to a Persian king, which is set in this very period. But Esther is a fiction, if that counts for anything—we deal with it in the next chapter. That we have used Ezra and Nehemiah for so many centuries to impede if not prohibit all intermarriages which do not include conversion of the non-Jewish partner reflects a more "modern" Jewish agenda.

6. Terms of Defilement[28]

Using a welter of biblical texts dealing with gentiles, rabbis long argued about whether foreigners were ritually impure or morally impure. Ritual impurity meant X, moral impurity meant Y. In either case, however, gentiles could renounce what had caused the impurity and consequently attach themselves to a Jewish community.

Ezra faced a situation in which "outsiders" who had converted—if such a thing were possible—or intermarried, or both, were allied with prominent Judean families and competing for leadership/governance of the entire country. Ezra's solution was the then-novel one that gentiles were genealogically impure, that is, impure by reason of being gentiles. And being gentile they could not be allowed to profane the "holy seed" of Israel.

We can better understand Ezra's position by comparing what happened in the Catholic Church in Spain after the arrival there of the Holy Office (popularly known as the Spanish Inquisition) in 1483. During the previous century some Jews, responding to bloody riots that began in Seville in 1391, had at least formally converted to Catholicism to avoid further persecution. Under the threat of expulsion, which finally took place in 1492, many more did so.

Many of these "New Christians" became influential in the Church, including ecclesiastical circles. This dismayed some Old Christians who resented them as parvenus and suspected that their conversions were only skin deep. One can understand the anxiety—or envy—of old line Spanish Catholics feeling that their church was in danger of being taken over or polluted by double-dealing New Christians. The Holy Office was invited to Spain not to harass Jews, but to make sure the New Christians were not secretly retaining and practicing their Judaism. The presence of such people, referred to by the disrespectful term Marranos ("swine"), must also have cast a pall over those Jews whose conversions had been sincere. And their children? Even today in some Spanish circles, *limpieza de sangre,* which equates to a desire to prove that one never had any Jewish ancestors, no matter how remote, remains important.

If Hayes is correct, Ezra and Nehemiah sought to close avenues into Israel that had been open since its very origin. The beauty of a doctrine of genealogical impurity was that it could not be appealed from, was not cancelled by conversion, and worked as well whether the gentile was male or female. Conversely, it is monstrous. Moreover, it flies in the face of what we know about Israel's origins and its own traditions.

Gen. Rabbah 39:14 commenting on Gen. 12:5, "the souls they had made at Harran," credits Abraham, already, with converting gentiles, though one has to ask what exactly there would have been for gentiles to convert to. What Scriptures did Ezra consult before making his rules and what commentaries did he discreetly overlook? If conversion had been an option, Ezra should have specifically commented as to why that solution to the problem wasn't acceptable.

More than fifty years ago, that is to say before our Civil Rights movement had peaked, Salo Baron called what Ezra proposed "racialism,"[29] but even if that epithet had been available to Ezra's detractors, it would not have made much of an impression on him. Desperate times call for desperate measures. In the following chapters, we hope to show why it was a good thing that they did not finally succeed.

7. Nehemiah

Nehemiah was also a Persian government official. His book identifies him as cupbearer to king Artaxerxes—but which king Artaxerxes? There are at least three by that name, hence the difficulty in deciding when, exactly, Nehemiah arrived. Scholars long held that Nehemiah preceded Ezra to Jerusalem, though in recent years the tide of scholarship has turned the other way. It makes the most sense to put both men's return to Israel in the reign of Artaxerxes Longimanus (465 - 425 b.c.e) or Artaxerxes II (404 -359 b.c.e.). Happily for our study, it really doesn't matter who was king or who came first, because the problem we're addressing, intermarriage, didn't change much in the period before the coming of Alexander the Great.

In any case, "cupbearer" was a very responsible position. It was the cupbearer who drank first from the king's cup to preclude the monarch from being poisoned. Given this physical nearness to the king, we have to wonder how Nehemiah and his people mixed socially while still in Persia. Were they totally free to intermarry, or, like Esther, only free if they concealed their Jewishness?

Unfortunately, Nehemiah's book is mainly concerned with his efforts to rebuild the walls of Jerusalem and his opponents' endeavors to prevent it, so we do not know much about other aspects of his governorship beyond the reconstruction and the political rivalries it involved. Among these rivals for control we find one Geshem the Arabian, about whom almost nothing is preserved, the aforementioned Tobiah, and Sanballat the Horonite. (Here again, "Horonite" is only a geographic locator, and three separate locations for it—including one across the river—have been suggested.)

One of Sanballat's daughters was married to Joiada, son of Eliashib the High Priest. Nehemiah 13:28 reports, "I drove him [Joiada] away from me." (NJPS) One wonders what effect this would have had on the boy's father, but even more why that particular marriage had taken place at all.

It appears to us that Eliashib must have been trying to remain on good terms with both sides, even all sides, marrying his children into influential families across the board so that he would not forfeit his position if he "backed the wrong horse" in the turbulent race for control of the city and of Judea.

This had happened to the priestly family of one Abiathar during the difficult times that attended David's succession. The family had wisely refrained from backing Absalom, but then threw its support to Adonijah. When, instead, Solomon succeeded David, he disenfranchised the family from the priesthood. Eliashib, apparently, knew his history.

Nehemiah 13:23, however, is unequivocal in his opposition to intermarriage with Ammonites, Moabites and Ashdodites (!) and is followed by a criticism of Solomon for breaking the rule. (See I Kings 11:1-3) It is to this chapter, too, that we owe the knowledge that children of Jews who had married Ashdodite women were growing up speaking Ashdodite and not Hebrew, another indication that some children at least took the culture if not also the religion of their mothers.

The clever reading by Rashi [Rabbi Solomon ben Isaac, 1040 -1105 c.e.] of Deut. 7:3, which gives us the legal basis for declaring that the religion of the child follows that of the mother, must have been either unknown or unacceptable to Ezra and Nehemiah.[22] After all, if that were the case, Jewish women who married out would be creating new Jews with every birth, so intermarriage of that sort should have been encouraged.

Conversely, what would have been the status of the children of all those Midianite virgins mentioned above? This seeming dilemma will be addressed when we discuss Israel's adoption of a matrilineal principle in the transmission of religion.

8. To What End?

Admittedly, there were those in Israel—the prophets—who had been pushing exclusivism in religion for more than four hundred years before Ezra's time, but they had made little headway. As we shall see, the reason for this was that for most of Israel's history the religion of women simply didn't appear as a threat to the dominant practice. It was, after all, a religion that centered upon successful childbirth and growth, hence, a goal that their husbands also had. If women had extra deities to whom they could appeal for help, so much the better.

We tend to back-read the modern difficulties involved in intermarriage, namely, stiff opposition from both sides, into biblical times. We presume that if intermarriage was rare and frowned upon until quite recently,[31] how much more so back then? The logic is defensible, but the facts that we have don't support it.

Consider this: even before Israel came into being, Ancient Near Eastern societies were tribal (as many of them still are). Protection or expansion of tribal territories depended upon maintaining tribal territories: on how many fighters a tribe could field and how well it succeeded in making alliances with other tribes, especially those that could threaten hostile neighbors from another quarter.

One way to cement alliances was by marriage between members of two groups, making them "family." In all of this, religion would have played little part. That is, neither side would have cared that the other had a different religion, even if they recognized the other as different.

The aforementioned Sanballat I, governor of Samaria, whose name means "Sin [the Moon God] has given life," had two sons with Hebrew theophoric names, indicating either that they were children of a Judean/Jewish wife or that Sanballat's family were polytheist. The first explanation, however, seems more likely. If Sanballat was a polytheist, how could Eliashib—the high priest who cooperated with Nehemiah in rebuilding Jerusalem's wall (3:1)— have married one of his sons to one of Sanballat's daughters?

Ezra's and Nehemiah's plea probably had only a limited effect in its own time. After all, Ezra 10 only lists members of ten families. Surely intermarriage must have been more widespread than that. Hayes says[32] an attempt to generalize the prohibition to include women and to apply it to all Israelites would be a "novel argument." Novel, indeed: it would be revolutionary. Ezra created a legal fiction in order to forward his particular political agenda. We also note that a blanket prohibition of intermarriage did not become normative in Judaism, another support for the proposition that Ezra's situation was unique.

At this point, the reader may be wondering why Ezra and Nehemiah proposed such a drastic solution to the intermarriage problem. Why not simply insist that the foreign women convert? Rabbi Joel Rembaum, writing in the new Conservative *Etz Hayim* Torah commentary says, "Since the option to convert the women did not exist at that time, removal from society was the only resolution."[33]

This assertion is congruent with the views of most modern scholarship, which acknowledges that conversion to Judaism was not an option until well after Ezra's time; no one would have known what such a thing was, or thought it necessary if they did, until much later. Still, Jewish tradition maintains that Asenath, the Egyptian wife of Joseph, converted *before* Torah was given to Moses, that Rahab the prostitute converted, that Ruth the Moabitess converted without benefit of clergy—still some centuries before Ezra's time.[34] Since Ezra was a priest and presumably had more authority to convert than Naomi, Ruth's mother-in-law had, we would have to inquire of tradition just when did the "option" to convert expire?

Clearly, those who follow a traditional line are too narrowly focused. The opposition to intermarriage manifested by Nehemiah and Ezra had less to do with religion or the actual unions of men and women and more to do with a desire to exert political control over Judea. Official opposition to intermarriage was a means to this end, but it was late in coming and does not seem to have become a permanent feature of Jewish law or practice.

To get a better handle on this we turn to two of the most famous women in Israel, the only two who have canonical books named for them: Ruth and Esther.

Notes to Chapter II

1. See Stanley N. Rosenbaum, "A Letter from Rabbi Gamaliel ben Gamaliel," in Beatrice Bruteau, ed., *Jesus Through Jewish Eyes*, Maryknoll, NY: Orbis, 2002.

2. The use of a capital letter here is a literary convenience, hallowed by time and tradition, but not dictated by history, as we shall see in ch. IV:1.

3. Saadia Gaon (892-942) in Nahum N. Glatzer, *The Judaic Tradition* (Springfield NJ: Behrman House, 1961, 1969), 318-21.

4. Donald B. Redford, *Egypt, Canaan and Israel in Ancient Times* (Princeton: Princeton University Press, 1992) 257ff. Redford represents those scholars, sometimes called "minimalists," who are most reluctant to accept anything the Bible says as fact without outside corroboration.

5. See Shemaryu Talmon, "Daniel," in *The Literary Guide to the Bible,* Robert Alter and Frank Kermode, eds. (Cambridge MA: Belknap Press of Harvard University Press, 1990) 357.

6. It is hard to decide when the term "Jewish" becomes appropriate. It derives from Judah, the kingdom named for Jacob's fourth son, but should be reserved to describe inhabitants of that kingdom only after the fall of the Temple and perhaps not until the return of the first exiles ca. 539 b.c.e.

The term "Jewish" is not an appropriate designation for inhabitants of David and Solomon's kingdom until after 722 b.c.e. when the kingdom of Israel, which had broken the Israelite confederacy, fell and only the kingdom of Judah remained independent.

7. Note, too, the curious addition at the end of the Book of Numbers which dictates that women who have no brothers and

hence are in line to inherit their father's property must marry men from within their own tribe so that the family property does not become alienated. We might ask why, if all the tribes were part of Jacob's house, such a thing mattered, but it did. A lot.

8. If scholars are correct, the Torah—the first five books of the Bible—was canonized about 550 b.c.e., the Prophets a century later. Hence, when Jesus speaks of the "Law and the Prophets," it is because the third section, the Writings, had not yet been added to the canon. The last part of Scripture was canonized ca. 100 c.e.

9. Michael Fishbane, *Biblical Interpretation in Ancient Israel* (Oxford: OUP, 1985) 123, cited in Hayes, *Gentile Impurities and Jewish Identities* (NY: OUP, 2002), 33. The *Encyclopedia Judaica* proclaims (7:410) that in the "later Second Temple period" Ezra's prohibitions were extended to include all nations, but gives no references to support its contention or even a clear idea of when during this 600-year period it happened.

10. Tikvah Frymer-Kensky counts Malachi as opposed to Ezra's demand for divorce and Chronicles as being more tolerant of intermarriage. *Reading the Women of the Bible* (NY: Schocken, 2002), 290-292, 340.

11. See, for instance, Saul Levin, *The Father of Joshua/Jesus* (Binghamton NY: State University of New York, 1978) 85. As presently read, the passage is a ringing charge that drowns out the fact that, at the time, ninety-nine percent of Israelites no longer lived in tents. Tradition could counter-argue that the phrase is meant metaphorically, but for centuries commentators were quite content with the literal understanding. Salo Baron, *Social and Religious History of the Jews* (NY: Columbia University Press), 1951 VII: 1XX. One might read Malachi, a contemporary of Ezra, as opposing divorce, but it is more likely

that he is using a metaphor à la Hosea to describe, and criticize, Israel's "divorcing" God to marry other gods.

12. EJ *mamzer* 11:840. An Aramaic cognate from the root /m-z-r means "bad eggs," which would be wildly appropriate here, though meant figuratively.

13. Joseph Naveh, "Graffiti and Dedications," BASOR 235 [1979] 27-30) translates the inscription: "May Uryahu be blessed by Yahweh my guardian and by his Asherah.

14. Josephus reports that people in Jerusalem attributed Herod's defeat not to his divorcing his wife, but for his killing of John the Baptist. Since the war took place in 35 c.e., one wonders if this suggests John actually outlived his more famous cousin, Jesus, despite what the Gospels say.

15. Some moderns think it was entirely composed by Judeans during this late period and reflects nothing of earlier reality. Bis Shaye J. D. Cohen, *Beginnings,* 248f.

16. For more on who the Benjaminites were, see chap. XX Choosing Up Sides

17. Note the recent dramatic falling off of Roman Catholic Church revenues in the United States due to popular disaffection with the Church's concealment of the acts of predatory priests.

18. Renfrew, *Archeology,* 211ff.

19. This could certainly be seen in Iraq even before the U.S. invasion of that country. Tribalism remains the biggest single obstacle to the creation of the nation-state.

20. Beginnings, 249.

21. See, for example, Robert Deutsch, "Seal of *Baalis* Surfaces: Ammonite King Plotted Murder of Judahite Governor," *BAR* 25 (Mar-Apr 1999): 44-49, 66. More in VIII. Choosing Up Sides

22. This would parallel what and be supported by the DNA evidence of people like the Lemba. Of course, here we're talking about refugees

23. Rosenbaum, *UBI*; noted, too, by EJ ad loc. KETUBBAH 17. Which has sparked a big, big discussion—e.g. in Jacob Milgrom, *Leviticus, a Book of Ritual and Ethics: A Continental Commentary* (Minneapolis: Fortress Press, 2004) 194f; Hayes, *Gentile Impurities, passim;* Fishbane, *Biblical Interpretation,* 114-123.

24. Hayes, however, argues that Ezra was taking the unprecedented step of democratizing the ban, extending it to all Israelites regardless of class or position, *ibid.,* 10ff. If that is the case, "prohibition prohibits previous practice;" ordinary Israelites must also have been intermarried. The relatively small size of Israelite ethnic units, for lack of a better term, might have necessitated a certain amount of intermarriage.

25. Reading *vav* as explicative, not conjunctive.

26. In 1965, Amram Blau, a leader of Jerusalem's ultra Orthodox Neturei Karta ("Guardians of the City") sect, was severely criticized by some of his own followers for marrying a convert after his first wife died.

27. ShemaryahuTalmon in King, Cult and Calendar in Ancient Israel: Collected Studies (Ancient Near East) (Lieden: Brill Academic Publishers, 1997), 599.

28. Christine Hayes' term; see Chapter XIII.

29. Baron, Social and Religious History of the Jews, I;147

30. Hebrew pronoun reference is notoriously ambiguous. Thus the phrase, "they will lead the children astray," which we think refers to all foreigners with whom marriage is contracted, is read by Rashi (7:3 ad loc.) to apply to the immediately preceding noun, foreign daughters. Cohen, *Beginnings,* traces this narrower interpretation back nearly 1000 years earlier. That's still centuries after Ezra.

31. Before 1960, some 5.9 percent of Jews married non-Jews; that rate tripled in the following five years. **Keren R.**

McGinity, *Still Jewish: A History of Women and Intermarriage in America* (NY: NYUP, 2009), 66.

32. Gentile Impurities, 10.

33. *Etz Hayim, Torah and Commentary*, David L. Lieber, ed., (Phila: Jewish Publication Society, 2001), 1378.

34. See Chapter III for Ruth's story, Chapter XII for Rahab's.

Chapter III. Guess Who's Coming to Purim?

"May you be like Ruth and like Esther." – Fiddler on the Roof

1. Ruth

That Ezra's drastic measure for protecting Israel was a one-off event, found neither before nor long after his and Nehemiah's time, might be inferred from considering the Bible's two arguably most famous females: Ruth and Esther, heroines of the only two canonical books named for and starring women. Two virtuous women, one gentile, one Jewish and… both are intermarried!

Ruth's story purports to come from the period of Judges, some seven hundred and more years before Ezra; more likely it comes from the ninth pre-Christian century, but still well before Ezra's time. He does not mention it—of course, it wasn't canonical in his time—but that's just as well. How could he know Ruth and still maintain his position against intermarriage?

Esther is post-Ezra by at least a hundred years. Their stories are so famous, each in its own way, that it may seem something of a disservice to consider them jointly. Yet while recognizing the divergent lessons that each story is designed to teach, we look here at both stories in the light of one thing not generally noted which they share, intermarriage. That is emphatically not the point of either story and, indeed, the song quoted above goes on to express the hope that Jewish daughters be kept from "the stranger's ways" without pausing to note—in what would be a supreme irony—that Ruth was a stranger herself or that Esther married one.

One may do this in fiction and, like *Fiddler on the Roof,* the story of Esther is fictional, that of Ruth probably so.[1] This actually works to our advantage. If they were simply true tales of two women in exceptional circumstances, they might not be as useful for positing principles of behavior or social usage. It is the latter that we are investigating. To do this, we look for incidental details that can give us insights into social processes, up to and including marriage/intermarriage, that the authors of the books thought acceptable.

For example, we note that Ruth meets the Israelite family of Elimelech, whom she joins because that family has crossed the Jordan River into her country, Moab. According to the book, famine drove them, but Moab is higher and drier than most of the land west of the river. If the Elimelechs wanted relief, they'd have probably found it closer to home by going west, not east. We therefore assume they may have had a reason more compelling than just a desire to find greener pastures, or that they didn't need a reason.

It is likely that the river constituted no real barrier to the movement of peoples in the ninth century, the more so if the Moabites had any stories, as the Bible does, that showed a blood-kinship between them. Taking the Bible (Gen. 19) at its word, the Moabites were related to Israel through Lot, Abraham's nephew. If people in Ruth's time, whenever that was, regarded Moabites as relatives, they would hardly have recognized the Jordan as more than a territorial marker, not a border in any formal sense. When her husband dies, Ruth returns with Naomi, her husband's mother, to the west side of Jordan.

Tradition reports that the two sons of Elimelech, Mahlon and Chilion, married Moabites only after their father died because he disapproved of intermarriage, but the Bible says nothing of the sort. In fact, it indicates that the marriages took place before Elimelech's death. What is important to us here, however, is that the tradition cannot claim that there were *statutes* prohibiting intermarriage because no such strictures existed. Of course, marriage is another way of establishing kinship.

It's hard to prove that the Book of Ruth is a fiction, but two things about it point that way. First, it begins with "In the days of the Judges," rather than telling us which judge(s) was (were) ostensibly judging in Israel.[2] This is not altogether surprising, since the book probably comes from the period of Elisha[3]—some two hundred years after the period of Judges. However, when we compare this beginning to the careful identification of the times of Israelite and Judean kings elsewhere in Scripture, we have to wonder why this seemingly knowable detail is absent.

According to the formalist-folklorist school of Vladimir Propp,[4] Ruth "follows a pattern common to folktales and as such cannot be a reliable source for information of a legal or historical nature." In other words, neither legal nor historical details are at the heart of such stories; "exemplary behavior" is.

Since Ruth was Moabite, her book comes, necessarily it would seem, well before any prohibition of marriage with Moabites. But how can this be? Genesis 19, with its story of Moab's illegitimacy, and Deuteronomy 7:3, with its blanket prohibition on intermarriage, are Torah, given to Moses on Sinai, hence before Ruth. Just as Ezra doesn't mention Ruth, we might ask why Ruth doesn't mention Torah? What is the chronological relationship of Ruth to Deut. 7:3 and to Gen. 19?

The Talmud[5] indirectly acknowledges the inherent contradiction here by cleverly excluding foreign women from the Bible's prohibition of intermarriages. But of course it had to, unless the transmitters of tradition wished to suppress known facts. Another example: Rehoboam, the son and successor of Solomon, had an Ammonite mother.

The Talmud might better argue that the prohibition of intermarriage was sometimes honored in the breach, especially in regard to women, but this would be no light matter. If children follow the religion of the mother, as Judaism later ruled, it would be better to argue that non-Jewish men were more welcome in the community than non-Jewish women were. So what is Ruth, the book, about?

One of the things it's about is women's desire to have children, but this would not differentiate Ruth, the person, from other Ancient Near Eastern women. It's also about the non-alienation of property, which was very important to agriculturalists. If the book is, say, post-Exilic but pre-Ezra (586 - 450 b.c.e.), locating its story in the pre-monarchic period might have had polemic purposes. That is, it might be meant as a plea to contemporary Israelites not to reject automatically what foreign people and, by extension, their cultures, had to offer.

2. Conversion in the Iron Age?

"He for God alone,
She for God in him." – John Milton, Paradise Lost

Beginning with Abraham, traditional Judaism assumes that a whole lot of people, especially foreign women who married Israelites, converted to Judaism and that only grandson Esau went the other way. The *Encyclopedia Judaica* (1971), however, and most modern scholars begin their discussions of the conversion process only with the Tannaitic period, that is, about the time Jesus would have been of bar mitzvah age, because before that time there was no conversion in any meaningful sense. Using the word "conversion" at any earlier time might be something of an anachronism. Whatever Abraham's new religion was, it probably bore little resemblance to the Judaisms of a thousand years later. We use a plural here to indicate how variegated Judaism had become by then.[6] But it would be wrong to think of it as essentially monochromatic before then.

Nonetheless, Ruth is honored as the "first convert," and for uncounted years she has been the popular poster-child for conversion to Judaism. That is unfortunate for two reasons. For one thing, we have to ask what exactly there was to convert to in this period? For another, what mechanisms existed for accepting converts?

It was just before Jesus's time that Rabbi Hillel told a would-be proselyte that to be Jewish all one had to do was live Jewishly, or, as Hillel put it, "What is hateful to you, don't do to others."[7] Since no Jewish woman would be ordained for another two thousand years, it's doubtful that Naomi, Ruth's former mother-in-law, enjoyed the same rabbinic authority as Hillel (but see below for a tradition-based empowerment of Naomi).

The answer to the second question we began with is that, of course, there were no community organs or standards for accepting converts, both of which are very modern notions, in the period of the Judges. It might be more correct to say Ruth is the first self-convert whose name we know,[8] but even that isn't entirely accurate.

In a sense, what Ruth offered to do—though probably neither she nor the woman to whom she first turned probably had a clear idea of it—was "to live Jewishly." After all, Judges ends with the ominous observation, "In those days there was no king so every man did what was right in his own eyes." (Judges 21:25) If there was no state, then there could hardly be a state religion. Hardly a situation in which conversion makes much sense.

At what point in Israelite history did conversion to Judaism become possible? As we noted above, most books on the subject begin around 10 c.e. But this brings up another question: at what point was there a (uniform) Judaism to which to convert? And if there wasn't, would different groups accept each other's converts as legitimate, in the manner of states in the U.S. honoring each other's laws? It's doubtful.

Consider: Jewish Orthodoxy in Israel today does not accept as converts any who were converted by the non-Halachic branches of Judaism. Indeed, it scarcely recognizes two newer branches, Reconstructionism and Reform, at all. If, then, a person converted to whatever Northern Israelites were practicing after or even before the kingdom split, let alone before any Israelite state ever formed, would such a person be recognized as "Jewish" all over? After 722 b.c.e., the answer would probably be an emphatic "No," because the Southerners viewed the subsequent Northern population as too mixed with peoples who had been forcibly settled there by their Assyrian conquerors to qualify.

However, we're not really talking about conversion here; rather, we are talking about one person leaving her own people and adhering to another.[8] Ruth puts her change in a most moving way, including "your people will be my people, your god, my god. Where you die I will die and there will I be buried." This last is perhaps the most important thing she could say, because most people believed that the successful transit of their spirit or soul to its eternal home depended upon being buried in their ancestral grounds. (Recall that Abraham felt compelled to buy his own field in which he could bury Sarah and not rely upon the kindness of strangers.)

Here Jewish tradition engages in a flight of fancy, retrojecting into history what would almost certainly not be the case for another thousand years at least: namely, the empowerment of Naomi to accept Ruth as a convert. It is worth quoting the traditional account:

> The rabbis of the Midrash[10] mark Ruth's statement to Naomi, "Entreat me not to leave thee," as "I intend to be converted, but I prefer it not be through another but through you." When Naomi heard this, she began to set forth the rules of conversion, saying also, "My child, it is not the practice for the daughters of Israel to go to the theaters and circuses of heathens." Ruth replied, "Whither thou goest, I will go." Naomi continued, "It is not the practice for daughters of Israel to dwell in a house that has no mezuzah." Ruth replied, "Where thou lodgest, I will lodge." (Ruth Rabbah 2:4)

Clearly, this exposition serves the purposes of its writers more than it does that of the historian examining "conversion" in the time of Judges. The same source raises the ante by identifying Ruth as daughter of Eglon, king of Moab, "proving" that Judaism in the period of the Judges was so recognizably superior to the Chemosh religion of the Moabites that a Moabite king would not stand in the way of his daughter's making such a career move.

Conversion to Judaism was very much a product of the Diaspora, the period during which more and more Jews lived outside of Israel until, at last, the majority of them did so. The Midrashim are roughly contemporary with the Mishnah, that rabbinic interpretation of the Bible compiled between about 200 b.c.e. and 200 c.e. Rabbinic writings strongly suggest that Jews were scattered throughout the world precisely in order to bring pagans to Judaism: in other words, to convert them.

There is an equally strong implication that, until long after the Exile, there really was no pressure on non-Israelites to convert.[11] Why should there have been? In a polytheistic culture one might add another god[12] to those already worshipped, but substituting one for all the rest would not have been required. "Strangers" were able to live and practice as Jews without much difficulty, and without converting, until the fourth century when Christian law forbade them.[13] These people were the *gerim,* "sojourners," whom we will have met already in Abraham's time.

Ca. 200 b.c.e. Is where we put the beginning of the original Sanhedrin, that gathering of leaders who codified and made laws concerning the community. Tradition places its start about 300 b.c.e. Either way, serious efforts at proselytism began well after the Exile. We also need to consider that accounts of early converts might have been invented by Pharisaic Judaism after it recognized emerging gentile Christianity as a serious threat.

One of the problems spawned like a long-dormant locust in this gray area is that of contemporary people who claim to be Jews simply on their own sayso.[14] To the best of our knowledge, no one claims to be Roman Catholic, Methodist or Presbyterian simply by deciding that's what they want to be. Such claims would be laughed at. But in Judaism the claim retains a shadowy half-life precisely because it has always been so difficult to establish criteria determining just who is and who is not a Jew.

Many modern Jews use Buddhist meditation techniques, but Buddhism is not an exclusivist religion in the Western sense, so there is no inherent contradiction here. On the other hand, we note the absurd claim of so-called Jews for Jesus. One cannot be a Liberal-Fundamentalist; some choices do exclude others.

Conversely, Jews who lived among others, as most eventually did during the long centuries of Diaspora, often adopted the names, language and culture, if not the religion, of those among whom they lived.[15] The outstanding example of this, of course, is Esther.

3. Esther and Social Integration

"Be a Jew at home and a man in public." – Moses Mendelssohn
(1729 -1786)

Esther is a late book, dating from as long as six hundred years after
Ruth was written and almost a thousand after the period Ruth
represents. Hence, the mores and customs Esther represents are
those of the Persian (539 -333 b.c.e.) or even the Greco-Roman
period (begins in earnest in 333 b.c.e. with the invasion of Asia by
Alexander the Great). Therefore, Esther cannot be expected to
mirror the culture of pre-monarchic Israel. Perhaps it is for this
reason that Frymer-Kensky has no sustained discussion of this, the
greatest of Israel's heroines.

Esther is mentioned by Frymer-Kensky only in passing, in a
discussion of "the many stories of marriages to outsiders [that]
dramatize the boundary issues that marriage presents."[16] This is
scant recognition of one whose heroic intervention to save her
people from extermination was even more critical than Ruth's
marriage to Boaz.

Of course, Esther is a fiction; it has to be. As Herodotus, who is
contemporary with Nehemiah—and hence with the setting of
Esther—tells us,[17] the queen of Persia was selected from the
daughters of seven highly qualified Persian families. To imply, as
the Book of Esther does, that the queen was chosen as a result of a
beauty contest and that, further, her background remained
unchecked, is absurd. Dressing herself with a gentile name would
hardly be sufficient.

In fact, Esther's Jewish name, Hadassah, comes only once in the
book (2:7). This leads us to suspect that it was added in later by
tradents who felt uncomfortable that our heroine be known by any

foreign name, let alone the name of a foreign goddess.[18] Just having a gentile name is some indication of Jewish integration into Persian society. Of course it is just possible that, like the German Reform Jews of the nineteenth century, Esther/Hadassah had two names so she could "be a Jew at home and a man in public" as Moses Mendelssohn would later counsel.[19]

Does Esther's double name acknowledge that, no matter where Jews live, there may one day arise a "Pharaoh that knows not Joseph" so that being able to "pass" becomes a life and death matter? That could hardly have been the case anywhere that Jews lived in the fourth century, especially after the coming of Alexander. However that may be, are we to assume that after the nuptials she regularly snuck off to synagogue services in disguise while her husband, the king, was occupied elsewhere? Such a wife should have been required to "convert" or, at least, to recognize and worship the local gods—as Daniel was, and refused to do.

(We should note here that, for all its pretense of antiquity, modern scholars have concluded that Daniel is a fiction that was composed about 164 b.c.e., making it the youngest of all the canonical books.)

However, as we have noted before, fiction is often more useful than what purports to be history because fiction mirrors the circumstances of the community in and for which it is written. So let's look briefly at the story's sequence of events. At the behest of her Uncle Mordecai, Esther puts herself forward as a contestant in a beauty pageant, the aim of which is to replace the disgraced Persian queen, Vashti. She does not enter the contest with the idea of intervening on behalf of her people; no threat to them has yet been issued. That being so, Uncle Mordecai must not have been terribly opposed to intermarriage, else he would have forbidden his niece the opportunity.

Reading between the lines, then, the Book of Esther tells several stories. One of them is a kind of rehabilitation for the Benjaminites, the tribe of Esther and her uncle Mordecai. Aggadah makes of her a descendant of Saul. (*Meg.* 13a) As we will see, the Benjaminites had been rather on the outs with the rest of Israel since Saul's defeat and death and the displacement of his line. That is of some consequence to the present work because it supports the idea that, after the return from Exile, the collectors of Scripture tried consciously to re-invent the notion of the essential nationhood of the Israelite tribes.

But wait. What were Mordecai and Esther doing in Persia in the first place? No matter which King Ahasuerus is intended, the period in question falls well after the return from Exile that was inaugurated by Cyrus of Persia; Esther and her uncle necessarily came from a family that did not choose to return.

In his twenty-ninth chapter, Jeremiah had written to the original exiles to hold on and to build lives for themselves because, he said, the Exile would be only as long as one person's lifetime. In this he was almost uncannily correct. The rededication of the Second Temple began almost exactly seventy years after the destruction of the first. The first Ahasuerus (Artaxerxes), however, did not begin his reign until fifty years later, so Mordecai's family would have had plenty of time in which to return had they so chosen. That they did not do so implies that they had found a comfortable existence in Persia—not unlike American Jews who remained in America after the creation of the modern State of Israel 1948.

Ezra contains a list of people who did come back from Exile. Counting slaves, they numbered only about fifty thousand, far fewer than the number who presumably went into Exile even without accounting for natural increase in the intervening period. Those who returned, then, were probably a minority of the whole and, as we know, the Babylonian community went on to become central in

Jewish life even before the destruction of the Second Temple. Did they mix with Persians? How much and how soon?

We may get some clue to the answers to these questions when we add in the experience of the Greeks who overran Persia in the fourth century. In the wake of Alexander's conquest of the Near East, "mixed marriages between soldiers and local women constituted a basic fact in the life of these new settlements, a fact often mentioned in various sources."[20] Of course, soldiers on the road for years without their families are one thing, entire communities could be quite another. How many of the local women were Jewish? We don't know, but the story of Esther opens a door for us.

Initially, perhaps, intermarriage would not have been common in the Exilic community. This is of a piece with Jeremiah's advice (above) to settle down in the place to which they had been brought, to build houses, raise families and work for the welfare of their new rulers. But after Cyrus allowed Jews to return, many nonetheless stayed and established lives for themselves in Persia. Did they then begin to marry local, that is to say foreign, women? This, of course, was exactly what Ezra found so objectionable. However, as we saw, he also had examples closer to home.

To be sure, Esther is not about intermarriage. She has to be and remain Jewish in order for the story to work, but in her case the *pshat*, the simple story line, gives way to *drash* —interpretation. The principle of behavior that is being taught here is that the welfare of the community is so important that an individual person, man or woman, can and perhaps should risk death in order to preserve it. We might say that Esther is an early literary example and precursor of the *Hofjude,* the "court Jew" who represented Jewish communities' interests and values at courts in the Middle Ages.[21] They were well placed to intervene on behalf of coreligionists, often taking on onerous tax burdens to keep their communities from being expelled.

Later Judaism evolved the doctrine that any commandment except those prohibiting murder, adultery and idol worship might be set aside to preserve life. Intermarriage was never in the same category as these. One might almost say that both stories, whether truth or fiction, make a case *for* intermarriage.

Esther: Because we do not know exactly when Esther was written, we don't know all the motives of its writers. If it comes from the Roman period (63 b.c.e. – 363 c.e.) it might be seen as a justification for intermarriage because, as we know, there was a good deal of intermarriage then, especially in places such as Alexandria in Egypt. This could have been a reaction to the harsh Hasmonean social restrictions of the immediately preceding period (164 b.c.e. - 63 b.c.e.)

Ruth: It is through her subsequent husband, Boaz, that Ruth becomes one of David's great-grandmothers. The Bible would not have thought about things in this way, perhaps, but without that sliver of Moabite genetic material, what would David have been? Probably just another singer, or a hired brigand, or maybe a college professor.

4. Guess Who's Coming to Purim?

Esther purports to come from the fifth pre-Christian century. It was probably not written until the second century b.c.e. or later and not included in the canon until about 250 years after that, that is, around 100 c.e. The collectors of Scripture argued about its inclusion because, they noted, it would be the only book in Scripture that did not mention the name of God.

We don't have the "minutes" of these discussions, but there may have been another reason as well. Esther makes a case for Jewish integration at all levels of gentile society. Why should she go by—and go down in history by—her gentile name, Esther, when she had the perfectly serviceable Jewish name Hadassah?

Esther invited the Jews' chief adversary, the wicked Haman, in for a dinner; of course, as queen, she would be expected to entertain. And no one knew, at the time, that she was Jewish. But there is also the barest hint, in Esther 9:27, that Jews grateful for being spared Haman's genocidal intentions invited their gentile neighbors in to help celebrate their ultimate deliverance at a festive meal. That meal might have been Passover, as Exodus 12:48 allows circumcised foreigners to share this meal. The context is one that implies Israel is at home, not in exile, but that shouldn't matter. Besides, inviting circumcised Persians in would have had the added advantage of showing the neighbors that Jews were loyal citizens and no danger to the host society. (Opening the door "for Elijah" at Passover also had this function during the Middle Ages—and how much earlier?)

The question that Esther poses for us, then, is this: how much social integration of Jews and gentiles does the story point to, either in the Persian period or earlier? For example, did Jews and gentiles ever eat together, and if so, under what circumstances? Here again, we must not be too greatly influenced by later Jewish law or custom. All of us are familiar with Jews who will not eat in any place or home that serves un-kosher food unless they can bring their own food with them—as Judith did when calling on Holofernes. But this seems to be later elaboration of texts, both biblical and non-canonical, that polemicize or can be made to support polemics against the practice.

Joseph's brothers did not initially eat with him in Egypt, though here the text seems to make it clear that this was an Egyptian choice, not because of any Jewish dietary restrictions. After all, the Joseph story precedes Moses and the giving of Torah in which these things were laid out.

Presumably Joseph's descendants were carrying his bones to the Promised Land when they stopped off, as it were, in Shittim (located very close to the place later fortified by Ammonite Tobiads) and participated in eating of a sacrificial meal offered by "daughters of Moab." This is the prelude to Pinchas' killing of Zimri and Cozbi, the Israelite man and Moabite woman whom he found together, which the Bible credits with stopping a plague then in progress—the main didactic point for the text's writer.

But consider: Israelites and Moabites eating together? Not only that, but eating food that was dedicated to Moabite gods? This indicates that all Israelites did not uniformly subscribe to monotheism immediately after Sinai. Additional support for this contention can be found in the book of Joshua, at the end of the so-called Period of Wanderings, when Moses's successor exhorts his brethren to choose between God and the gods of their ancestors. It is hard to imagine these once-and-future Israelites declining to dine with each other on the grounds that they had different gods. But let's not lose track of the fact that this incident comes two hundred years after tradition tells us Torah was handed down at Sinai.

Continuing religious pluralism within Israel should not surprise us. The stories of Ruth and Esther, because they are fictions, seem to countenance some intermarriage precisely because intermarriage is not the main point of either story. As we shall see in the following chapters, the founding family of Abram, Sarai and their descendants had or represented a variety of religions. Hence, many of their marriages were intermarriages and this situation continued for many centuries thereafter.

Notes to Chapter III

1. At the very least, part of it is written much later than the period it purports to come from, since it shows David as Ruth's great-grandson. See Jack M. Sasson, "Ruth," in Robert Alter and Frank Kermode, *The Literary Guide to the Bible*, Cambridge, MA: Harvard University Press, 1987, 320.

2. Similarly the story of Joseph does not tell us which pharaoh(s) ruled Egypt during his remarkable adventures there.

3. Thus EJ, ad loc

4. Quoted by Sasson in Alter and Kermode, 320.

5. Yev. 8:3 clearly abandons the *pshat* (simple story line) when there is, in fact, no problem with it that would compel finding a different explanation.

6. On Judaisms: Edelman, *Triumph of Elohim*, *passim*.

7. One recognizes that Jesus's so-called "Golden Rule" is a commentary, a *drash* on Hillel.

8. Lowell K. Handy, "The Appearance of the Pantheon in Judah," in Edelman, *Triumph*, 27ff.

9. Hayes, 229

10. Ruth Rabbah 2:22

11. The circumcision of the Shechemites in Gen. 34 might be seen as an exception, except that it was done for the purpose of disabling the menfolk to facilitate their slaughter. See Chapter V for a refutation of the notion that Jews in Egypt were serious proselytizers.

12. As Israelites themselves did (Num. 25) with the Baal of Peor in Moab. Hayes concurs.

13. Jacob R. Marcus, *The Jew in the Medieval World* (NY: Atheneum, 1969 ((1938)), p. 4. The law of Constantine applied to "Jews, Samaritans and Heaven-Worshippers." Marcus terms the

last-named group "a sect closely allied to Judaism." We think it denotes those gentiles who had attached themselves to Judaism without formal conversion.

Why not go whole hog, so to speak? Precisely because some gentiles would have balked at dietary rules, others at circumcision. It was in large measure by waiving these "requirements" that early Christianity managed to "undersell" Judaism.

14. Which is to say that the modern Orthodox Israelis' refusal to recognize conversions performed by Reform or Reconstructionist rabbis has an historical precedent. But we speak here of the occasional aberrant individual or group that one often finds in Jerusalem, not denominations claiming hundreds of thousands of adherents over decades or centuries.

15. The gentile world ultimately resorted to bogus racial theories in support of their policies of exclusion or extermination. In *The Thirteenth Tribe* (Arthur Koestler, Fawcett: 1975), attempts to show that all European Jews are descended from tenth century Crimean converts, hence not "racially" Jewish at all, making Nazi efforts at extermination a tragic mistake, to say the least.

16. Frymer-Kensky 334/5

17. Herodotus 3:84

18. Victor Tcherikover, "Social Conditions," in Abraham Schalit, ed., *The World History of the Jewish people: The Hellenistic Age* (New Brunswick: Rutgers University Press, 1972), 87f.

19. We are familiar with later generations of European Jews who gave their children both a Jewish and a gentile name, like the authors' revered teacher (z"l) Nahum Norbert Glatzer, a.k.a. Norbert Nahum Glatzer, before having the wisdom to leave Germany for Palestine and then the United States.

20. Schalit, 45.

21. See *EJ* on *Hofjude*. Not only then, as the story of Joseph in Pharaoh's court and the very real career of Henry Kissinger in

Nixon's attest. Of the two, most Jews would agree that Joseph did the better job. Aggadah says Esther hid her Jewishness even from her own people so they would not relax and assume they were safely represented at court.

It might be counter-argued that with the rate of intermarriage in this country approaching or even passing fifty percent, soon almost everyone will have Jewish relatives. Hence any Nazi-like attempt to extirpate Jews would not be able to get off the ground.

Tradition could respond, Yes, but intermarriage is a cure that is worse than the disease. Some argue that by the end of this century there will not be enough Jews left here—a mere ten thousand or so—to be able to defend themselves. Intermarriage, they say, is acceptable only as long as the non-Jew converts, and that according to Orthodox procedures; but the same rabbis who say this would not accept a modern Ruth, or anyone else, as a convert based merely on an expressed desire to join the Jewish people.

Chapter IV. The Patriarchs and Their Significant Others

"We have met the enemy and he is us." – Walt Kelly's Pogo

1. "Canaanites" and "H"ebrews

Canaan is simply a geographical designation given by Akkadians of Mesopotamia to that stretch of land lying between the Jordan River and the Mediterranean. People living there could be called Canaanite, of course, in the same sense that people living in the USA are called Americans, except for one thing. There was never a native government in place in throughout the area called Canaan until it was organized by our biblical ancestors. No one living there at any previous time would have called him/herself "Canaanite."

The name seems to derive from an Akkadian word which could denote either the purple dye that came from there or a reddish-purple sunset. "Amorite," from *amurru* = "westerner," would seem to support the latter, while the later Greek designation of Phoenicians based upon the murex-derived royal purple dye they were famous for supports the former.

The Bible uses "Amorite" or "Canaanite" almost interchangeably, as, for example, in Gen. 15:16 where God tells Abraham that his descendants will have to stay in Egypt for four generations until the "iniquity of the Amorites" is cleansed from the land his children are to inhabit. Likewise, "Canaan" just happens to be that grandson of Noah who is cursed and declared the slave of his brethren. (Why Canaan should be cursed for the sin of his father, Ham, is a question that is beyond our scope.)

All of this is in order to differentiate the so-called native inhabitants from the narrative's heroes, the Israelites—also known

103

to us as Hebrews—and perhaps to soothe those of conscience among the latter who might object to forcibly dispossessing others. But if "Canaanite" is an artificial term, what shall we say of "Hebrews"?

Paradoxically, it is a bigger, but probably no longer correctable, mistake to capitalize this word. "Hebrew" has been used for centuries as an identification of our biblical ancestors, and to "demote" it to lower case now would be seen as an attempt to delegitimize Israel, biblical and modern. Consequently, we will retain the capital "H."

That said, one reason for this false formalism is that we tend to retroject modern[1] notions of "insider-outsider" back into history. Israelites are insiders; gentiles are outsiders. Jews—for so we often, if erroneously, refer to the biblical ancestors—worship the One God; gentiles—of whatever stripe or time—worship idols.[2] Even if today's Jews no longer believe this,[3] the current state of the State of Israel versus its Muslim neighbors greatly reinforces this "Us *v.* Them" mentality.

In biblical times, the situation on the ground was not nearly so simple. Who was "inside," who "outside"? Scripture's story of familial relationships may be a later cover for what actually happened, namely, the confederation of somewhat disparate groups of people, thereby producing what Van Wyck Brooks called a "usable past." For the Jews, that past emerged from the mists of history after 586 b.c.e: they knew Israel as a nation, divided or no, from time out of mind. There were no written records from patriarchal times, no clear memory of a time when this was not so. But perhaps we should be grateful that the rabbis who finally collected Scripture did such a poor job of homogenizing their sources; this allows us to shed light on what history lies beneath them.

If Israelites had been a separate, distinct and intrusive group, we might expect them to have left cultural remains that differed in several noticeable respects from those of the cultures they allegedly displaced. But this is not the case. Except for the relative absence of pig bones[4] in sites that we can confidently claim to be Israelite, there isn't much to differentiate among contemporary inhabitants. So unless startling new finds are made, archaeologists proceed on the assumption that the earliest Israelites were cut from the same goat's-hair cloth as many other Ancient Near Easterners. But isn't this, really, what a careful examination of Scripture reveals?

In Deuteronomy 26:5 Moses says, "My father [Jacob] was a fugitive Aramean." (NJPS) Even in Exile, Ezekiel (16:3) still recalled that Israel's origins were foreign and mixed. "Your father," he says, "was an Amorite, your mother a Hittite." These observations are not simply poetry, but real historical memory. So is Isaiah's (19:18) offhand identification of the language spoken by Israelites as "the language of Canaan." That is, he doesn't know the word "Hebrew" as denoting a separate language.[5]

The word 'ivri (Hebrew) seems to derive from 'apiru/habiru and denotes a social status which, it must be said, stood rather low on the scale. We'll discuss at greater length just what 'ivrim (the plural) might have been, but we note here that of Abraham's line only himself, Isaac and Jacob are so identified.

2. Patriarchs and Their Significant Others

"Four matriarchs; three patriarchs..." – "Who Knows One?" a Passover song

Counting all spouses and children of Abraham, Isaac and Jacob along with those Patriarchs themselves gives us thirty-two people. We have titled this section "Patriarchs and Their Significant Others" and not "Patriarchs and Matriarchs" in order to point up that those people whom the Judeo-Christian tradition regards as Israel's ancestors are a judicious selection of fewer than one-quarter of those people who might have qualified for the titles, and to inquire as to Israel's relations with the rest of the family.

Abraham had eight named offspring, but as we indicated above, only one is considered Israelite! Hagar's son, Ishmael, is disowned at Sarah's request, though it takes a literal "act of God" (Gen. 21:12) to set aside what is apparently the customary adoption of the children of one's concubines when one's wife is barren. It is great-uncle Ishmael's people, apparently grown mightily in number in just two generations, who buy and transport Joseph to Egypt without either side to the transaction commenting on their kinship.

Sarah gets her name changed from Sarai, presumably when she adopts her husband's new religion. But here, as elsewhere, neither name includes a divine element indicating deity. In Sarah's case, it's not even certain that the two names have different meanings.

Abraham's other families followed disparate paths. The six named children from Abraham's later wife—she is also referred to as his concubine—Keturah, are not exactly Israelite, either; that is to say, they do not inherit property from their father. Almost perversely, all four children born to Jacob of concubines Bilhah and Zilpah are Israelites and did inherit alongside the sons of the first-

106

rank wives, Leah and Rachel.[6] As we'll see below, even this doesn't do justice to the situation's complexity, and we've yet to consider the other relatives.

It does not matter that there is as yet no reliable evidence for the existence of any one of these people. Names such as Abram, Jacob and Laban are found in Late Bronze Age texts, but even if no proof of their individual existence is ever forthcoming, the stories that Jewish tradition tells, like those of Ruth and Esther, are even more instructive than the raw history would be. They tell us what our Israelite ancestors remembered or thought their ancestry to have been.

The first thing we note is that Israel did not claim to be God's first created people.[7] Unlike Egyptian or Mesopotamian kingships, Israelites recognized (Gen. 10) that they were relative late-comers on the world scene. Further, they understood themselves to be in no sense a uniform group by acknowledging foreign—that is, Amorite, Aramean and Hittite—ancestry. This is not at all the "Us v. Them" of so much of later Jewish history.

Judges 10, the story of some Gibeonites who tricked Joshua into letting them join the Israelite community, testifies to the Gibeonites' foreign origin; they may have originated in Greece. Numbers adds 32,000 Moabite or Midianite virgins absorbed into Israel. With no mechanisms for conversion or, indeed, any need to convert, what religions did these people bring to the mix that was becoming Israel?

The religious situation was made infinitely more complex by the presence of polygamy within Israel. If men took wives from different nations/ethnicities, as many did, what "religion" were their various children? It is not our purpose here to weigh in on the question of whether or not polygamy was the norm in Israel.[8] It is enough to note that some polygamy did indubitably exist.

As proof we may adduce Deut. 21:15-17, which forbids a man from favoring the son of a more-liked wife when, in fact, a son of the less-liked wife is the firstborn. Of particular interest in this regard is Joshua's contemporary Caleb, who had two wives but married another when one of them died. (I Chron 2:18) Is this exceptional, or does it tell us something about the prevalence of polygamy?

Even if monogamy were the norm, one would expect a lot of "serial monogamy" in Israel, and of this the Bible gives some evidence, beginning with Abraham himself.[9] Nor should we be surprised that this seems to be the case. Consider: until the nineteenth century it still took six pregnancies to produce two children who lived to adulthood. What was the ratio in the Bronze Age, with what we presume were even less sophisticated medical techniques? And this says nothing of the many women who must have died in childbirth from ailments we can only now successfully attend?[10]

So if a man had three wives, as both Abraham and grandson Esau did, and each produced two sons (first generation) who then repeated the process, there would be thirty-six full or half brothers already in the second generation and over three hundred in the third. Now, if that man's wives came from three different groups as Abraham's did, what "religion" would his various grandchildren have?

Perhaps a more important question at this point might be, why did Abraham have children with foreign women? The answer is that either the religion of womenfolk didn't matter much in the patriarchal period, or family/clan/tribal affiliations were more important than theologies and their attendant rituals. Recognizing this, perhaps, biblical and rabbinic tradition are quick to minimize the women's foreignness.

An example of a traditional perspective: Hagar just happened to be Egyptian; she might have been anything; adopting her child as Sarah's as well as his own was what mattered. Some interpreters went further, suggesting Hagar was Pharaoh's daughter, whom he had given to Sarah as a servant,[11] an absurd proposition. As we saw earlier, Egypt accepted foreign princesses into inter-dynastic unions, but the notion of giving a daughter of Pharaoh as a servant to a "vile Asiatic" is beyond belief.

Other interpreters, disturbed by even Abraham's apparent serial monogamy, proposed that Keturah was none other than Hagar herself, brought back after Sarah died. No matter that Hagar-Keturah, too, would have been well beyond normal childbearing age when she bore Abraham six more children.

These are *aggadot* ("stories"), traditional embellishments that have no more historical value than the decorated letters of medieval Bible manuscripts. But they have value for us. They show that later Judaism recognized and remembered the foreign origin of much of Israel and so took steps to make it less so. Either way, the Bible does not entirely forget or suppress this information.

Recognizing that early or proto-Israelites were a diverse group should, but doesn't always, lead scholars to the next logical conclusion. The story of Abraham and his three families represents that element within Israel which made its living through trade. It's true that the three uses of "Canaan[ite]" as "trader"—Zeph. 1:11; Ezek. 16:29, 17:4—are all late texts, but the designation goes back to the Bronze Age.[12]

As we noted in the Introduction, Canaan is a natural crossroads, and trade in the area antedates the rise of Israel by many centuries. When our ancestors finally settled there, they became ipso facto Canaanites. As we'll see below, some of the ancestors were already "native" Canaanites who might very naturally have made their living in trade. And by trade, we don't mean just sitting on trade routes and collecting tolls.

Whether or not Abraham was an historical character, his story seems to represent the people whose place in society as teamsters led them to be on the road for long periods of time; that of his three women schematizes what might have been a profitable triangular trade route plied by Canaanites. They would carry foodstuffs, Dead Sea salt and sulfur to Arabia, trade them there for the aromatic spices needed for embalming, take these to Egypt—or back to Israel (Jer. 6:20)—and sell them for gold. This triangular trade route necessitated contact with at least three ethnicities, so at least two of his wives, Hagar and Keturah, represent intermarriages.

Other commodities one might find on the road included everything from mutton to tin for the making of bronze weapons. The latter was particularly valuable, so traders went far, far afield to find sources. Given the distances involved and the amount of time traders spent on the road,[13] it would not be unusual for them, like nineteenth century seamen, to have "a girl in every port." And since polygamy was by no means frowned upon, these could easily be more than casual partners.

Again, we are not attacking the historicity of the Bible story; rather we are using the names to point to the complex of ethnic interrelationships that the Bible admits to. Another of these is represented by the story of Jacob's only named daughter.

3. The Dinah Incident

Dinah, whom we first met in Chapter II, is the only named daughter of Jacob. That he should have had twelve sons and only one daughter by his four women is something of a statistical improbability, but that's not what concerns us here. Nor are we concerned that Dinah's story is, if not a fiction, then unsupported by any other proof, but that which its inclusion in Scripture offers.

Daughters, such as Dinah and David's Tamar, tend to get ink only when they are involved in something "worthy of saga."[14] Dinah is remembered because a prince of Shechem wished to take her, literally as well as figuratively, as (a) wife. Since cohabitation even following abduction was recognized as a form of marriage, Dinah was, however briefly, intermarried.

Fiction or no, the incident contains a couple of points that have the ring of truth, even placing the story near the time when it purportedly takes place. The first point that connects this story with knowable history may be derived from Herodotus's observation that Asiatics were in the habit of stealing each other's women and that, generally, nobody made a fuss about it.[15] To the extent that this applies to biblical peoples, it would indicate that a good deal of intermarriage, albeit unwilling on the part of the women, took place.

The second is that families, especially royal families, often arranged intermarriages in order to facilitate trade. This is what the Romans later termed *connubium et commercium*, figuratively, "Now we're married, so we're family and we can do some business." We know that it happened hundreds of years before Rome was founded.

In the Bronze Age, Shechem was the queen city of the northern plains,[16] and control of it gave whoever was in charge a strategic position, even a stranglehold, on the chief north-south trade route through Israel. It would have been to the Jacob family's advantage to have a marriage alliance with the Shechemites.

However, this is not the way the Bible sees it.

The Bible considers the Dinah incident as rape. In response, two of her brothers, Simeon and Levi, say, "Our sister should not be treated like a whore," and exact a terrible vengeance, not just on the alleged princely perpetrator but on every male in Shechem. This, of course, clears the way for a Jacobite takeover of the place and its attendant monopoly on toll-collecting. Not surprisingly, the Bible is mute on this last point.

We generally remember this story only because of its aftermath, the bloody and excessive reaction of brothers Simeon and Levi.[17] But a couple of other things need to be noted here. First, in negotiating with the Shechemites, the family of Jacob never said that they were forbidden to intermarry. Hence, we may assume that they were not opposed in principle. Second, the aftermath of what we call "the rape of Dinah" was to demote Simeon from family headship and Levi from land ownership, thus promoting Judah, the fourth born, to be first in line, despite the tribal founder's marriage to a Canaanite woman!

The story serves additional functions for later rabbinic writers.[18] In the aggadic literature it is used to "blame the victim" for being out alone where she should not have been, just like her mother— something of an anti-feminist perspective, if we may use that term of so ancient a period. Later still, in First Jubilees, a first-century Palestinian work, the authors use Dinah's story as a pretext for a polemic against all intermarriage that God expressly gives to Moses:

And you, Moses, command the children of Israel... Israel will not be free from uncleanness while it has one of the foreign women or if anyone has given one of his daughters to any foreign man.[19]

We may be fairly certain that what the commentators wrote tells us more about their own times than it does about the time they purportedly describe. For us, however, the bottom line remains this: marriage in Israel was not just an alliance between a man and a woman, but rather reflected the desire to create a tie that would allow trade between the now-related families or the groups they represented.

That this is in fact the case might be inferred from evidence gathered in Europe, specifically from two cemeteries near Heidelberg that date back over 7,000 years. By examining the ratio between Strontium isotopes in the remains, paleontologists concluded that intermarriage between incoming farmers and pre-existing hunter-gatherer communities took place. [20]

As we said in the introduction, the women themselves might have been considered commodities[21], as distasteful as the notion is to us. Certainly, their religious "labels" were of no importance. We will return to this point later.

4. Your God Shall Be My God?

Some marriages—for example that of Abram to Sarai, Isaac to Rebekah and Jacob to sisters Rachel and Leah—were unions made between members of previously related families, children of the same grandparents, even, in the case of the first couple, children of the same father (Gen. 20:12). These three unions, seven of Israel's "starting eleven," have been hallowed as Patriarchs and Matriarchs for so long that we overlook a startling fact: *all these were mixed marriages.*

Sarai's name is changed to Sarah in Gen. 17. She is not quoted concerning what she thinks about her husband's new religious allegiance, but her name change indicates that she, too, must have been practicing some other religion—Abram's previous one or some other—for her first sixty-five years. And did she just quietly go along with her husband's religious switch? Such a change would not be required for her marriage. Further, the people whom she left when she accompanied Abraham to Canaan, her relatives and his, would have continued to practice as they had done.[22]

As to Abraham, the founder of Judaism himself, a question to which scholars are only beginning to pay attention is this: what religion did Abraham follow before God contacted him? The name change Abram < Abraham (Gen. 17:5) indicates a change in religious allegiance, even as such changes often mean just that today among Catholics, Muslims, etc. A famous midrash[23] suggests that Abram—his given name—was but a lad working in his father's idol store when he had the revelation of monotheism. The Bible, however, explicitly states that he was seventy-five when he left for Canaan. To make a long story short, all indications point to the Moon (*Sin*) as the principal deity in both Abram and Sarai's families.[24]

Tradition regards Genesis 24:3, Abraham's charge to his servant Eleazar to find a wife for son Isaac from among Abraham's own people, rather than from among the Canaanites among whom they dwelled, as the earliest prohibition of intermarriage, but that would be stretching things. Marrying one's relatives as Abram did per force excluded all "outsiders" regardless of religion. Here tradition assumes that Abraham's wishing to find a wife for Isaac from among the relatives means that all those relatives had quickly come over to the newfound faith which had been the occasion of his leaving home in the first place. But of this the Bible says nothing and it is highly unlikely that any such thing occurred.

Though Isaac's years numbered more (180) than either his famous father's (175) or his equally famous son's (147), there is little space devoted to him in Scripture. Some scholars, in fact, think that the story of Isaac is a complete fiction designed to show a family relationship between Abrahamic (Southern) and Jacobite (Northern) tribes that were not related by blood.

Certainly, if they weren't originally related, than some such story would be necessary, but this strikes us as smacking too much of a circular argument. Besides, truth is somewhat less important than fiction. If we could prove the two groups were originally separate, it would support our case for extensive intermarriage within Israel. Meanwhile, what the Bible says of this hinge Patriarch tells its own tale.

The wife that is found for him, Rebekah, is a sister of Abraham's wily nephew Laban, who, we may be certain, was not a convert to Abraham's new religion. If Abraham "made many souls" (= converts) in Harran (Gen.12:5), Laban wasn't one of them; else why would his daughter Rachel pilfer the family god(s) on her way south with Isaac's son, her cousin Jacob?

Another "highlight": Rebekah conspires with favorite-son Jacob to defraud Esau of the family birthright. This is partly due to her higher esteem for the younger of her twins, but also, Scripture implies, because of exasperation with Esau's having married Hittite women. Predictably, tradition uses this as an argument against intermarriage, obscuring the fact that Rebekah herself had come from a household in which many deities were worshipped.

Support for this contention comes from the story of her nieces, Laban's daughters, whom their cousin Jacob married.

5. North Towards Home: Jacob Becomes Israel

North Towards Home – Willie Morris

Jacob gets his famous and enduring new name by wrestling all night with a divine messenger, an angel if you like (Gen. 32:4 ff.). What is this story designed to show? Two things suggest themselves. The first is that, as with grandfather Abram/Abraham, it signifies a change in religion. It is possible, of course, that Abraham's monotheism was not inherited whole and unchanged by his favored son and grandson. Could Isaac, for example, wholeheartedly adopt a faith that came so close to requiring his sacrifice? But to suggest this is to poke a hornet's nest of tradition.

Another suggestion is that the acquisition of the name "Israel" generates an ethnicon,[25] a people-identifier that the new-formed Israelites could use over against the other, established nations among whom they would shortly settle down. This would be useful in masking the fact that Israel's constituent elements come from several different sources.

Consider: of the children born to Jacob, some are born of Leah's concubine, Zilpah, after Leah had borne him children. Now, surrogacy was the recourse of barren women; why did Leah give a concubine to Jacob *after* she had borne him her own sons? Even the traditional commentaries are at a loss for words here.[26]

The names Bilhah and Zilpah do not tell us much, but those of their children—Gad, Dan, Naphtali, Asher—do. First, we note that all the tribes mothered by Jacob's concubines are clustered together in the North; this is highly suspicious. What this tells us is that one-third of the original twelve tribes were probably what we would now call autochthonous Canaanites. Two others, Zebulon and Issachar, are Northern, too, but born of Leah after she had stopped bearing, a highly suspicious circumstance.

The Hebrew of the psalm quoted above suggests that the various groups/tribes gathered around a single, possibly totemic standard. We might compare this to "rallying round the flag." In any case, it is acceptance of or allegiance to the same totem rather than a birth/blood relationship that makes these groups "brothers."

The designation of Northerners as "autochthonous" is not entirely fair, of course, because we lack any independent stories from any of them that might tell when their ancestors first entered the land. Here is what we do know:

Asher—Jewish tradition's association of the name with Hebrew *'asher*, "happy," is itself a happy coincidence. The name is curiously close to *asheri,* the name of a Canaanite group known to Egypt already in the Amarna period—that is to say, the fourteenth century: even before Moses's time, by most people's reckoning.

Calling Asher (and Issachar) the "first wave of Hebrew conquerors" as the *Encyclopedia Judaica* (3:702) does, is either wishful thinking or posthumous body-snatching. According to Scripture, Asher's territory extended far to the north of Tyre, something that would be reasonable to say if Asher were SA.GAZ, "nomads," which is how they are identified by Egyptian sources.

Most likely, they infiltrated from further north and east.

Dan—There is a wordplay on the tribal name Dan and the Hebrew verb "judge" (d-y-n) in Gen. 49:16, the Blessing/Testament of Jacob. Dan "will judge his people as one

118

of the tribes of Israel." A closer look should focus on "as," indicating that, in origin, Dan might not have been a coalition member. Frank Moore Cross is so uncomfortable with this idea that he emends the text to read "first among" the tribes of Israel,[27] but there is no need. The text isn't broken; it doesn't need fixing.

It is probably not coincidental that Samson, the "Hebrew Hercules," was a Danite. The Danites may well have been Greek-speakers. The names Denyen and Danuna are remembered from among the groups of Mediterranean migrants who inundated the lands further east at the end of the thirteenth pre-Christian century,[28] the same time that the Bible says Israel left Egypt and that Mycenae fell. According to the Bible, the tribe of Dan originally settled on the coast, but was forced inland; does this tale contain a real historical memory?

Judges 5:17, which is in one of the admittedly oldest pieces of Scripture, remembers a time when Dan dwelt by its ships. In fact, it criticizes the Danites for remaining by their ships when other Israelite elements were fighting with Canaanites inland. May we conclude from this that Danites were a Greek-speaking coastal trading colony isolated by the destruction of their mother country, hence increasingly vulnerable to pressure from native neighbors and finally forced to move inland?

Alternatively, original Danites might even have been refugees from the earlier explosion of Santorini (Thera) who eventually settled inland because it was a convenient location for their extensive metalworking industry, as reported by Avraham Biran, who has excavated there for nearly thirty years.[29]

Bronze Age tombs from the site of Tel Dan contain imported Mycenaean and Cypriote wares, which one might expect if the inhabitants of the city, at that time still called Laish, were from the Mediterranean. More tellingly, some of the tombs' skeletons "anthropologically, did not belong to the local Canaanite population."[30]

Judges 18:30 mentions that the Danites set up some sort of idol; the Hebrew word indicates a sculptured image, hardly what one would expect of Abraham's great-grandsons. The bottom line is that there is an outstanding possibility that the Danites were originally foreigners, so that any marriages between them and other Israelites would be intermarriages: for example, the Danite who married one of Hiram's craftsmen (2 Chronicles 2:13).

Gad—Again, the name is ambiguous. It is "the name of the god of good fortune and good luck in several Ancient Near Eastern cultures."[31] *Etz Hayim*, the Conservative Jewish Torah, is demythologizing when it says that to Leah it just meant "luck." The location of Gad across the Jordan River means that they would have common borders, if not overlapping land claims, with both Moabites and Ammonites.

This probably proved unlucky, as Jeremiah 49 indicates that by or before his time some Ammonites had overrun Gad. Of course, we don't know exactly when this might have taken place, but Judges indicates Ammonite oppression in the first half of the eleventh century. Parenthetically, none of Israel's Judges is identified as coming from Gad. Chronicles includes them with those exiled by Assyria around 745 b.c.e., and this tribe is dramatically underrepresented in the genealogy of First Chronicles.

For our purposes, then, they seem to be a non-factor.

Issa(s)char—We have spelled it this way to show there's another letter Shin in the Hebrew word. In Scripture it is silent, the only time this happens, and not found in most transliterations; clearly, it's a foreign name.[32] We find related names among the list of Asiatics employed in Egypt in the nineteenth century. James Pritchard's *Ancient Near Eastern Texts* translates[33] Jacob's words on this son as "Issachar is a (resident) alien donkey driver...." For this original reading Albright could get support from an unlikely source, Rashi. The great French rabbi indicates in his translation of the end of the "blessing" that he, too, feels Issaschar carried merchandise. And, clearly, the end of 49:15 unambiguously reports that "he became a slave at forced labor" (RSV) ("toiling serf" NJPS), something that could be expected to happen to such a low-status group.

Naphtali—here, as so often, the Bible supplies an etymology—"my struggle," i.e. that between Rachel, through her handmaid Bilhah, and Leah for the favor of Jacob—but it is hard to sustain. Names of its clans aren't places, though it lay athwart one of the most fertile regions of the north, and was crossed by major trade routes. *EJ* suggests there may have been a fusion between Naphtali and Dan. Naphtali produced Barak, who fought under Deborah against the Canaanite general Sisera.

Zebulon—Michael Astour[34] connects the name with Ugaritic Zebul, a divine name. It may also indicate "border dwellers," which could be congruent with Astour's suggestion; that is, the name may be that of a mountain deity associated with Mt. Tabor. Tabor is a solitary hill rising nearly 2,000 feet, about six miles east of Nazareth, where it could serve as a border marker/sacred site for the tribes of Zebulon, Naphtali and Issaschar. (Cf. Tolkien's Three-Farthing Stone.) Given our human propensity for connecting deities with the high places of the earth, I have no doubt that Mt. Tabor was sacred to whoever lived in its environs from the dawn of time.

As Northerners, they would have been less susceptible to the drought-induced famine that led their Southern "brethren" to take refuge in Egypt. Despite the Bible's meticulous, if exaggerated, census of those returning from there in the Book of Numbers, it is doubtful whether the Northern tribes ever went. Also, these tribes are remembered for having exceptional difficulty in expelling the "previous residents" of their assigned territories. This would make sense if they were breakaway Canaanite elements themselves, allying themselves with the incoming Israelites.

According to both Genesis 46 and I Chronicles, the "kosher" half of Israel wasn't pure, either. Simeon had a son, Shaul, by "a Canaanitish woman" (Gen. 46: 8) and the tribe seems to have made marriages with several of the surrounding peoples. The tribe of Simeon subsequently disappeared within the boundaries of Judah, which, as noted above, contained more non-Israelite elements than all the other tribes combined.

Manasseh had Asriel by an Aramean concubine (I Chron. 8:14). Judah had a Canaanite wife and of his descendants one married Bithiah, another (!) daughter of Pharaoh; the Simeonites had extensive marital connections with Edomites, Moabites and Midianites. It hardly matters whether Chronicles is history or just story. Its editors/writers would hardly chronicle such extensive intermarriage if a) such were not the memories passed on to them and b) such unions were already beyond the pale.

Of all the twelve/thirteen original tribes of Israel, the one that most commands our attention is Benjamin. From the story of his birth to the war with the other Israelites that almost led to the tribe's demise, Benjamin has more "press" in Scripture than any tribe save Judah.

6. Archaeology and the Biblical Record

We get more and more help determining the culture of the inhabitants from their material remains from the science of archaeology. But for those who hold to the traditional stories, the news isn't good. For one thing, it seems to indicate that the tribe of Judah did not begin its existence until after David's time.

In 1937, the Wellcome-Marston excavation of Jericho led by John Garstang announced that it had found the walls Joshua's trumpets had blown down. This kind of thing was just what the excavation's conservative religious backers wanted to hear. The connection was not unusual. For most of the previous century, American excavations had been financed by individuals (Rockefeller at Megiddo) or groups that were interested in proving the Bible's veracity.

Even today expeditions to find Noah's Ark, or claims that it has been found, are made. It has taken a very long time to wrest the science from the hands of religious partisans and establish it as anything like an impartial tool for evaluation (as witnessed by *EJ* 14).

One way to do this has been to get away from the excavation of big mounds—the tels under which ruined cities sleep—and into field surveys of smaller, less sexy sites. Of course these sites, many in Judea and Samaria (the West Bank to some), have only been available since 1967 and not continuously even then. These places can often tell us how many people the land could sustain and whether it was occupied serially by different groups with recognizably different layers of culture.

Discoveries such as the four-room house and the collar-rim jar have led some to posit that incoming Israelites represented a different culture, but most scholars do not find these, or anything else, significantly different from the artifacts of other peoples in the area.

One result of recent surveys is the startling conclusion that the tribe of Judah, which the Bible assigns to the central hill country, cannot have existed before twelfth/eleventh century b.c.e. According to Israel Finkelstein and Neil Asher Silberman, the settlement density in that area was around 4500 people at the beginning of the Iron Ages (ca. 1200 b.c.e), not nearly enough to sustain a tribe and not at all up to the count of the Bible's Book of Numbers.[35] The Bible may contain some hint of this; it lists Judah as the fourth-born of Leah, a position that needed "disqualifications" of the three older brothers in order to succeed to family leadership.

Traditional religious groups still want to believe that the Israelites were a unified invading force, albeit with an inferior material culture to that of the Canaanites whom they displaced. The record on the ground doesn't seem to support this notion. Consequently, there are several attractive alternative theories afield about who the Israelites were and where they came from.[36]

The older school—following the Bible—presumes they were outsiders, the newer schools that all or many came from disaffected elements within Canaan itself. Without pausing to evaluate their respective claims, we may posit that there is no single right answer here; the evidence is ambiguous because the Israelites derived from several sources and didn't operate as a unified group until the kingships of Saul, David and Solomon. Of course, the more sources, the more intermarriage. This was in fact the case, as the following example demonstrates.

7. Judah and Tamar

The story of Judah and Tamar deserves special attention for several reasons, not the least of which is the amount of space—all of Gen. 38—that the Bible assigns it. Briefly, Judah, is seduced by his daughter-in-law, Tamar, after her first two husbands, his sons, die and he refuses to promise her the third. When she is found to be pregnant, he takes her to court for prostitution, but she proves that he is the father and the court finds for her.

This would be an extraordinary story if only for its outcome, the legal victory of a woman over a man, and not just any man, but one of the patriarch Jacob's sons. Despite being Jacob's fourth born, Judah (whose name derives from a root that means either "cow-tender" or, by extension, "low class") becomes the leading tribe in what will become Israel's Southern Kingdom, eventually giving his name to the word "Jew."

What is really extraordinary, however, is that Tamar has legal standing in court. The Bible doesn't tell us much about her. She is probably also Canaanite, as was Judah's wife. (But cf. Gen. Rabbah, making her a daughter of a priest, Shem.) Of course, Numbers 15:14 says, "You shall have one law for yourselves and for the stranger who dwells among you." But that pronouncement is Torah; that is, it comes from a later period and does not necessarily apply to women. So it must be that both it and the Judah/Tamar story come from a time after Torah had become known. In any case, we are left with the idea that here, at least, Israelite law worked the way it was supposed to.[37] Just as well, too.

The children of Judah borne by Tamar were Zerah and Perez. Perez was an ancestor of Boaz, hence an ancestor of David. Our ancestors might not have given much thought to genetic inheritance, but we are free to wonder how history would have unrolled had Tamar not prevailed.

This raises a most interesting question. If the Israelites were not unified politically or religiously until relatively late in their history, did any of them subscribe to the idea that their gods were married? Since such were the beliefs of surrounding nations in Mesopotamia and Egypt and later in Greece, it would be surprising if the answer were "no." In fact there is evidence, which we will examine later, that suggests some in Israel believed God was what we would term intermarried!

8. The Egyptian Experience

Of those who did go down to Egypt, many strange tales are told. One is Jacob's adoption of his own grandsons, Ephraim and Manasseh, whom his son Joseph had from his Egyptian wife, Asenath. Why would such an action be necessary, especially since later Jewish tradition informs us that Asenath had converted to Judaism? It might be argued that by promoting them by one generation, Jacob was effectively giving a double portion to the oldest son of his favored wife, in defiance of Deut. 21:15 (quoted above). But could Jacob know this law, which even by the most conservative standards could only have been given after his death?

Another possibility is that this story establishes and justifies the tribes of both Ephraim and Manasseh's being considerably larger than Benjamin, a tribe that might have claimed the double portion on the principle of ultimo geniture (the rationale of which is the supposition that the youngest will survive longest). Saul was a Benjaminite and, as we shall see, his people contested for Israel's kingship even after his death.

Asenath herself is the subject of much Jewish legend.[38] She is held to be the daughter of Dinah, hence Jewish, and according to one source, to have rescued baby Moses from the water and defended Joseph from the false accusations of Mrs. Potiphar. (We should note here that Mrs. P. refers to Joseph as a Hebrew in a context that is clearly derogatory of the lad.)

Obviously these legends are not mutually compatible. Joseph lived about a century before Moses. How old must Asenath have been? And we must ask: If the Egyptian woman had converted[39]— to what, exactly, would she have converted and under whose auspices?

The problem with conversion before Moses is particularly knotty if we stop to examine Leah's and Rachel's own religious pedigree. They could only be considered "Israelite" in the religious sense if their father, Jacob's uncle Laban, had at some point converted to the faith of <u>his</u> uncle, Abraham. Laban's household seems to have been matrilineal (Gen. 24:28), indicating a different religion than Abraham's newly founded one. For Laban's conversion the Bible provides absolutely no hard evidence, while rabbinic sources seem intent on outdoing each other in identifying Laban with various enemies of Israel, most notably Bilaam.[40]

It could be suggested that Laban adopted Jacob because Laban had no sons, and that this motivated Rachel's later theft of her father's *teraphim*—on this reading, "family gods"—when he later wished to renege on the agreement. We're not sure what these objects were, but we note that most modern Jews and Christians would have objections to the very notion that the *teraphim* could be family gods of the Laban family. This dogmatic denial is unnecessary.

Shaye Cohen writes, "The foreign woman who married an Israelite was supposed to leave her gods in her father's house, *but even if she did not*, it never occurred to anyone to argue that her children were not Israelites."[41]

On any straight reading of the text, Laban already had male children when Jacob came on the scene. Jacob's joining Laban's family would mean that, if anyone, it was Jacob, not Laban, who should have changed gods, as brother Esau apparently did when he married Hittite women. By either reading, Leah and Rachel began life with a different religion than their future husband's.

And note that it is these women who give names to their children; does this indicate that, as Judaism later decided, the religion of the child follows that of the mother?

To sum up, we may state with some certainty that all four of Jacob's matrimonial arrangements were what we would today call intermarriages. Having said this, we need carefully to differentiate what we mean by the term from what it might have meant then. For this we need to examine the place and importance of women in marriage at the end of the Bronze Age, which we will do in the chapter on Joshua and Judges.

9. Adding Things Up

Stories of the Patriarchs are just that. How much historical truth they contain is almost impossible to ascertain in the absence of enough corroborating evidence. But they do contain a number of what we might call "social truths" that hold at least from the time that the stories were collected, edited and written down. This, scholars think, happened about the middle of the sixth pre-Christian century.

Can these social truths be retrojected into Israel's history of six to seven hundred years before? We think they can. Marriage to one's own half-sister or to two sisters became illegal in Israelite law. But Jacob's story does not give much ammunition to those who might have opposed marriage to sisters. Why, then, would someone make up such a story in regard to him (and he is not the only one)?

Similarly, identifying Judah's daughter-in-law as Canaanite adds little to their story. One might counter that such details are what story-tellers use to make their tales seem more realistic (following Kermode), but such literary touches surely would not outweigh Israel's later aversion to intermarriage. As we have seen, the patriarchs from Abraham onward are intermarried even though their wives are their relatives!

Nor does intermarriage stop with the adoption of Torah.

Notes to Chapter IV

1. See, e.g., Max Weber, *The Sociology of Religion,* Beacon Press, 1964.
2. "It should come as no surprise, therefore, that the overriding view of the non-Israelite world expressed in the Hebrew Bible is negative." Rembaum, 1377. Not until the 13th century did Judaism declare Christianity and Islam to be monotheistic faiths. See Menachem Meiri, *Beit HaBechirah.*
3. In Jerusalem in 1968, I was told by an American-born Orthodox Jew that Christians and Muslims worshipped "trees and stones." On reflection, I think he must have meant the Cross and the Ka'aba, respectively. Ned Rosenbaum
4. On the relative absence of pig bones: William Dever, *What Did the Biblical Writers Know & When Did They Know It?* (Grand Rapids MI: Wm. Eerdmans, 2001), 113.
5. Ben Sira, 2nd century b.c.e., is first to identify Hebrew as a language: 53:6.
6. First rank wives: As we shall see when we come to discuss Solomon & Co.
7. Nahum M. Sarna, "Paganism and Biblical Judaism," in *Studies in Biblical Interpretation* (Phila: Jewish Publication Society, 2000), 13ff.
8. Monogamy is thought to have been the norm except among royalty and the wealthy. Mayer I. Gruber, "Private Life in Ancient Israel," Sasson, *CANE,* I:644. Pastoralists, however, would have the "example" of their own animals to teach them that one male could service several females.
9. Serial monogamy: Isaac was 37 when his mother died; Keturah must have been at least 63 unless, as has been suggested, she was bearing while Sarah was alive. Richard Elliott Friedman calls her

"The most ignored significant person in the Torah": *Commentary on the Torah* (NY: Harper and Row, 2001), 85.

10. The Bible mentions only one such unfortunate wife, Rachel, but there's no reason to suppose that the death rate for mothers giving birth or after was any lower then than at any other time in history before the nineteenth century.

11. Sarah servant: Louis Ginzberg, *Legends,* I:237

12. Gösta Werner Ahlström, *History of Ancient Palestine* (Sheffield, UK: Sheffield Academic Press, 1993), 234: Amenhotep captive list.

13. A round trip into Anatolia might take a year: hence, Esau's Hittite wives.

14. We borrow this phrase, as well as much else, from our teacher Cyrus H. Gordon, z"l, then of Brandeis.

15. Herodotus, *Histories,* 4.

16. J. A. Soggin, *Old Testament and Oriental Studies* (Rome: Biblical Institute Press, 1975), 23.

17. So excessive is their reaction—rape is not punishable by death even to the rapist in later Jewish law—that one wonders whether this part of the story doesn't have the ulterior motive of disqualifying these two older brothers of Judah from family headship. Not all of Jewish tradition sees the reaction as excessive. See: Frymer-Kensky, *Reading,* 341.

18. James Kugel shows how tradition turns this grain of ugly sand into a beautiful pearl. *The Bible As it Was* (Cambridge, MA: Harvard, 1997), 231-44.

19. Jubilees 30:11-14 cited in Kugel, 236f.

20. Lemche, *Ancient Israel,* 73, on tribes that had to trade women for hard currency or other goods.

21. Brian Fagan, The Long Summer: How Climate Changed Civilization (NY: Basic Books, 2004), 117.

22. For Handy in Edelman, 27ff, a pantheon is as at home in Judah as anywhere else.

23. *Genesis Rabbah* 38:13; more on this story below.

24. On *Sin* as deity, see C. J. Gadd, "The Harran Inscriptions of Nabonidus," in *Anatolian Studies* VIII (1958), 46ff. "I raise my hands towards Sin, king of gods, imploring with reverence." (My translation.)

25. Ahlström, *Who Were the Israelites?* (Winona Lake, IN: Eisebrauns, 1986), 60, for YHWH as toponym.

26. R. E. Friedman, *Commentary on the Torah* (New York: Harper and Row, 2001).

27. In Frank Moore Cross and Helmut Koester, *Hermeneia—a Critical and Historical Commentary on the Bible* (Minneapolis: Fortress Press, 1971).

28. Nahum M. Sarna, "Paganism and Biblical Judaism," in *Studies in Biblical Interpretation*, (Phila; Jewish Publication Society, 2000), writes, "Mediterranean peoples, especially from the Aegean area, invaded from the sea," 13.

29. Avraham Biran, *Biblical Dan* (Jerusalem: Israel Exploration Society, 1994). 24, 29.

30. *Ibid.,* 114.

31. *Etz Hayim* 176.

32. W.F. Albright, *YGC* 265f.

33. Astour, *Hellenosemitica*, 47.

34. *Ibid.* 284.

35. Israel Finkelstein and Neil Asher Silberman, *The Bible Unearthed: Archeology's New Vision of Ancient Israel and Its Sacred Texts* (New York: Simon & Schuster, 2001), 141. Numbers 1:27 claims 74,600 heads of households for Judah. If we assume a family of five persons for each, the total is almost 375,000. See also "State Formation in Israel and Judah," NEA 62 (1999): 35-52.

36. For a recent discussion, William Dever, *Who Were the Early Israelites and Where Did They Come From?* (Grand Rapids MI: Wm. Eerdmans, 2003), among many others.

37. Alas, this was not always the case, as the text of Amos 2:6-16 makes abundantly clear. See S. N. Rosenbaum, *Amos of Israel; A New Interpretation,* (Macon, GA: Mercer University Press, 1990).

38. Victor Aptowitzer, "Asenath, the Wife of Joseph: A Haggadic Literary-historical Study." In *Hebrew Union College Annual* I (1924) I 239-406.

39. According to some Jewish sources, she didn't have to convert, as she was the daughter of Dinah. This explanation has the advantage of precluding the question of why Asenath did not exchange her Egyptian name for an Israelite one.

40. e.g. *Sanh.* 105a.

41. *Beginnings,* 265; emphasis added.

Chapter V. Who Was (Were the) Mrs. Moses? Or: Was Moses Intermarried?

1. Constructing a context

The short answer to the above question is, "Yes." And why not? There would have been no compelling reason to avoid intermarriage in the thirteenth pre-Christian century, the period when most people think Moses lived. By any account he could not have gotten the Torah on Sinai with its strictures against intermarriage before he was at least eighty years old—and already married. Despite, or perhaps because, the Jewish tradition takes such trouble to deny or disguise the fact, it is safe to conclude that Moses was intermarried. More pertinent questions would be: to whom was he married and how many wives did he have? That is the question this chapter will presently address.

Although he allegedly grew up in Egypt, no Egyptian source mentions Moses. On the one hand, that's no surprise given the number of foreigners in Egypt at any given time. The Disney movie *Prince of Egypt* does a terrible disservice by implying that Moses was THE principal pal of Pharaoh's only son. On the other hand, his alleged exploits should have earned him some notoriety, at least.

For better or worse, we have no source of information on the great lawgiver other than what the Bible tells us, though it is interesting to see what later Jewish sources make of his story. Convoluted attempts to alter the account tell us more about the Jewish establishment's agenda in rabbinic times than they do of Moses's actual presumed time. In any case, how much credible information is here?

To answer this, we should examine the "case of Moses" in its presumed historical context. That some once-and-future Israelites spent time in Egypt is beyond question. Egyptian records confirm "Asiatics" in Egypt for centuries before Moses's time, though it is not until about 1200 b.c.e. that we have what seems to be an Egyptian mention of an "Israel" in Canaan.[1]

Which and how many Israelites went down to Egypt and how long they stayed is a matter of some dispute, since the Bible gives self-contradictory evidence.

In our view, the stay in Egypt lasted about four twenty-year generations, not 430 or even 400 years, as the Bible reports in separate places. Serah bat Asher is not a matriarch and does not rate an entry under her own name in the *Encyclopedia Judaica*. Her claim to fame is that she is listed both among those going down to Egypt and among those coming back! Noting this, the rabbis of Jewish tradition made of her a figure of Elijah-like proportions.[2] Of course, no mathematical gymnastics are necessary if one posits that the people who left Egypt had only been there for four generations, no more than eighty years.

After all, Moses was the son of Amram, whose father, Kohath, was a son of Levi, one of the sons of Jacob. Joseph, if he is a real character, should have been alive when Moses was born. For that matter, since Jacob himself lived to be 147, did he know of Moses's birth? The Bible is silent about these two, saying only that Moses honored his great-granduncle Joseph's request that his bones be carried back to Canaan for burial there; again, we see the importance of being buried in one's own land among one's ancestors.

By the time of Moses's birth, Egypt had been an empire for almost 1,500 years. During that time "vile Asiatics," as the Egyptians usually referred to people living further East, were often imported or captured in war to serve as menials. Some "sons of princes" were brought to Egypt partly as hostages and partly to be educated in the high culture of Egypt, even given Egyptian names,[3] all so as to provide friends of Egypt when they returned as chiefs to their native lands. As we shall see, not all did.

Other Asiatics were compelled to seek refuge there when agricultural conditions in their own countries became intolerable; the Nile Valley was the surest producer of food in the entire Near East and, of course, Egypt lay just next door to Canaan. Famine in Canaan, the Bible tells us, was the cause of Moses's great-grandfather Jacob's migration.

It is just as likely, though, that Hebrews were habitual wanderers, which made them suspect among more sedentary populations just as hoboes, gypsies or other transients are looked at with suspicion today. The Middle Eastern version of suspicious transients—called "desert Arabs" in the Koran—that endures into our times are the Bedouin. In this regard, it is interesting to note that the word "gypsy" mistakenly labels those so called, the Romany, as coming from E-*gyp*-t, the same place Abraham, Isaac and Jacob visited.

Moses was third-generation Egyptian-born[4] and carried an Egyptian name, leading Sigmund Freud to conclude that he was an Egyptian. This tack represents the views of those nineteenth century scholars, and they were many, who felt that Hebrews learned whatever was good or useful that they had from outsiders. That is, if the critics didn't simply dismiss Moses as a pure literary fiction of the type all too often associated with Ancient Near Eastern or Greek heroes.

For its part, Scripture provides a bogus Hebrew etymology for Moses's name. We say bogus because it is somewhat improbable that an Egyptian princess would be sufficiently fluent in Hebrew to give the foundling Moses a Hebrew name—and that based on a wordplay, yet—or that she would dare do so after her father had decreed death to all Hebrew male infants.[5] That the Bible goes to such trouble to construct an acceptably Hebrew name for Moses does imply that a real human being lurks beneath it.

Freud's suggestion does have the advantage of explaining why Moses's father, Amram, was able to marry his own aunt, Jochebed, something that is in contravention of (later) Jewish law. For the proto-Israelites, however, this part of the story serves as a convenient explanation for Moses's Egyptian upbringing and his Egyptian name. But we should not get lost in details.

As an immediate backdrop to the story of Moses we must first assert that the Exodus is a composite of several tales, that is, an example of historical compression, concerning the exit from Egypt of "vile Asiatics." We think there was no single Exodus event. Rather there were a number of times when Asiatics were expelled or escaped from Egypt, incidents that can be confirmed from Egyptian records. Over time, the Bible's storytellers compressed these events into the single, moving tale that Jews still repeat every Passover.

To say that there was no single Exodus, however, is not to say that the story has no truth in it, rather that one has to prospect for truth in Scripture like a miner panning for gold. One piece of truth-bearing ore is the Bible's observation that Egypt feared its Asiatic slave population might side with invaders. The Pharaoh who "knew not Joseph" says (Ex. 1:10), "Let us deal shrewdly with them so that they may not increase; otherwise in the event of war they may join our enemies in fighting against us and rise from the ground." (NJPS)

(A note suggests the last phrase may mean "from their wretched condition"; RSV has "escape from the land." Expelling Asiatics would be one way to prevent this internal fifth column from forming, but either understanding fits with the identification of these Asiatics as *habiru,* a term we will discuss below.)

Just such a thing may have happened about four hundred years before Moses, namely, when Asiatic invaders whom we know as Hyksos not only invaded Egypt but maintained control there for about two hundred years. (It was once thought that Joseph owed his exalted position to their patronage of other foreigners.) A reprise of this situation would have been a legitimate fear in the last decades of the thirteenth century, when invaders whom the Egyptians called "Sea Peoples" redrew the map of the eastern Mediterranean and nearly took over Egypt, as we know from the fine Egyptian wall-paintings at Medinet Habu of the decisive battle.

We don't know exactly what these people called themselves, but one of the invading groups was called *pilishtim* by the Egyptians. The Bible knows them as Philistines, and it is they who, with thanks also to the Romans, have given the name "Palestine" to posterity. Repulsed by Egypt, they settled to the east....

2. Exodii: Expulsions and Explosions

It requires a bit of imagination to unravel the strands that the Bible has so artfully woven into THE Exodus story, but some speculation may be useful. An early flight of Asiatics from Egypt might be coincidental with the Egyptians' regaining control of their own country from the Hyksos around 1550 b.c.e. That was contemporary[6] with the most cataclysmic event seen in the eastern Mediterranean in historic times, the explosion of Thera.

Thera, also known as Santorini, was a small volcanic island about sixty miles north of Crete. About 1550 b.c.e. it simply blew up. This was the greatest natural cataclysm the world had seen since the Mediterranean had flooded the Euxine (Black) Sea four thousand years before. How big was it? Well, the size of the explosion can be judged by comparison with the volcanic island of Krakatau, which exploded in 1883. For this latter explosion we have eye-witness accounts of "darkness at noon," of a tremendous tidal wave and of particulate matter so thick in the atmosphere that it colored sunsets for a year, to name a few of the aftereffects. Now, imagine that Thera's explosion is estimated to have been anywhere from three to ten times greater than Krakatau.[7]

Immediately one thinks of the "pillar of cloud by day and fire by night" that guided the biblical Israelites on their way East. Thera could not be seen from so great a distance, but we estimate that the explosion would have produced a dense cloud roughly the size of Montana, which then drifted slowly southeastward and become visible all over the eastern Mediterranean. Though the explosion must have taken place centuries before Moses, it could have been the occasion of an earlier expulsion of Asiatics. If so, it has been integrated into the Exodus story along with many other details from intervening expulsions from Egypt by the process of historical compression. That is, events which took place even at vastly different times are often compressed to the point where they seem contemporary, or at least sequential.

There is one other aspect to this story that is important for us here and that is the psychological effect of the catastrophe on the fleeing Asiatics, whether proto-Israelite or not. The Egyptians might have seen the explosion as a signal to reclaim their country, but some Asiatics might have concluded that the paroxysm was arranged specifically for their benefit. And what force could have dealt so devastating a blow to Egypt, with its many powerful gods? One answer would be that there was a higher god, one above all those of the Egyptians and against whom the Egyptians could not prevail.

If monotheism had not yet been born, the explosion would serve as a momentous midwife to the idea.[8] If it had been born, such an unprecedented event would give it a powerful boost. Even so, the new religious idea would not immediately sweep away belief in other gods. The Bible's own history of Israel demonstrates that, among Israelites, polytheism was almost impossible to root out for centuries after Moses's time. It is hardly to be wondered at, then, that Moses, at the (far) shore of whatever body of water he thought God had controlled on his behalf, says (as we still do in Jewish Sabbath service), *Mi camokha b'elim, 'adonai* (Ex. 15:11): "Who is like thee, O Lord, among the gods?" (RSV)

"Gods" has proven a bit strong for Jewish translators. "Who is like you, O Lord, among the celestials?" So NJPS asks, and offers "mighty" as an alternative. Apparently, the translators were unwilling to see Moses even as acknowledging the existence of other gods, never mind that he considered them inferior to his. As we can see, the Jewish translation tradition is still sensitive about calling this spade a spade.[9]

141

But rooting out the other gods would not have been entirely necessary. Another way to deal with them was by what we could call a "friendly takeover," what scholars call syncretism. This seems to be attested in an early divine revelation to Moses.

Though not first in the present biblical ordering of things, Exodus 6:2 relates that God tells Moses that he was known to the patriarchs as *'el shaddai*. We translate this as "God Almighty," but this generalization does not reflect the Hebrew. Admittedly an obscure phrase, the Hebrew *'el shaddai* may well reflect a god of fecundity or nurture.[10] This conjecture assumes a connection between *shaddai* and *sod*, the Hebrew word for "breast."

This should not be surprising. Prominent among the statuary/idols found all over the Ancient Near East are female figurines with prominent breasts, sometimes cupped in their hands as though to give suck to infants. Female deities, or any that could be appealed to for fertility and increase, would be high in the pantheon of Near Eastern cultures. Assigning that function, too, to the one God would be a necessity in a monotheistic system.

3. Zipporah and Circumcision

"Surely, a bridegroom of blood you are to me" – Exod. 4:25 RSV

Long before Moses reached the borders of the Promised Land, however, he had acquired at least one wife, Zipporah. Who was she and what was her religion? Although mentioned only three times in Scripture, Zipporah has been the object of an intense scrutiny. Unlike Moses', her name is unexceptionable; it is the feminine form of "bird." (One thinks of Edith Piaf, the celebrated French singer, though "sparrow" was not her given name.) So even though there is a Moabite named Zippor, father of King Balak, we can't assume from her name that Zipporah was foreign.

But Jewish tradition does. Midrash Tadshe[11] considers her Egyptian, but we also know her as the daughter of one Jethro, a Midianite, hence clearly foreign even if from a related people.

Here we must pause to remind the reader that our biblical ancestors thought everyone was related: how not? Are we not all children of Adam and Eve or, closer to their time, of the three sons of Noah? Edomites are sons of Esau, Jacob's outdoors-loving twin brother; Ammonites and Moabites are the children of Abraham's nephew, Lot, by his own daughters. In the case of the Midianites, they are also called Ishmaelites—that is, descendants of Abraham's son by Hagar, Ishmael. They are called by both names in the narrative of Joseph's sale to Egypt. Joseph, of course, was Moses's great-granduncle.

Returning to Zipporah, interest in her[12] centers on her part in the circumcision of Moses's and her son, but which son? What is really odd about this story is that it is Zipporah who does the circumcising. Rabbinic sources excuse Moses's delay in performing this ritual on the grounds that he had been too busy with other aspects of the trip from Midian to Egypt and worried about the effects on the boy that such an operation might have! But how old was the boy? Circumcision of adolescent boys or men is debilitating; it should not be so for infants, though the possibility for infection is probably greater. But Scripture is silent on this, nor does it say anything about the effects of a 140-mile trip across the northern Negev on a woman who had, presumably, just given birth.

In the end, it is impossible to understand exactly what it is the Bible wishes us to learn here—NJPS terms vv. 25-26 "uncertain"— but it might mean that Moses's family had been sufficiently "Egyptianized" that they had left off a practice the Egyptians disapproved of, at least on the popular level.[13] Admittedly, this is an heretical suggestion, but consider: the text says nothing about Moses being circumcised—an argument from silence, to be sure— which traditionalists could counter-argue: Wasn't his being circumcised what allowed the woman who found him to recognize his being Hebrew?

We have the much later example of Jews in the Hellenistic period who tried medical procedures to hide the fact that they had been circumcised because the culturally superior Greeks were not. Might there have been Hebrew families in Egypt who opted not to circumcise their newborns for the same reason, aping their betters as they did in choosing Egyptian names for their children?

If this is so, then we might have a situation very like the well-reported modern one[14] in which nominal Jews marrying gentiles are consequently moved to re-identify with their religion. Did marriage to a foreigner re-enforce in Moses the need more fully to identify with his own people? After all, had not his killing of an Egyptian who was beating a Hebrew been the immediate cause of his flight?

In any case, all of the above invites a brief discussion of circumcision.

Of the many explanations offered for circumcision, that of Julian Morgenstern[15] seems most plausible. It is, he says, derived from the earlier practice of sacrificing the first-born to the god who had engendered it. The Bible commands (Num. 18:15), "What opens the womb is mine....." and demands its sacrifice. Initially, this might have meant sacrificing the first-born (son) of every wife, then of just one wife (the first to give birth?) as sufficient to redeem all subsequent children[16] and, finally, over time, into taking a part, the foreskin, of each male child as a substitute for the whole.[17]

On a purely human level, there is another aspect of the practice, however, that wants to be explored. Circumcision is a blood-ritual, the "covenant in the flesh" that bound Israelite men together as it does Jewish men to this day. Why should this be deemed useful, even necessary? Can it be because, absent this practice, they were not related before?

4. Hebrews: A Band of Blood Brothers

Most Near Eastern peoples practiced circumcision, but we have no evidence to suggest that it was universal among their males. Universal infant circumcision might be seen as a blood-brotherhood ritual for males who were otherwise unrelated. Modern groups favoring such practices include pirates, the Ku Klux Klan and the Mafia. Admittedly, these groups are not very exalted company for our ancestors to be compared with, but the comparison is not without merit. The early Hebrews were not a group with high social status: just the opposite. Remember Pharaoh's concern about their "rising from their wretched condition."

We noted in Chapter IV that the name Hebrew ('*ivri*) itself seems to denote both a lack of status and no necessary blood connection among those so named. Again, the Bible is at some pains to connect it with Abraham's distant ancestor, one Eber, but saying "I am Abraham the Eber-ite" would not be a very useful or even intelligible identification to make with foreigners to whom Abraham might introduce himself and neither he nor anyone else in his genealogical line does so. In fact there is only one verse (Gen. 14:13) in which he is referred to as a Hebrew.

Siting Abraham late in the Bronze Ages, as we do, makes him almost contemporary with the *hab/piru* brigands of whom the Canaanite client/vassals of Egypt complain.[18] The word was not rediscovered until 1887, with the finding of the first Amarna Letters. These were a series of letters directed to Egypt from vassals in Retenu (Canaan) complaining of harassment or even armed attacks by *habiru*. This invites the question, "Who are those guys?"

From the texts that have come to light, we deduce that *Habiru/hapiru/'apiru* denoted a social class whose occupations ranged from donkey-driving when times were good to brigandage or selling their children or themselves into slavery when they were not.

Early commentators crowed that here, at last, was extra-biblical evidence of the Hebrews and their conquests. On the other hand, here is Gosta Ahlström's characterization of them: "outcasts, refugees, fugitives, rebels, slaves and mercenaries;... robbers and raiders..."[19] This kind of evaluation has a chilling effect on some people; after all, is this an ancestry to take any pride in? It makes sense to connect 'ivri (hebrew) with habiru/hapiru, but how exactly?

The term habiru seems to be equivalent to the Sumerian ideogram SA.GAZ and as such is found, already, in the period scholars call UR III (2050 -1930 b.c.e.). The SA.GAZ are identified or described in ways that makes Ahlström's characterization of them apt, but at the same time, not a description some people would be comfortable assigning to Abraham.

Writing for a series called *The World History of the Jewish People,* Moshe Greenberg was very circumspect in making the identification. He calls the SA. GAZ (=habiru) "freebooters," then allows himself to say, "The possibility—and it is no more than that—remains that the Patriarchs—as individuals and families—may have been hapiru."[20] And why not? Did Abraham not have his own effectively military force of 314 men with which he rescued his nephew Lot? This makes one think of the under- or unemployed German soldiers of the various *Freikorps* after World War I. (We don't know how large or well-organized habiru groups were, but Egypt might well have had reason to fear theirs; *Freikorps* soldiers formed the backbone of Hitler's support in the 1920s.)

Traditional explanations of the word 'ivri that try to distance Abraham from the habiru, saying, e.g., that Abraham must have "crossed over"(/ ' b r) many rivers, or that, religiously, he was on the other side from every one else, are farfetched. Of course, these traditions were constructed well after Abraham's time and well before the Amarna Letters came to light. Let's just say that, for a number of reasons, Hebrews were wanderers. It's no more than what Scripture admits to in Deut. 26:5: "A wandering [thus RSV; NJPS has "fugitive"] Aramean was my father."

We may wonder if by "fugitive" the translators wished to suggest that the patriarchal ancestors habitually operated "outside the law." This would fit Ahlström's characterization of *habiru* noted above.

Abraham is called *'ivri,* (Gen. 14:13), which we translate nowadays as Hebrew, and understand from other uses in Scripture as an ethnic marker. But as we have noted, this is misleading, as are many terms in Scripture for which we supply unwanted capital letters. Abraham is *habiru,* even if not one of those *habiru* complained of in the letters; he lived at least a century before that time. The *hab/piru* were ubiquitous in the second millennium, and the word is sometimes used to designate "enemies of the state" in the same way the late Soviet Union called all of its internal opponents "hooligans" *(khuligan).*

We have Hebrew as a self-identification from the Book of Jonah, where *'ivri* clearly is intended to indicate an ethnicon[21] as well as a worshipper of the One God of Israel. And so it has continued to be used ever since. There is no intent to deceive here, it is simply that Jonah was written so long after Abraham's time that his descendants will have likely forgotten what *'ivri* originally meant and accorded themselves ethnic status, "like the nations."[22]

Not all Israelites were *habiru,* of course, and not all *habiru* became Israelites, but some connection is widely accepted in scholarly circles.[23] It is not too much to suggest that, even if *habiru* were a minority element in Israel's formation, they ultimately gave

148

their name to the group as a whole, as, for example, the Franks have to France.

Furthermore, since some *hapiru* became constituent elements of Israel, it is to be expected that they would have brought their Canaanitish ways, including their religions, with them. What exactly these were is hard to tell, but that they were polytheists is indubitable.

The Bible (Judges 9:4) criticizes the half-Canaanite judge-wannabe Abimelech for surrounding himself with "worthless fellows." Although the word *habiru* is not found in this text, it does say that he hired them, something that would fit what we know of the *habiru*. Some of David's early supporters, apparently, were of the same stripe. Samuel reports, "And every one who was in distress, *and every one who was in debt,* and every one who was discontented, gathered to him; and he became captain over them." (I Samuel 22:2, emphasis added)

This is in keeping with our proposal that the birth of Israel represents a re-tribalization from disparate elements. To the extent that this was the case, any marriage between people of two constituent elements would likely be intermarriage. Needless to say, intermarriage could reach well beyond tribal boundaries as well.

5. Black Is Beautiful

"I am very dark, but comely...." - Song of Songs 1:5 (RSV)

This phrase from Song of Songs may come from the pen of an African wife—the Egyptian wife (I Kings 3:1)?—of King Solomon. If so, it will not have been the first time that we can connect prominent biblical men with African women, maybe.[24]

NJPS, omitting "very," has only "dark" in what we feel is an attempt to minimize the woman's *racial* difference—which would be of no consequence for biblical people—and appease Jewish tradition or later Jewish audiences to whom race did matter. The Hebrew here, *shahorah,* is ambiguous, but the text continues "like the tents of Kedar," that is, the tents of Bedouin that even today are of goatskin dyed a deep black.[25]

Moses is credited with two, or perhaps three, fathers-in-law, but tradition glosses this by saying they were all names of Zipporah's father. The issue here is whether Moses had a second wife and, if so, was she Ethiopian=Cushite? On this point, rabbinic sources take extraordinary steps to offer different explanations. The first is that Zipporah herself was the Cushite and that Miriam and Aaron were exercised on her behalf because Moses had left her behind before going to encounter God, even giving her a conditional *get* (divorce document) against the possibility that he would not return.

But the divorce document is not known in Israel for centuries after Moses's time and, anyway, identifying Zipporah as Cushite is a difficult premise to maintain when the Bible identifies her as Midianite. The Midianites occupied areas probably on both sides of the Gulf of Aqaba, hence they can only be called African by a geographical stretch. And they probably were not black.

Nonetheless, Jewish commentaries do their best to explain her away, in one place even suggesting that "Blackie" would be a pet name for a most fair (white) woman. This won't wash. Jeremiah 8:18, which identifies the then-residents of Ethiopia as different in color from Canaanites, precluded their claiming that the residents of Ethiopia in Moses's time were racially the same as Moses's own people.

The rabbinical balloon-barrage of denial itself smacks of racism, but it really is not. Rather, the rabbis who concocted these explanations thought it unseemly that Israel's premier leader, prophet and law-giver should have "married out"—religiously, not racially—as if this were a relevant category of thought in Moses's time.

All of this explaining away of an uncomfortable fact bends if it does not break one of the rules of interpretation which informs traditional commentary, namely, if the *pshat* (simple story line) carries water, there is no need for other explanations. In our terms, if it ain't broke, don't fix it. Cush is almost certainly Ethiopia and the inhabitants then probably pretty much as they are today.

Another tack taken by tradition is to posit that Moses wouldn't have had two wives because monogamy was mandated on the basis of...the story of Adam and Eve![26] Despite this reading—one that is popular with feminists who would like to see women more as partners than commodities—monogamy was probably not the rule.

In any case, using Adam and Eve for any historical purpose raises more questions than it answers. Even if the text mentioned the First Parents' daughters, one would wonder why the incest taboo, so prevalent in later Judaism, was not operating here or how and for how long this tight-knit family avoided the deleterious mutations that accompany inbreeding.

Adam and Eve works better as an etiological story explaining the relations between men and women (the allegorical level of interpretation) and humankind's need to obey God (the homiletical level). Again, if monogamy is mandated it took a very long time for that ideal to make its way into law. It was not until the early fourteenth century, that is, easily 2,500 years after Moses's time, that Levi ben Gerson, a French rabbi, issued the decree that became normative, at least in European circles. (Some Sephardim, e.g., the Yemenites, brought polygamy with them to Israel in 1948, and the Israeli government had to grandfather it out.)

It's important to establish that the Cushite was a second wife, because if Moses were married to a Cushite and a Midianite, there is virtually no way that he would not have been intermarried at least once. Two marriages are certainly consistent with Moses having two fathers-in-law rather than one with two or three names.[27]

6. Moses's Appeal

As we have noted, the fact that the Bible goes to such lengths to provide a kosher name for Moses is some indication that the man actually existed. Even if Moses did not exist, the religion that we associate with him would have enormous appeal across a broad range of peoples. It is not the "vertical" religion of a single ethnic group with a built-in hierarchy, but a "horizontal" faith that insists on fair and equal treatment for everyone, viz.:

> -- Do not favor the rich because of their wealth or the poor because of their poverty. (Lev. 19:15)
> -- Defend the widow, the orphan, the stranger who lives among you. (Lev. 19:34, 35:25)
> -- Punishment for crimes fits the crime and does not depend on any difference in social status between perpetrator and victim. (The much-maligned Lev. 24:19's "eye for an eye, tooth for a tooth.")

All of these things are quite revolutionary when seen against the background of previous ancient near Eastern legal codes.

More important, they would appeal to those people who had been at the bottom of the social-economic ladder, regardless of ethnicity; think *habiru*. In other words, Moses's religion is tailor-made to knit together the lower-class people of various ethnicities. We might also note here that the practice of universal circumcision, reserved for priests in Egypt, makes sense of Exodus 19:6's "You shall be unto me a nation of priests and a holy people."[28]

The Bible refers to the people he led as including a "mixed multitude" (Ex. 12:38), but in truth, Israel was its own mixed multitude. Here we have Philistines and other Aegeans,

153

misplaced Mesopotamians and native Canaanites along with soon-to-be Israelites led by Moses and inspired by the idea that there was only one God converging on the New Jersey-sized piece of real estate that later Jews would call Israel.

Notes to Chapter V

1. The Mer-ne-ptah stele, after the pharaoh of that name (ruled ca. 1225-1200 b.c.e.), tells us, apparently, that an "Israel" existed, because it claims this Israel has been utterly destroyed.

2. Serah bat Asher: Leilah Leah Bronner, *From Eve to Esther*, 53.

3. E.g., Joseph's name was changed to "Life-giving North Wind."

4. Even Yehezkel Kaufmann, a paragon of orthodox scholarship, sees this and prefers it to the 400 or 430 years found elsewhere in Scripture. See *Religion of Israel,* abridged and translated by Moshe Greenberg (Chicago: University of Chicago Press, 1960).

5. The young woman, princess or no, would have likely forfeited her own life for this transgression.

At best, the name "moses" is paranomasia, a play on the verb " to draw up." Taking it as Egyptian, however, it makes sense as a hypocoristicon, that is, what's left when you take away the divine element from names such as those of pharaohs Ahmose, Kamose and Ramses. Hebrew has such names, e.g., *Jo*-nathan, Dani-*el*, Jeremi-*yah*, but "Moses" isn't one of them.

6. Scientists who study tree-rings (dendrochronology) have confidently identified 1628 as the date.

7. The reader may wish to meander through Simon Winchester's book-length account of the explosion of Krakatau, known to us as Krakatoa. (*Krakatoa: The Day the World Exploded: August 27, 1883,* HarperCollins, 2003).

8. As over against those scholars who hold that Abraham's generation was, already, monotheist.

9. See Jon D. Levenson's commentary in *Sinai and Zion: An Entry into the Jewish Bible* (New York: HarperCollins, 1985), 60.

10. Shaddai in Tikva Frymer-Kensky, In the Wake of the Goddesses: Women, Culture, and the Biblical Transformation of Pagan Myth (MacMillan, 1992), p. 97.

11. *Midrash Tadshe, Ozar ha-Midrashim* [ed. Eisenstein] (NY: Reznick, Menshel & Co., 1928), p. 474.

12. Oddly enough, Nahum Sarna, *Exploring Exodus* (Schocken, 1986), is supremely uninterested, mentioning Zipporah only once and her circumcision of Moses's son not at all.

13. In most cases; there is evidence that some Egyptian priests were circumcised.

14. See Rosenbaum and Rosenbaum, *Celebrating Our Differences: Living Two Faiths in One Marriage* (Shippensburg, PA: Ragged Edge Press, 1994).

15. Circumcision in antiquity may not have been the radical procedure it is today, but the removal of only as much skin as was necessary to free the glans: see Julian Morgenstern *Rites of Birth, Marriage, Death, and Kindred Occasions among the Semites* (Cincinnati: Hebrew Union College and Chicago: Quadrangle Books, 1966), 64ff. Other explanations exist, some of which are mutually contradictory, as for example that circumcision increases or diminishes a man's sexual pleasure. See also J. Sasson, "Circumcision in the Ancient Near East," *JBL* 85 (1966), 473-6.

16. The further attenuated modern version of this is *pidyon ha-ben*, in which parents "ransom" their first-born son from their rabbi, literally from the rabbi's arms, by making a special contribution to their synagogue.

17. One can easily imagine how this would have affected court politics in monarchic times as the families of the king's various wives would maneuver to safeguard the child of their respective daughters.

18. They seem to be those people complained of by Ahmose III of Egypt, whose name for them is "vile Asiatics."

19. Ahlström, *History,* 235.

20. Moshe Greenberg, "Hab/piru and Hebrews, *World History,* B. Mazar, ed. (Rutgers UP, 1961), 200.

21. Greenberg, *ibid.* This proves nothing, as Jonah was written centuries after the Amarna Letters, long enough for the term *habiru* to have acquired its present, metamorphosed status.

22. The quoted words are those of the people to Samuel (I Sam. 8:5), asking the prophet to give them a king. As to the name, who nowadays would remember that the name Fletcher originally meant one who puts feathers on arrows? We do ourselves a disservice by using our English capital letters on words that we take to be proper nouns, making them so whether or no.

23. A. Malamat, *Mari and the Early Israelite Experience* (New York: Oxford University Press, 1992, 1989), makes it cognate with Hebrew /h- b- r, from which we get the words "friend" and "fellowship."

24. Nor the last. Recent DNA studies of the Lemba, a Bantu-speaking African tribe presently living in South Africa and Zimbabwe, suggest that they are descendants of Israelites! *Judaising Movements: Studies in the Margins of Judaism,* Tudor Parfitt and Emanuela Trevisan Semi, eds., (London: RoutledgeCurzon, 2002), 39-51.

25. The black Jews of Ethiopia, called Falashas by their detractors, claim descent from Moses. It's not impossible, but more likely they are descendants of Jews who fled from the Babylonia invasions in the sixth pre-Christian century.

26. *EJ* 11:844. This inference is not itself invalid, but it pales before the black letter law of Deut. 21:15, with its instructions to a man not to favor one of his wives' children over those of another. For all that, Jewish legend has it that Eve was Adam's second wife, the first being the infamous and egalitarian Lilith.

27. Reuel, Hobab and Jethro (the two-name supposition applies to some kings, but I don't know of it elsewhere): tradition gives him seven names; see J. H. Hertz in *The Pentateuch and Haftorahs* (Brooklyn: The Soncino Press, 1960). Is this a balloon barrage designed to distract us from the fact of Moses's multiple marriages?

28. Friedrich Nietzsche (1844-1900), the German philosopher, was no Bible scholar, but he saw clearly—and roundly rejected—the radical Judeo-Christian notion that the weak rather than the mighty should, somehow, inherit the earth.

Chapter VI. Joshua and the Judges

If the time of the Judges—from Joshua to the monarchy—seems less glamorous than the two periods that flank it, it is every bit as important. Overshadowed, at least in the popular mind, by Moses on one side and David on the other, the period is often neglected, the more so by those who are embarrassed at the seemingly bloody extirpation of Canaan's native inhabitants. (Evidence is accumulating that the emergence of Israel was in fact largely peaceful.)

We are speaking here of a period of about two centuries, from around 1230 to 1020 b.c.e. That is much longer than Moses's whole life and twice the duration of the united monarchy. It was two hundred years during which what became Israel was very much in the process of formation. Before the establishment of even Saul's monarchy, Israel was hardly homogeneous. And as we shall see in this chapter, the variety of its constituent elements has a bearing upon the history of intermarriage.

1. Becoming Israel: The Historical Context

Two biblical books,[1] Joshua and Judges, contain the story of this period and Israel's attempt to occupy—or re-occupy—the "Promised Land." It used to be called "The Conquest," following the account in Joshua, but the two books differ greatly on the nature of Israel's entrance. Was it warlike or peaceful? Was it an invasion or rather more of a displacement of people already living there from the cities to the hill country?

However one answers these questions, both books are narrowly focused on the same subject, Israel in Canaan. But just here it is vitally important we expand our field of vision beyond the Israel-centric to see how the emerging Israelite people(s) fit in to their historical and social context.

While Joshua tells a tale of military victories following each other in close order, Judges seems to revel in revealing how unsuccessful Israelites were in expelling "natives": extirpating or enslaving them in the South; sometimes being enslaved by them, especially in the North. Other national "histories" never relate failures; why should Israel be different? Well, it may be just a later, Judean criticism of Northern tribes and hence exaggerated. Finkelstein and Silberman, however, buy into this characterization to such a degree that they write, "in the south there were no Canaanites left, no Canaanite women to marry and to be influenced by."[2]

It's hard to imagine what period they are referring to, but this particular bit of fatuousness overlooks what the prophets were complaining about down to the time of Jeremiah, namely, Israel's continuing worship of other, especially female, deities. The underlying reality is that various ethnic groups lived cheek-by-jowl with Israel at all periods, with all that implies. Ruth's story shows just how close relationships could be. And this just at a time when the "neighborhood" was changing radically.

Toward the end of the thirteenth century, a time contemporary with what religious tradition once thought was the period of THE Exodus, there was an almost unprecedented displacement of eastern Mediterranean peoples. What neither Joshua nor Judges mentions—what neither book, apparently, knows—is that the period of the Judges coincides with a time of the greatest human migration that the Near East had seen in almost four hundred years: that is, since the explosion of Santorini.

We have lists of migrants from various Egyptian sources, and from these we can identify, in addition to Pilishtim[3] (the Bible's

Philistines), Shardana, Tjakker (Troad) and the Danuna (Argolids).[4] Amos 9:7 knew of Philistines coming from Caphtor (Crete) but this was probably their last stop before entering the eastern Mediterranean. We can expect that many migrants came from further northwest, namely, from the Asiatic coast of Turkey and from Greece. Frustrated in their attempt to invade Egypt, some of them settled on the coast to the northeast and established the Philistine pentapolis of Gaza, Ekron, Ashkelon, Ashdod and Gath (Goliath's hometown).

What caused this movement of peoples? Difficult to say. It may have been exacerbated by famine and the epidemic diseases that accompany it. According to Brian Fagon,[5] overpopulation was suddenly undercut by a long drought and subsequent food shortages. A need for food would make Egypt an inviting takeover target. In any case, the movement of these "Sea Peoples" coincides with the breakdown of what we might call the "Ancient Near Eastern economic community," that is, the trade network that tied the empires of Egypt, Hatti and other trading partners together.[6]

The problem with the ANEEC, as with any global network, is that the larger it grows the harder it is to protect trade routes. Domestically, this meant dealing with *habiru*, who could usually be contained. But the partners had no way of interdicting the unprecedented hordes of needy migrants who completely overran the Hittite lands, rattled the gates of Egypt and changed the map of Canaan.

In Canaan, the newcomers might have had little contact with hill-dwelling Israelites but for one thing: Philistines brought with them iron technology that the Israelites lacked. The Bible helps here by reporting (I Sam. 13:19ff): "Now there was no smith to be found throughout the land of Israel;..." so Israelites had to descend to the Philistine cities to have their tools tended.

It seems to have been a cash and carry business, but we wonder if the Philistines might have accepted foodstuffs in payment for their services. In any case, we have to ask how often Israelite farmers going to get tools sharpened would have encountered Philistine women. Would they have been kept in or even hidden, like Mexican women and girls in the movie *The Magnificent Seven*?

On the other hand, as we will shortly see, an alliance with Philistines was one of the tricks in David's bag as he schemed to supplant Saul. How intimate were these relations? Finkelstein and Silberman put one and one together and get... Samson and Delilah, observing only that "intermarriage was not unknown."[7]

Samson had occasion to visit the Philistines and so provides a link with which to begin exploring the extent of social interaction between Israelites and others. Here, as elsewhere, it is of no consequence that Samson seems to be a completely fictitious character. His actions should be considered representative of the countrymen who left no records.

2. Samson and Whatshername

"Make Love, Not War" - Viet Nam War era peace slogan

Samson is the last of the twelve or thirteen (counting Deborah separately) judges to be mentioned in the Book of Judges, but more space is given him than to any of the others; Judges devotes four whole chapters to the adventures of this Danite judge/hero, and yet he is the least likely of the group to have been historical!

Sir James G. Frazer got off a nice, cheap shot a century ago when he said, "I doubt that he [Samson] particularly adorned the bench."[8] This misses the point. We have to say at the outset that "judge," with its implications of legal training, is not a good translation of the Hebrew *shophet*. "Justice of the peace" would be better because *shophtim* (the plural) had no legal training. They did have the authority to decide altercations such as, say, a boundary dispute between two farmers; none of them had more than local or, at best, regional authority. The Book of Judges would have us believe that a handful of them served as *ad hoc* military leaders, but if so, none led a coalition that included all the tribes.[9]

Returning to Samson, his tribe, as we saw above, is probably Greek-derived, so seeing Samson as a Hebrew Hercules is no stretch. A story like Samson's would be very much at home among people with Greek origins. Including it in Scripture would give Danites a stake in the broader community.

Alternatively, Samson's name derives from a Semitic root for "sun," leading nineteenth century commentators to assume he began his career as a sun myth. In this vein, Hertha von Dechend and Giorgio de Santillana present a better case[10] for Samson being derived from Orion, the blind hunter of the skies. However, this is not germane to the present study, so we must leave it here.

163

In his biblical incarnation, Samson is famous for berserk, splenetic exploits that ended with his killing more Philistines by his own death—three thousand—than he had in his lifetime. And what were the circumstances that led up to this bloody end? In a word, intermarriage.

It's hardly necessary here to retell the story of the wily Philistine Delilah (his second or third Philistine wife, by the way), and how she caused him finally to fall into the hands of Philistine enemies. If their story were a movie and Samson's parents were being played by, say, Billy Crystal and the late Carol Kane of *The Princess Bride,* their refrain would be "I told you so." This might be preceded and followed by, "So you couldn't, maybe, find a nice Jewish girl to marry?" The first line is fanciful, but the second is merely an updated version of Judges 14:3:

His father and his mother said to him, "Is there no one among the daughters of your own kinsmen and among all our [Heb. my] people, that you must go and take a wife from the uncircumcised Philistines?" (NJPS)

That's what they said; what didn't they say? They did not say that marriage of Israelites to Philistines was forbidden or that a Philistine wife would be expected to convert. Even though the Philistines are not in the lists of proscribed peoples in Exod. 33 and Deut. 7, it might be assumed that marriage to the "uncircumcised' was even more outside the law than that to one's Semitic kin. Apparently, it wasn't.

That is to say, intermarriage between/among the members of some groups might have been discouraged and therefore rare, but it was not forbidden. In this particular case, perhaps it didn't have to be. By the time the Bible came to be written, the Philistines had all but disappeared as a coherent group. Some of them may have been absorbed by Israel, as we'll see when we come to discuss David's retine.

It might be argued that Samson's is simply a cautionary tale warning that foreign women may be counted upon to lead Israelite men astray. Later Jewish tradition suggests gentile women often lured Israelite men with sex as bait and then required them to change gods.[11] In these scenarios, the men are described as particularly vulnerable to this approach. But in this instance, it is Samson who goes looking for a wife among the Philistines, rather than the other way about. And his first spouse did nothing, apparently, to cause him to stray from the truth path of righteousness—aside from marrying her, that is.

3. You Can't Tell the Players Even with a Scorecard, or: Beware of Greeks Bearing Whatever

Tradition looks at this period (ca. 1250 -1020 b.c.e.) as one in which Israelites tried to expel, exterminate or enslave the previous inhabitants or at least erect barriers between themselves and the people they found in Canaan on their arrival. They were by no means always successful, and the Bible reports that they continued to live among Canaanites, sometimes as masters but sometimes as subservient to them.

But scholars no longer accept the "us v. them," Israelite v. Canaanite model the Bible proposes. The distinctions among these groups was far hazier than Scripture indicates or tradition remembers. Louis Epstein says it well: "[T]he distance between a Hebrew and a heathen was merely an extension of that between *a Hebrew of the tribe of Judah and one of the tribe of Benjamin.*"[12] [Emphasis added]

For one thing, many previous inhabitants joined the Israelites, notably the Gibeonites of Joshua 9. In this unusually detailed story, the inhabitants of Gibeon approach the Joshua-led Israelites pretending to be from far away and wishing to conclude a mutual non-aggression treaty. They—four cities of them—were in fact from just over the hill and wanted to escape the fate that had reportedly overtaken so much of Canaan. But Joshua falls for the ruse and, even when the truth comes out, he cannot go back on his word. Gibeonites are punished by being made "hewers of wood and drawers of water": end of story. But we're not satisfied. We would like to know who these people were.

Evidence, including the offer of a non-aggression treaty, suggests that the Gibeonites were of Greek origin. That suggestion is strengthened by the fact that in the aftermath of the treaty, they were attacked by "Canaanites." Since they were thus cut off from their erstwhile neighbors, we then have to wonder what their subsequent social relation was to the rest of Israel. Louis Epstein gives a convincing description of marital relations among peoples in this period. Here is the context for the above quote:

A mild attitude to intermarriage was natural for the Jews during the early settlement in Palestine. The nation was just being formed out of tribal groups and the distance between a Hebrew and a heathen was merely an extension of that between a Hebrew of the tribe of Judah and one of the tribe of *Benjamin*. [Emphasis added] Religious formulation was still in process. Political and social mingling between the Hebrews and their neighbors was inevitable; covenants of friendship and mutual assistance were necessary for political security and peace. The Hebrews... saw little objection therein save the breach of the general rule of endogamy.[13]

Epstein aside, we cannot accurately assess whether or not Hebrews were, in principle, endogamous or exogamous: that is, whether they were inclined or even compelled to marry inside or outside of their own groups. There is Scriptural evidence to suggest that both routes to the acquisition of wives were present within Israel, and that reinforces our idea that Israel was not a uniform people.

A recent wrinkle in the theories of Israelite origins has it that the earliest of our ancestors were pastoral nomads living on the eastern fringes of Canaan's arable land, depending on its city-states for grain to supplement their and their livestock's diets. At the end of the Bronze Age, when the city-state system collapsed, their erstwhile providers could no longer produce surplus grain; consequently, the pastoralists were pretty much compelled to settle down and raise their own.

This they did, according to Finkelstein and Silberman, in a series of about 250 villages comprising a population of perhaps 45,000, in the central Judean hills.[14] They chose this region because it was sparsely populated. Hence, there was no "Conquest" as the Book of Joshua has it.

Though served by a fair amount of crop and grazing land, the actual villages were usually small, perhaps an acre in size, populated by perhaps fifty adults and fifty children.[15] Villagers would have kept pretty much to themselves; they pretty much had to. Topography of the hill country did not make travel easy; there were no international trade routes close by, not even many local routes. Moreover, initially most villages were composed of subsistence farmers with little to trade.

However, they would have faced two critical shortages. One, as we saw above, was the iron tools so necessary to break stone that they used to terrace the hills for farming. Terracing helped produce an agricultural surplus that could be bartered for other needed goods. The other shortage, as we shall shortly see, was that of suitable partners for their children to marry. And this would get worse with the adoption of laws prohibiting marriage between people too closely related by blood.

Villagers may, of course, have adopted the ugly, but almost universal, practice of murdering excess female infants. We know this practice from present-day China, but it is also as reported by the Palestinian woman known only as "Souad" in her book, *Burned Alive: A Victim of the Law of Men*. She writes:

Two or three girls at most are needed for the housework, to work on the land and see to the animals. If more girls are born, it is a great misfortune and they should be gotten rid of as soon as possible.[16]

She writes of her own horror when she realizes that her mother has killed unwanted female infants, her sisters.

168

It is hard to imagine the value of girls being greater in antiquity than now, especially if their farms were no larger than present-day ones, but since Hebrews and others practiced concubinage perhaps that was the preferred way of finding places for otherwise superfluous females and would go hand-in-hand with polygamy.

We don't know the extent to which polygamy was practiced, but Joshua's contemporary and fellow spy, Caleb, married another woman after wife Azubah died. Interestingly enough, he already had another wife; what does this tell us? It is consistent with Israel's being, in the beginning, anything but a uniform group in regard to marriage practices.

Finally, as we noted in Chapter IV, capitalizing "H" in Hebrew is a mistake. It is a mistake so old that it can't easily be corrected, but we should keep in mind that the term does not initially refer to any sort of ethnic or tribal groups. It seems rather to delineate a social status that cut across ethnic or tribal lines. Therefore, it is incorrect to see "Hebrews" as standing over against other, necessarily foreign, peoples.

Theoretical support for exogamy includes the idea that "marrying out" effectively avoided incest,[17] a real possibility in small villages. Would intermarriage also result in a net population gain or a net loss for them? Would they care? Perhaps even a net loss would be less harmful to the tribe than what was gained, namely, the right to engage in trade with those who were now "members of the family."

4. Trading-partners, Trading Partners

Scholars disagree about whether the artifacts—e.g., pottery, house structures and arrangements—identified as "Israelite" were significantly different from those deemed "Canaanite." The balance presently seems to tilt in favor of those who find little or no difference. Linguistically, if one examines the few inscriptions dating from that period, Israelites seem to have been indistinguishable from their Canaanite neighbors.

This blending is unconsciously noted later by First[18] Isaiah (19:18) who refers to his people's language as *s'fa'at Cana'an*, "the tongue/language of Canaan." This will not be, as some have suggested, that Hebrews learned it as we now do English in order to get along with our neighbors. Rather, it was the native language of some, perhaps many, within Israel. That being so, the parameters of acceptable marriage-mates might be extended far beyond the local village. It almost had to be.

Just imagine: a family composed of a father and his two wives, two unmarried daughters, three sons with two wives each and three children by each wife would total over thirty persons. Add a few stray relatives and the total approaches three dozen, all related; the Hebrew term that describes this is *mishpachah*, usually translated "family." Three or four such families might constitute the entire village. Would there be enough eligible people for all the children to marry? It depends.

The small size of villages might explain, in part, why marriage between children of one father but different mothers was initially allowed in Israel. Iron Age villagers were light years away from understanding genetics. Even the physiological role of the mother in reproduction was not understood. It would be useful to know whether or not elements of Israel were ever close enough to the

Egyptian experience of royal brother-sister marriage to reject sibling marriage outright on what we would call medical grounds. That is, did they have the opportunity to observe the higher incidence of birth defects and deleterious mutations that resulted from such unions? It's doubtful (though they might have inferred some connection from animal husbandry).

More likely, they will have blamed things like congenital defects on the "sins" of parents or grandparents, as Exodus 20:5 threatens. But these sins would not have included marrying someone too closely related by blood. We can and will trace a development away from the practice of allowing half-siblings to marry which comes to a head in Amnon's attempt forcibly to marry his half-sister Tamar.

5. Hoshea bin Nun

The title-name of this section may be unfamiliar to most people, but it is the name Joshua carried before Moses renamed him (Num. 13:16). It happened just before Joshua and eleven others were sent to spy out conditions in Canaan prior to a projected Israelite incursion. The attack never happened, but only Joshua was renamed, and this immediately raises the question of why the name change took place and what it meant.

Here, as usual, Jewish tradition scores an "own goal" by proposing patently absurd reasons for the change. One such proposal is that Moses didn't change Joshua's name, but prayed (the verb in question can be read both ways) that Joshua would not be adversely influenced by the negative reports of the other spies *before their mission began.* This cure is worse than the disease. If Moses knew the reports would be negative, why send the spies in the first place? Something else is apparently going on.

Name change here, as so often—e.g., Abram < Abraham, Sarai < Sarah—indicates a change in religion. We suggest that Joshua was an Ammonite from across the river; that is, he was not an Israelite until he and those he led joined Israel on the eve of its (re-)settlement in Canaan. This assertion leads in the direction of denying that Joshua spent any time in Egypt, but as that is not relevant to this work, we will not pursue it here.[19]

Further, we think Joshua was a devotee of Nehushtan, the bronze serpent that is ascribed to Moses in Numbers 21:9ff. This is of a piece with the later friendship of David with one King Nahash of Ammon, whose name also comes from the root "serpent."[20]

What all of this says is this: just as we saw in considering the story of Ruth, the Jordan did not always constitute an ethnic barrier even if it was something of a physical barrier between peoples. Later Jewish tradition seems to be aware of Joshua's non-Israelite origin (Num. Rabbah 8:4), claiming that he was the descendant of Asenath, the Egyptian wife (and according to tradition, proselyte) of Joseph.

However, there's little possibility this knowledge would have remained underground, as it were, for the thousand or so years between Joshua and the midrashists. Ironically, their speculation (or subterfuge) is really unnecessary; the rabbis were playing a winning hand, they just didn't realize how strong their cards were.

A religion that did *not* assume that whatever your condition was, it was deserved—even ordained by God—and there was nothing you could do to ameliorate it, would appeal precisely to those at the lower end of the socio-economic scale. And not only to them. May we not assume that, just as the cause of the American colonies attracted the support of some high-level foreign soldiers such as von Steuben and Lafayette, so the religion of Moses-led Israelites was attractive to some people who were not part of the flight from Egypt?

For all his putative adventures, we know little about Joshua after Israelites enter Canaan. No sons succeed him; in fact, Scripture does not mention his having a wife. Later Jewish traditional says that he married Rahab, the Jerichoan prostitute who hid the spies he sent when he was reconnoitering the land for Moses (Josh. 2). Further, their descendants included the prophet Jeremiah and his female prophet contemporary, Huldah.[21] Oh yes, and by the way, Rahab converted.

It probably never crossed any rabbi's mind that Rahab and Joshua might be of the same ethnic group and it was that tie,

173

rather than her foreknowledge of the impending Israelite victory, that accounts for her behavior. (Jericho is right on the Jordan River, on the west side but almost midway between Jerusalem and Amman.)

In any case, the notion that Rahab converted is fanciful. That is, it's hard to imagine that such information would have stayed alive but remained underground for over a thousand years until "the rabbis" thought to write it down. But even so, what does it tell us? That some rabbinic authorities felt adherence to her husband's religion could make any woman kosher.

Such a notion is a kind of patriarchal imperialism that does not describe the biblical reality, as we shall see. Women's place in Israelite society was such as to keep alive a religion of women, so to speak, that had probably been practiced in the Near East in one form or another for 30,000 years, too long a time to be simply uprooted by monotheistic fiat.

The Book of Joshua ends, sort of, with a plea to the soon-to-be-invaders to drop their previous polytheism and unite behind the One God. Interestingly, except for Deut. 20, Ammonites are not among those whom the invading Israelites are about to dispossess and, as we've noticed, absent from the lists of proscribed nations in Exodus. Again, let us remember that the term *b'nei 'ammon* does not describe a single people, but groups of people who happened to live on the east side of the Jordan.

Here the Bible reveals that, even on the eve of the so-called Conquest, Israel was a people encompassing many different religious beliefs. If that is so, unless members of one religious-belief unit, clan or tribe or whatever, married only within their own group, Israel would have been a heavily intermarried society. Given the relatively small size of the units in question, strict endogamy would have been unlikely.

174

Again, let us emphasize that the people we are writing about would not have seen it this way, that is, would not have seen marriage across tribal lines as *religiously* mixed. Until exclusive monotheism became even an ideal, let alone the norm, differences in religious practice and belief among married people would have been inconsequential.

6. The Judges and Their Families

Judges is not much interested in the families of Israel's early leaders, less in their religion(s) and not at all in the religion of their womenfolk. There is however, one tantalizing story of the last that may be mentioned in this regard, the rather detailed account of Jephthah's daughter (Judges 11). Briefly, Jephthah is compelled to sacrifice his virgin daughter because of an ill-advised vow he makes before going off to war. The young woman accepts this fate, asking only that she be given two months to go off and bewail her virginity upon the mountains (11:38). Doing what? We don't know. Nor do we know what women in Israel did during the four days every year when it became a custom to celebrate her sacrifice (vv. 39-40).

We have much more information concerning orgiastic female rites of the Greek Bacchanalia, but no way of connecting the two. Still, Judges contains the refrain that, often, Israel worshipped other gods and was therefore punished by the One True God with subjugation by foreigners. Only after they repented did God relent and send another judge to rescue them. Who were these judges?

In many cases, those of the so-called minor judges, we know nothing of the judges themselves except their names. It is even possible that some names have been added to the total—Samson (above) comes most immediately to mind—to give us a number, thirteen, that reflects the thirteen tribes (Joseph splits into Ephraim and Manasseh) of Israel. (That this is not merely fortuitous is demonstrated by the fact that Jesus has thirteen disciples, though only twelve at any one time, and that both the Old and New Testament schemes reflect the 12/13 lunations in a given solar year.)[22]

What we do know of minor judges is not without value. One was named Shamgar ben Anath, and both of his names suggest foreignness. "Shamgar" may be Hittite, but 'Anath is certainly the goddess/consort/sister of Baal in the Ugaritic pantheon: she who resuscitates her brother (killed by the god Mot = "Death") every fall, coincident with the fall harvest. The two names together mark him as foreign, the more so because Scripture does not assign him membership in any tribe.

Abimelech, a judge-wannabe, had a Canaanite mother, a concubine of his father, Judge Gideon. Baal Peor, like Shamgar, is not given a tribe, and this is interesting because it seems to indicate that his ethnicity/religion passed through his mother. Was this a function of class difference or something else? It was Abimelech who hired (*habiru?*) mercenaries to kill his siblings and thus consolidate his hold over Shechem, and it was his mother's people to whom he appealed.

Abimelech shares his name with a king of Gerar who is identified as a Philistine, but the connection may be fortuitous, as the name itself is not essentially Philistine. Judge Jephthah, son of Gilead, was also the son of a prostitute, but of what ethnic group the text does not say. One wonders, however, how he got to be a judge while Abimelech did not.

At best, only two judges came from Judah,[23] the others from various corners of the land north and east of Judah. Unlike Joshua, none is reported to have led "all Israel" in battle, which bespeaks a loosening up of Israel's putative national unity under Moses. In fact, as we shall see, all Israel was generally busier with infighting, most notably against the tribe of Benjamin, than against people identified as foreign. This is noteworthy for many reasons. The first of these is that the first[24] judge was Ehud, a Benjaminite.

He seems to have been one of the 700 left-handed fighters in the tribe (Judg. 20:16) and he uses this sinister advantage to kill king Eglon of Moab. Unfortunately for our purposes, nothing is known of his family beyond his father's name, Gera, but this is not without interest.

David and Solomon's chief Benjaminite opponent was one Shimei ben Gera. Now, Shimei lived some three hundred years after Ehud, but if they belong to the same family it shows a continuity that should not be surprising. I Chron. 8:7 makes him a great-grandson of Benjamin by his first-born, Bela, which would be some indication of family strength and prominence. David put Shimei on the "hit list" that he passed on to Solomon, and Solomon took advantage of what we would call a parole violation in order to kill this rival.

There was also a king of Edom named Bela (with the same spelling) whom Gen. 36:33 identifies as having ruled in Edom before any kings ruled in Israel. That would make him roughly contemporary with Ehud's father. No one has suggested that the Benjaminites ever had an independent kingdom in Edom, but such a thing might explain why Ehud was the person chosen to bring Israel's tribute to the Moabite king whom he killed. And it would also give strength to the theory that Benjamin had its own foreign policy.

These intramural differences, however, have been largely buried under a history of oppression by various gentile nations that did not bother with differences among their Jewish victims, differences that Jewish tradition itself had long forgotten.

Notes to Chapter VI

1. The Book of Ruth purports to be from this time but was probably written at least three centuries later and, in any case, says nothing about the period's politics.

2. Silberman and Finkelstein, *Bible Unearthed*, 150. If they were right, it would be genocide. If not, the population would have been assimilated.

3. The Philistines (Pilishtim) ultimately gave their name, Palestine, to the region we now call Israel. The rendering is still preferred by many Muslims.

4. Donald B. Redford, *Egypt, Canaan and Israel in Ancient Times* (Princeton: Princeton University Press, 1992); p. 146 has a set of lists.

5. In *The Long Summer* (NY: Basic Books, 2004), 82ff.

6. The fourteenth century b.c.e. shipwreck found off the coast of Turkey at Ulubarun in 1982 had items from all over the Ancient Near East, headed for Greece.

7. Op. cit. 98.

8. Folk-lore in the Old Testament: Studies in Comparative Religion, Legend, and Law (London: Macmillan and Co., 1919); Vol. 2, p. 98.

9. See Lawrence Stager, "The Song of Deborah: Why Some Tribes Answered the Call and Others did Not" in *Bar* 15:1 (1989), 50-64.

10. Hertha Von Dechend and Giorgio de Santillana, *Hamlet's Mill* (Boston: David Godine, 1977); 165ff.

11. E.g., at Peor in Numbers. See Frymer-Kensky, *Reading the Women of the Bible: A New Interpretation* (Schocken, 2002); 215ff.

12. Marriage Laws in the Bible and the Talmud (Harvard UP, 1942); 168f.

13. Ibid.

14. Finkelstein and Silberman, 83ff.

15. Cf. the description of Izbet Sarta in Finkelstein and Silberman, 110-111.

16. "Souad," *Burned Alive: A Victim of the Law of Men* (Warner Books, 2004), cited in *World Jewish Digest,* Calumet City, June, 2004 1:10, 23.

17. See, e.g., Frazer, *Totemism and Exogamy* (London: Macmillan and Co., 1910); Vol. 4, p. 167.

18. We generally refer to most of chs. 1-39 of Isaiah as "first Isaiah" because of the scholarly consensus that the hand of at least three authors is visible beneath Isaiah's words.

19. See Rosenbaum, *Understanding Biblical Israel* (Mercer UP, 2002).

20. To his credit, Rashi goes so far as to wonder "out loud" what Joshua is doing in some of the wilderness narrative. He could not, of course, have suggested that Joshua bits were inserted into the narrative to cement his position as Moses's successor, but the idea probably crossed his mind.

21. Matt. 1:5 includes her in his genealogy of Jesus; thus, her genetic contribution enriches both Judaism and Christianity.

22. Rosenbaum in *UBI.*

23. Othniel of Judah, though he is not explicitly called a judge, precedes Ehud. Some scholars feel the Othniel story was added precisely to deny Benjamin pride of place as providing the first judge. See Baruch Halpern, *The First Historians: The Hebrew Bible and History* (Harper & Row, 1988/Pennsylvania State University Press, 1996), p. 125ff.

Chapter VII: Hannah and Women's Religion

"It is becoming for a wife to worship and to know only the Gods that her husband believes in." –Plutarch, Advice to Bride and Groom[1]

The anthropomorphic nature of human thought is abundantly evident when we consider how the ancients thought of their cities. Cities were feminine. How not? Cities nurture and protect their inhabitants, sometimes with walls in which there is but one, guarded gate. How very like the '"gate of horn" through which all of us pass at birth. For the Greeks, the city was one's *mater polis*, "mother city," from which we derive our word "metropolis." For Hebrews, too, the word for city is feminine. But the presence of the feminine in religion far antedates the creation of cities.

1. Women's Religion: It Wasn't Rocket Science

We know from the heartwarming story of Hannah, mother of Samuel the prophet, with which the Books of Samuel begin that women had reason to engage in private prayer. For what did they pray and to whom? In Hannah's case, the answers—children,[2] especially sons,[3] and to the God of Israel—seem well-nigh indisputable. Or are they? Since a woman's place in Ancient Near Eastern society depended so much upon her bearing children, especially sons, the object of Hannah's prayer is not surprising. But the desire/need for children far pre-dates the arrival in the world of Israel's God. To whom did women pray before Hannah's time? If intermarriage means the union of a man and a woman who follow

181

different religious beliefs, then, in order best to assess the extent of intermarriage in the Bible, we should examine what might reasonably be called the world's oldest religion: women's.

Why oldest? The earliest signs of religion that we can see speak to us of the worship of female deities[4] or male gods that ensured female fecundity. These include the myriad representations of snakes[5] or statuettes of females—some of which go back thousands of years—pregnant or with exaggerated vulvae or cupping their breasts. The Bible's Shaddai (now linked with masculine El and called by us "God Almighty"), whom we discuss below, probably began life as a female deity who presided over lactation!

By way of contrast, the earliest date for the emergence of Israel and its self-proclaimed aniconic monotheism is about 3,000 years ago. So whatever religion women may have held had about a 25,000-year head start over monotheism and a mountain of momentum on its side. As we know from Scriptural evidence, elements within monarchic Israel needed a lot of persuading to give up their iconic deities. If that is so hundreds of years after Moses's time, what was the case before? To put it simply, armed with a logic the Greeks and we, their descendants, would reject, pre-monotheistic religion worked tolerably well.

Much early religion, we think, is founded on the observation that what comes after must be caused by something that came before. Thus, in Solomon's prayer of dedication for the Temple (I Kings 8:33), the new king theorizes that military defeats, when they happen, will be the result of Israel's having sinned. To Roman philosophers, this is known as the logical fallacy of *post hoc ergo propter hoc* and their classic example is the crowing rooster... which supposedly causes the sunrise that so soon follows.

For people who didn't exactly know how nature worked, much less have familiarity with Greco-Roman philosophy, it was their prayers and rituals that caused salmon to return to the rivers to spawn, crops to grow, and babies to be born. As to the last of these, the notion of value-neutral "congenital birth defects" did not exist. Defective or stillborn babies were, necessarily, the result of sin, either of the parents or grandparents or even great-grandparents, if one reads the Ten Commandments literally.

There God promises to visit the sins we do on the heads of our great-grandchildren. Now, we are taking this snippet out of its ameliorating context and much more could be said here. But many people, Jews and Christians, have taken the verse literally; indeed, they have both used it to justify (Christians) or explain (Jews) the Holocaust. If such outrageous opinions can exist in our time, how much more so in the times we are talking about?

And with thousands of years in which they had witnessed good and bad results from their previous practices, the ancestors accumulated much spiritual capital to invest in resisting any calls for exclusive worship by upstart monotheists.

No wonder, then, that Plutarch, writing in the first Christian century, can only advise, á la Miss Manners, that women give up their gods/goddesses when they marry. He does not, of course, hold any brief for monotheism. What this bit of advice tells us is that women and men in Plutarch's world did not necessarily worship the same set of deities. Now, it might be argued that Plutarch's world was still mostly pagan and so his words are of no value in assessing the situation in Israel a thousand and more years earlier. The opposite is true.

As we saw in the Esarhaddon Vassal Treaty, male and female deities were plentiful. To this we may add Jeremiah's contemporary criticism of the women of Israel for baking cakes to the crescent moon. Recall that Jeremiah lived to se the destruction of the First Temple. After the destruction, some in Judah blamed Jeremiah for interdicting this worship. Nor should this surprise us.

Monotheism was both a new and a geographically limited faith for a long time after its conception. Of Abraham's eight sons (and how many daughters?), only one followed his revolutionary path. Why? For one thing, the Israelite version of the new faith became increasingly transcendent. It deprived worshippers of the realia of religious belief: that is, the animals, trees, standing stones and icons which gave the believer something to see, to touch, to pray to and which had done so for time out of mind.

By itself, we doubt whether monotheism could have carried the day. But Abraham's faith had the advantage of coming at a time when the paradigm that allowed such a prominent place for women's religion, for the goddesses to whom women prayed, had already been changing for over a thousand years.

Some time after the beginning of the Bronze Ages (3500 -1200 b.c.e.), male gods came to supplant goddesses. Why? The Bronze Age gave men weapons of bronze, and farming tools, too, which only those with the requisite upper body strength could wield. (About 1200 b.c.e., bronze gave way to iron, a stronger metal but harder to work.) We know of two later instances, on Crete and in Assyria, where warriors actually deified their weapons! It is not too much to suggest that this early technological revolution had the unlooked-for effect of accelerating what Tikvah Frymer-Kensky describes as marginalizing of the goddesses.[6]

Nowhere is this more visible than in the Enuma Elish, the Babylonian creation myth that showcases Marduk, the male god of Babylon, in a successful fight against Ti'amat, the female deity of the briny deep, who is bent on destroying humankind. But though banished from the center of religious activity, those deities who were seen as necessary for reproduction and nurture continued to have a place in women's hearts. And in their practice.

184

2. Serpent, Venus, Moon

If ever I saw the light shining
The moon on its course in full glory,
And I secretly succumbed,
And my hand touched my mouth in a kiss,
That, too, would have been a criminal offense. – Job 31:26-8
(NJPS)

As Stewart Guthrie observes,[7] much of human religion is anthropomorphic; that is, it describes the world in terms derived from our own selves and our experiences. Consider: the Greeks, whom we consider pillars of sophistication—the very word we use is of Greek origin—had 3,673 gods, all of whom were related by blood or marriage.[8] If the countrymen of Socrates, Plato and Aristotle could believe that Zeus impregnated human women and even animals, how much less sophisticated might we expect the religion of the Semitic pastoralist of five hundred years before to be?

It seems impossible that the farmers of Israel could have adhered to a system so abstract, so devoid of symbols for such important matters, so lacking in emotional outlets for their concerns.[9]

And what about the religion of Mrs. Pastoralist? Tirzah Firestone asks[10] whether women had "their own ways of accessing the Divine that went unrecorded." The answer is an emphatic "Yes," but she's wrong to state that they went unrecorded. Scripture records many elements of women's religion, though always in contexts of disparagement.

Even assuming complete validity for the Bible's story of God's revelation to Abraham, the monotheistic "revolution" thus engendered came very late in the history of the Ancient Near East. By the most conservative of estimates, Abraham will have lived only 4,000 years ago.[11] So we may ask, how much of their religion was retained by non-monotheistic women after marriage to monotheists in the pre-Mosaic period?

Well, we have the story of Rachel taking her family's *teraphim* from her father, Laban's, house when she went off with husband Jacob and sister/co-wife Leah. We don't know exactly what this was/these were, but Jewish tradition understood them as objects of worship; Gen. 31:30 says as much. Rashi (Gen. 31:19) alibis Rachel saying that she stole the *teraphim*—which Rashi understands as plural—not to worship them herself, but in order to wean her father from *his* idol worship. Can we imagine Laban arising next day and saying, "Drat! My teraphim have gone missing; guess I'll have to become a monotheist"?

As we will shortly see, the shoe is very much on the other foot.

First, we would like to suggest that *teraphim* may be construed as a plural of majesty.[12] We've been led astray by translations which, apparently, presume that "pagans" are polytheistic and so any plural form is, well, plural. But just as *'elohim* (God) is a formal plural that we translate as singular (LORD), so *teraphim* may also be used as a singular.

Further, we think /t-r-p/ may be a dialectal or by-form of /s-r-p/ = "burn," the root from which the word *seraph* = "poisonous snake" (lit: fiery serpent) comes. Consequently, we can posit that what Rachel pilfered was that oldest of all earthborn gods, the snake. This should not surprise us. The famous faience snake goddess from Crete, now in the Boston Museum, dates from the fourteenth pre-Christian century, roughly contemporary with the story of Rachel. If Rachel did not know that particular representation, there would have been plenty of local examples that she did know.

Here we might ask: why a serpent in the garden and not, say, a monkey or a tree toad? Obviously, more needs to be said on this subject.

At the Scopes "monkey trial" in Dayton, Tennessee in 1925, Clarence Darrow, speaking for Scopes, mockingly asked William Jennings Bryan how the snake, which God condemned to crawl on its belly like a reptile, had gotten around before that fateful curse. If Bryan had had any knowledge of herpetology he might have answered Darrow's question by pointing out that the python has vestigial hind legs, indicating that its ancestors did indeed walk or could at least stand upright.

Not coincidentally, it's a python at Delphi that the *pythia,* or Delphic oracle, consulted for centuries, answering the questions of kings and commoners. This must have been known to the writers of the Bible. Hence, one of the purposes of putting a serpent in the garden as man's rival[13] is to remind all of us, but especially women, not to listen to their forked speech; that is, not to worship snakes.

What the parameters of snake-worship in Laban's house might have been we don't know, but there are many possibilities. At various times and places snakes have been held responsible for fertility in cows, wisdom, wealth and the power to resuscitate dead children. So prevalent and enduring is the snake as an object of worship that Marija Gimbutas, who identifies the snake as a goddess, reports its service as still being alive and well in her mother's Lithuania at the beginning of the twentieth century.[14]

Would Rachel's continuing to practice her family's religion have been of much concern to Jacob? In other words, would Jacob have been overly concerned that Rachel continued to practice ancient snake rituals associated with women? As we saw earlier, Shaye Cohen doesn't think so. His is a scholarly view; traditional Judaism insisted that foreign women had, indeed, followed Plutarch's advice and "converted," even if we may question what there was to convert to. In this case, tradition is aided by conveniently forgetting that, though related, Rachel and Leah were religiously foreign to Abraham and Jacob.

Nor, in all likelihood, was the snake the only deity worshipped *chez* Laban. The name Laban ("white") itself, in its feminine singular form *lavanah,* means "moon." Moon-worship would comport very well with what we know of the names, both personal and place—e.g., Terah, Jericho—of the larger family of which both Laban and Abram were a part. However, as we indicated above, monotheists made moves to incorporate pagan practices that could not be immediately done away with. Thus, *rosh hodesh,* the New Moon (actually "no moon"), has been incorporated into Judaism... as a women's holiday, of course.

The most remarkable example of incorporation, however, concerns another serpent. To cure people bitten by poisonous snakes (Num. 21:9ff.), Moses makes a bronze serpent so powerful that merely to look upon it is to effect a cure. (Parenthetically, those afflicted concluded that the snakebites were punishment for their previous sins.) How is this possible so soon after the Ten Commandments, with their prohibition against "graven images"— that is, the representation of any living thing—have been handed down that Moses violates God's law? Remember, at this point Israel hasn't even reached the Promised Land.

Tradition falls to haggling about whether God intended Moses to use bronze in the construction or not, but this is beside the point. It's still an image. Moses's defenders might claim, "It was an emergency situation. People were being killed by these poisonous (*saraph*) snakes so God made an exception to his own rule—just this once." This, however, is bogus, but to prove our contention we have to examine what the serpent really was.

First, we have to realize that this "bronze serpent" is actually two serpents; the word *nehustan* should be understood as having a dual ending: that is, indicating something that comes in pairs. Given this, it's not hard to see what Moses made; we can still see it on cars in any hospital parking lot in America. It, of course, is the caduceus, that most powerful symbol of healing that we (erroneously) ascribe to the Greeks.[15] That Nehustan was considered poisonous may be gathered from Deut. 8:15 and Num. 21:6, where it is used with *saraph* in apposition. What deals death also gives life.

As we saw above, Moses was not the first person to make it, either. Rather, worship of the snake as healer was so old, so ingrained in the people who formed Israel, that it simply could not be extirpated even by divine fiat. So it was "kosherized," syncretized into Israelite religion, where it remained a presence for another 500 years. For this we have the witness of II Kings 18:4, the laconic description of *nehustan*'s destruction by King Hezekiah (reigned 716 - 686 b.c.e.).

He also broke into pieces the bronze serpent Moses had made, for until that time the Israelites had been offering sacrifices to it; it was called Nehustan. (NJPS)

Early Church fathers did their own hatchet job on the snake, a character assassination that modern political candidates might envy. The Roman Catholic interpretation of Gen. 3:15 has Mary, the mother of Jesus, stepping on the head of a snake, one of that brood of vipers that is Satan's. And so the transformation of what had once been a healing god to complete identification with the Prince of Darkness was complete. Talk about your makeovers.... It is instructive, though, that even this didn't stop snakes from being used in worship.[16]

3. Holy Hannah!

We get a clue as to what women's religion in the Iron Age was all about from the story of Hannah in the Book of Samuel. Hannah, as we know, went to the shrine at Shiloh maintained by Eli, the resident priest, to pray for offspring. But let's begin at the beginning.

Hannah and a woman named Peninah were married to one Elkanah. Here is another indication of the prevalence of polygamy in early Israel, but that's not the issue here. Hannah had no children. Tradition reports that, after ten years of barrenness, it was her suggestion, á la Sarah, that Elkanah take another wife.[17] When this other wife, Peninah, had children she taunted her co-wife for continuing barrenness, a common response in the region even to this day. The pseudonymous Palestinian writer Souad writes, "A wife must first produce a son, at least one, and if she gives birth to only girls, she is mocked."[18]

Hannah didn't produce even girls, but her husband generously continued to love and support her. Since he was content, why was she not content to overlook the taunting, forego the tribulations of childbirth and help raise her co-wife's children? It just didn't work that way.

As indicated at the beginning of this chapter, a woman's status in biblical society, even her continuation in marriage, was usually dependent upon producing offspring, male preferred. So important was this that the maternity dispute so cleverly solved by Solomon concerning which of two women was the mother of a live baby overshadows the fact that the two were prostitutes fighting over possession of a child. Given their profession, one might think children something of an encumbrance.

Rabbi Firestone asks, "Why did women put up with being kept, from earliest times, on the outer circle of formal tradition?"[19] The answer, again, derives from the fact that in the Ancient Near East, even married women might be divorced for barrenness;[20] in later Jewish law the period of barrenness was set at ten years, but we doubt men in Elkanah's time needed to wait that long. The question for women, then, would be how to insure that they had children.

In one famous case, barren Rachel gave up her "turn" to sleep with husband Jacob in order to obtain mandrakes collected by her sister (and co-wife) Leah's son, Reuben. Because of the bifurcated shape of their roots, mandrakes were considered pregnancy-producing agents. But for this purpose women had recourse to agencies more powerful than things found growing in their fields.

4. A Garden of Earthly Delight

If the Bible has any idea of women's real physical contribution to conception, it certainly doesn't say so. To the best of our knowledge, this discovery was made by the Greek Galen (Galenus Claudius c130 - c200 c.e.). In the biblical period, then, women's role in pregnancy was almost certainly unknown. At most, they were seen as gardens in which men planted seeds,[21] an easy analogy for people who had been planting and harvesting crops since Neolithic times. To insure that the seed took root, women had recourse to things in nature that seemed to govern the production and health of offspring. Their roster will have included Venus, the morning and evening "star."

In the Ancient Near East, the planet we call Venus was worshipped in various places as Ishtar, Astarte or Ashtoreth because its apogee (highest point above the horizon) in the spring was and is when domestic animals mated. (It's no coincidence that, 1,500 years after the fall of Rome, we still recognize Venus as the goddess of love.) Our ancestors would have seen spring pregnancy as causation not coincidence; things that precede cause things that follow.

As important as Venus and snakes are, however, women's religion might be said to center on the moon and, we would guess, has done so since the dawn of human consciousness. How not? Is there a society that has not noticed the menstrual cycle in women corresponds with the cycles of the moon? Further, even today when women live together, as they do in college dormitories, they quickly get on the same menstrual schedule! In ancient times, menstruation would have taken place in the dark of the moon—when there is no moon, or, as we now call that period, the new moon.[22]

This is certainly more powerful "magic" than mandrakes, to be sure. It practically ensures that women would pray to the moon to show them that they were carrying: in other words, to "give" them a child. A thirteenth century b.c.e. shrine at Hazor, the one fortified city that the Bible reports Israelites captured, features a small basalt block clearly showing a pair of hands reaching up to a full and a crescent moon.[23]

The passage from Job quoted above shows that moon worship by women or men, though apparently proscribed in the time those verses were written, was still done, if only in secret, with the hope that God somehow wouldn't see. It would not matter whether the moon itself were conceived of as masculine or feminine, and in fact it has various genders in Ancient Near Eastern cultures. In Hebrew it is masculine.

Until very recently,[24] scholars were reluctant, perhaps embarrassed, to acknowledge this dependence upon the moon's regulation of menstruation as a foundation of belief. But if we're embarrassed to discuss such intimate details, we're not alone. The Bible itself euphemizes when it declares that a captive woman should be allowed to wait a month before being subject to sexual relations to "mourn her father and mother." In fact, the word used in Deut. 21:10-14 isn't month, it is "moon," and the meaning is, plainly, wait until the next new moon shows them that they aren't pregnant so that there will be no questionable paternity for offspring born in captivity.[25]

Worship of astral divinities was not exclusive to women. As we saw above, names like Laban, Abram's ancestor Terah (m.), and places like Jericho (Lot's abode in Canaan), both the latter from the root /y-r-h = moon, show that moon-worship was rife in Abraham's family before the turn to monotheism.[26] Those not in Abraham's direct line—for example, Lot and his daughters—would presumably maintain the old religion, as we noted above.

What happens when, say, a moon-worshipping woman marries a monotheistic man? Perhaps not too much at first, because the question just asked begs another. It assumes that devotees of one deity were somehow cut off from worshipping any others. This, however, is a Western conceit, though of considerable antiquity.[27] Many polytheistic societies still exist and their adherents have no difficulty in worshipping multiple deities. It will have been likewise in antiquity.

And is this really so different from what we do now? We have our patron saints, guardian angels and more veneration of ancestors than we care to admit. When monotheism did make headway in Israel, it was often done by absorbing the celebrations of the land's inhabitants and syncretizing other gods into aspects of Israel's One.

(The most obvious case of syncretism or, at least, metamorphosis, is that of the Great Goddess of prehistoric times into the Blessed Virgin Mary of Roman Catholicism. And why not? For all of our patriarchal posturing, females are more important than males. The female principle should be recognized in our religions. In Judaism, this is represented by the Shekinah, the Divine Presence that emanates throughout the world, but Jewish championing of the Shekinah is relatively late, having gotten its first big play only in seventeenth century Hasidism.)

Syncretism or "covering" is also reflected in Israel's religious calendar. The Bible's three pilgrimage festivals (Passover, Shavuot and Sukkot) are all based in agriculture—they are harvest festivals—but we are given historical reasons for the Israelites' celebrations of them. Passover celebrates the escape from Egypt, Shavuot the giving of the law on Sinai, and Sukkot the moveable dwellings of the forty years of wandering. Similarly, when God tells Moses that he had previously revealed himself to Israel's founders as 'el shaddai—without capital letters, of course—a name that

194

probably denotes a fertility function, that name becomes just another appellative for God. But there is a lot more here.

We usually write El Shaddai, translate as "God Almighty," and don't give it a second thought. But as we saw in the chapter on Moses, *shaddai* probably derives from a root that, in Hebrew, gives us the word "breast." El Shaddai is a mountain deity and, just as mountains bring rain,[28] or seem to, so breasts give milk, or it is to be hoped that they will, else our offspring will die.

Consider this: a normal woman who began menses at thirteen and died at the usual age[29] of under forty would be either pregnant or nursing for nearly half her adult life even if she only had the six pregnancies that would produce two living, adult children. In addition to the four and a half years of pregnancy involved, six living babies would require at least twelve years of nursing. Any deity that could be successfully appealed to for help in this most important aspect of human life would have a loyal following.

To conclude: from the Paps (= "breasts") of Jura off the coast of Scotland to the Grand Teton in the U.S., the similarity of mountains to breasts, both in shape and function, has been universally noticed. As Guthrie says, much of religion is anthropomorphic.[30]

In Israel there is a pair of mountains, Gerizim and Ebal near biblical Shechem (modern Nablus), that are so close together that they do, indeed, resemble a pair of breasts. Samaritans—that is, the Northern Kingdom of Israel—had a temple there, but these peaks were doubtlessly worshipped long before any proto-Israelites set foot upon them. And so let us return to Hannah at her prayers.

Eli rebukes Hannah, thinking her drunk. Though we don't know for sure to whom she was praying, there is no indication that it was improper for her to be praying. The Bible reports that she prayed to her and Elkanah's god, to Yahweh, for a son who, she promised, she would then dedicate to Him. In due course her son Samuel was born and not only was he dedicated to God, he came to supplant Eli at the very shrine where his mother had prayed for him.

All very neat. But if Hannah was a Yahweh-worshipping monotheist, she was both early and, I think, of a minority among biblical women. As some proof of this we note that few of the Bible's women have names in which Israel's god (*'el* or a variant of *yah*) is manifest. Instead, we have women named "bee" (Deborah), "rock-badger" (Huldah), "ankle-bracelet" (Achsaph), "palm tree" (Tamar), "snake" (Nehusta) and the like. These are among the names that we can at least translate.[31]

Yael, a heroine of Judges 5 whose name might seem to indicate early Yahwhism, is in, fact a Kenite or hanger-on, and her name is consonantally indistinguishable from the word for "mountain-goat." That would be in keeping with the usual nomenclature for women noted above.

Moses's mother, Jochebed, has a name that some have connected with Yahwhism, but the connection is far from certain. She, the reader will recall, married her nephew, Amram, which is against (later) Jewish law. The most prominent female who bears an indisputably "kosher" name is Athaliah, Queen of Judah in the ninth pre-Christian century and... daughter of Ahab and Jezebel, his Phoenician wife, hardly a religiously pure lineage. None of David's wives have identifiably Yahwistic names. What are we to make of this?

It's true that the women's names are not generally construed with the names of other deities, either, but the majority were still involved with those their mothers had worshipped from time immemorial. And they continued to do so even as the wives of kings in Israel and Judah, as we'll see in the next chapter.

Another object of worship was the *'asherah*. This seems to have been a pole or perhaps an evergreen, the symbol of undying reproduction. As such it/she was known in the Ugaritic pantheon as the wife of El, the head of the pantheon. Worship of this phallic symbol, for so we may interpret it, was so prevalent that even after periods of monotheistic reform, e.g., that of King Asa of Judah—who dismissed his mother, Maacah, from the office of Queen Mother because she caused one to be set up—the practice resurfaced again and again.

Maacah, it should be noted, was an Israelite woman, not a foreigner upon whom idol-worship could be conveniently blamed.

In part this is because Asherah was not as great a threat to the Father God of Israel as were the various Baals of Tyre or Peor or elsewhere. In fact, the names of Asherah and Yah are linked at the Sinai caravan station of Kuntillet 'Ajrud. As a result of the contest on Mt. Carmel where Yah vanquished Baal, some in Israel, especially in the North, might have concluded that God had succeeded to Asherah as his consort. This would parallel David's taking of Saul's widow, though, except for Baruch Halpern,[32] no one so far thinks that David arranged Saul's death in order to do so.

Alternatively, there may have been a Canaanite/Israelite Asherah who was there all along. We will return to this possibility at the end of this work, asking the question: Was God Ever Intermarried?

As we indicated at the beginning of this chapter, women's religion wasn't rocket science, but that goes for men's religion as well. It is possible to see the struggle between men's and women's religions, or more precisely the monotheism that we associate with Abraham and previous polytheisms, as a struggle between conceptions of immanent gods and goddesses *vs* the one transcendent God. In theory, the One God is invisible and cannot or at least ought not to be represented iconically, whereas the many dwell with their devotees, in or with or near their icons.

Notes to Chapter VII

1. Cited in Cohen, *Beginnings,* 170fn.

2. We see this indirectly in the Esarhaddon Vassal Treaty with Urakazabanu in which "Belet-ili, the Lady of all creatures [is invoked to] put an end to birth-giving in your land so that the nurses among you shall miss the cries of babies in the streets." ANET. Pb 63.

3. Below, women giving birth to daughters might be mocked and their infant daughters killed.

4. Marija Gimbutas and Joseph Campbell, *Language of the Goddesses* (London: Thames & Hudson, 1989).

5. Gimbutas writes, "Representations of the snake are known since the Upper Paleolithic and continue in the Mesolithic and Neolithic." *Language,* 122.

6. E.g. in In the Wake of the Goddesses: Women, Culture, and the Biblical Transformation of Pagan Myth (Macmillan, 1992).

7. Stewart Elliott Guthrie, *Faces in the Clouds: A New Theory of Religion* (NY: Oxford University Press, 1993) *passim.*

8. Harold Newman and Jon O. Newman, A Genealogical Chart of Greek Mythology: Comprising 3,673 Named Figures of Greek Mythology, All related to Each Other Within a Single Family of Twenty Generations (Chapel Hill: University of North Carolina Press, 2007).

9. Frymer-Kensky, *Wake,* p. 153.

10. Firestone, *Receiving,* 18.

11. The actual date is probably closer to 3,500 years ago.

12. Article by Theodor Noldeke in Brown-Driver-Briggs, *Hebrew and English Lexicon of the Old Testament* (Oxford: Clarendon Press, 1906).

13. Gimbutas *passim*. We say nothing here of the obvious phallic association of the snake.

14. Gimbutas, ibid. Had St. Patrick been sent east instead of west, Lithuania might not have had this problem. It was not snakes alone that Patrick drove from Ireland, but worship of the snake goddess.

15. Astour, *Hellenosemitica* (Leiden: E. J. Brill, 1965), 236.

16. Astour, "Two Ugaritic *Snake* Charms," JNES 27 [1968] 19-21. Note that Asclepius, whose symbol the caduceus is, was the product of the union of Apollo with a human woman. Is this what the Bible refers to when it says, "The divine beings saw how beautiful the daughters of men were and took wives from among those that pleased them"? (Gen. 6:2 NJPS)

17. In Hebrew, "child" and "son" are expressed by the same word, indicating the preference for male children. PR 43, 181b cited in *EJ* 7:1270.

18. *World Jewish Digest* June, 2004, I:10, 23. The present distress of the Japanese Emperor's wife shows that such things are by no means confined to the Middle East.

19. Firestone, *Receiving*, 18.

20. This is still the case in the Middle East. e.g., beautiful Queen Soraya of Iran was divorced by the Shah for failure to produce a male heir. The prevailing rabbinic view regarding the commandment to "multiply" holds that one needs two sons and a daughter to fulfill it.

21. In the Ugaritic poem titled "The Wedding of Nikkal and the Moon," "The prospective groom... promises to... cultivate his beloved, even as a farmer transforms a field into a fertile vineyard." Cyrus Gordon, *Ugaritic Literature* (Rome: PBI, 1949, 63). For all that, in modern India if the result is a girl, the mother is blamed.

22. Dr. Katherine C. Baker, personal communication.

23. Yadin, *Hazor* (NY: Random House, 1975), ill. P. 45.

24. Judy Grahn rips the lid off this suppressed connection in *Blood, Bread, and Roses: How Menstruation Created the World* (Beacon Press, 1993).

25. Or even after a three-month wait; see Tosefta Yevamot 6: 8.

26. See Michael Astour's article in *Genesis,* Anchor Bible, Vol. 1, E. A. Speiser, ed. (Doubleday, 1964) 85ff.

27. Ephraim Feldman, *Intermarriage Historically Considered* (Cincinnati, 1905), compares the ancient Greeks, who were expected to be loyal to a single city though they might maintain multiple allegiances within that city.

28. In Israel, rain falls on hills/mountains first and then on the seaward side. The sacrifice of young girls on the high slopes of Peru's Nevado de Ampato shows how seriously people take the need for rain.

29. Philip J. King and Lawrence E. Stager, *Life in Biblical Israel* (Louisville, KY: Westminster John Knox Press, 2001) extrapolate this figure from David Noel Freedman's calculations in "Kingly Chronologies, Then and Later," *Eretz Israel* 24 (Jerusalem: Israel Exploration Society, 1993, S. Ahituv and B. A. Levine, eds.).

30. Stewart Elliott Guthrie, *Faces in the Clouds: A New Theory of Religion* (NY: Oxford University Press, 1993) *passim.*

31. We owe the idea for this to Ms Corinne Kline, a student of Prof. S. N. Rosenbaum's at the University of Kentucky.

32. Baruch Halpern, *David's Secret Demons: Messiah, Murderer, Traitor, King* (Grand Rapids, MI: Wm. B. Eerdmans, 2001).

Chapter VIII. Choosing Up Sides: Who's In, Who's Out

1. "Have we not all one Father?" (Malachi 2:10)

The prophet's question is theological-rhetorical, assuming the answer "Yes." On the human level, Israel's answer is the same even if it had three different mothers, as did the eight children of Abraham. Anterior to Abraham we have Noah (Gen. 6 - 9) and his wife, and standing before Noah there were Adam and Eve. Scripture understands that, however different we may be in physical appearance, we are all descendants of one family.

If that's the case, we all ought to have one religion and one language. Gen. 11, the story of the Tower of Babel, which follows Noah pretty closely, explains why we speak different languages. It is, like so many of the Bible's accounts, etiological—that is, designed principally to explain why a certain thing is the case: here, why we have different languages. The other differences, including religion, are a bit more complex. (We deal with them in Chapter X, Contours of Israel's Religion)

We know from the Table of Nations in Gen. 10 that Mr. and Mrs. Noah's offspring spread out quite a bit. The Hamites went to North Africa, some Semites settled in the East, and the Japhethites inhabited the Greek islands. Thus the three sons' families represent the three areas with which the collectors of Scripture were most familiar.

The Table has seventy nations and, while seventy is a conventional number, the list is notable for the myriad peoples it omits, from Aleuts to Hmong. Christian or Muslim fundamentalists may strain credulity by trying to integrate all the people we now know into the Bible's list, but it's a futile exercise, the more so because these same people usually want to fit all of human history into less than 6,000 years.

The Bible doesn't really explain how all of Noah's descendants became and remained polytheists until Abraham, some ten generations later, but we may essay a suggestion: our notion of Deity has evolved in the last 40,000 years, that is, the time during which paleontologists tells we've had recognizable speech and, consequently, the ability to think.

Even the above-mentioned fundamentalists have to admit to something like "progressive revelation," because their own movements are so very dependent upon it. Neither occupies more than five percent of the time during which we may assume our human ancestors had religions.

We have to keep in mind that the knowable period of history in the Ancient Near East had been going on for at least 1,500 years before Abraham's time and for more than 2,000 years before the first stirrings of exclusive monotheism. Here we might use the insights of Thorkild Jacobsen[1] concerning the period from 4000 b.c.e. onward. Dividing history into millennia, Jacobsen says that the gods went from being providers (4,000 - 3,000) to rulers (3,000 - 2,000) to parents (2,000 - 1,000). These changes reflect the evolution of the Near Eastern societies that espoused them. Those people whose descendants became Israel would have participated in this progression, but it was in Israel that the next big change took place.

2. My Big, Fat Greek What?

The Bible's prophetic literature[2] is chock-a-block with oracles against foreign nations or groups because of their religious beliefs and their practices, and even more because of their ill-treatment of Israelites. Taken altogether, they could be considered as an indication of misanthropy, a hatred of all humans who aren't Jews (and even including some Jews as time went by). That is, in fact, something Jews have indeed been accused of, for example, by the Greeks of Alexandria somewhat before Jesus's time. What is particularly amusing about this accusation is that a fair percentage of early Israel seems to have been... Greek in origin.

This is something that the Alexandrians would not, could not have known. The Jewish community of Alexandria commissioned the first translation of the Bible into Greek in the third pre-Christian century, the Septuagint (LXX), to counter the misconceptions of its Greek-speaking neighbors, but already by that time the Greek origin of some of Israel was all but forgotten. However, as we saw in previous chapters, there seems to have been more than a little of Hellenism in the original Israelite mix. We think, in fact, that Greek elements may already be represented among the sons of Noah.

We know that the names of some of the descendants of Japheth, such as Rhodanim and Javanim, represent Greeks of the island of Rhodes and of Ionia, respectively. But the name "Japheth" itself may be a derived form of *yaphlet*, "refugee." Chronicles lists one Japheth as a descendant of Asher, but the older Josh. 16:3 knows of "Japhethites" living on the seaward side of Joseph. It may be that Gen. 9:27, "Japheth dwells in the tents of Shem," contains a distant echo of the displacement of Greek islanders that must have accompanied the explosion of Santorini.

Whenever they came, both the tribe of Dan and Joshua's Gibeonite adherents seem to be of Greek origin. In Chapter XIII we'll see that, upon a time, David was employed by one King Achish, whose name means "Achaean," and that David employed Cretan mercenaries as part of his bodyguard when he became king.

Putting all of these things together, we can be reasonably confident in proposing that a fair amount of Greek genetic material found its way into the Israelite body politic even if we can't judge how many big, fat Greek weddings there were in the early period. The coming of Alexander of Macedon to the east had an impact that we can at least estimate.

The first of the Greeks to come were, of course, soldiers, and many of them married local women.[3] The policy of Alexander's successors in Egypt, who ruled Palestine for over a century after his death, made it easy to do so.[4] In the wake of the conquest, more Greeks came. "As in all periods of emigration, the majority of these emigrants were males, especially young and unmarried."[5] Shall we suppose that Judean women, alone among all other females, were able to withstand the charms of these newcomers, or that their families prevented them from meeting strangers?

We think that Ezra's reforms did not withstand the tide of Hellenization that followed upon Alexander's conquest, and this for two reasons. The first is that the reforms were only meant to confront an acute, immediate problem: the battle for political control of Jerusalem/Judea. It was only long after that Jewish authorities felt the need to invoke them anew. The second is that the culture of the Greeks was so attractive that it was taken up by many Jews, along with the other peoples of the Near East.

In this regard we may invoke the stories of Tevye by Scholem Aleichem, stories of Tevye forbidding his daughter from marrying a Russian gentile... and failing. If it is objected that we are wrong to retroject the attitudes, and failures, of 19th century Jewish

Orthodoxy back into the biblical era, we might respond: Why should Jews of the Persian period manifest such close-mindedness? After all, there is no record of them murdering excess female children and, if the principle of matrilineality had been established, each Greek man to marry in would produce more Jewish children. Were they familiar with the story of Esther or had they, in fact, written it?

The point we wish to make here is a simple one: a fair amount of population mixing seems to have taken place in Israel after the canonization of that part of Hebrew Scripture called *nebi'im*, "Prophets," approximately during Ezra's time. It is in the prophets that we find excoriation of foreign nations; the prophets might not have approved of this post-Alexander mixing, but none of them lived to see it.

3. Israel's Enemies, the A-List

"Even paranoids have enemies." – Delmore Schwartz

Israel's geographical position at the crossroads of the Ancient Near East meant that it was often overrun by more powerful neighbors. And at one time or another, almost everyone else in Israel's neighborhood was more powerful. Consequently, the country suffered grievously at the hands of people for whom our Geneva Conventions would have made absolutely no sense. One might almost say that carrying a grudge became biblical Israel's favorite indoor sport, but that would be trivializing a very serious situation.

Writing in the eighth pre-Christian century, the prophet Amos excoriates three foreign nations: Tyre, Damascus and Gaza, and then does the same for Ammonites, Moabites and Edomites, all blood-relatives of Israel. Amos's list is carefully arranged.[6] The six are objects of God's wrath for what we might call "crimes against humanity."

Amos is doing more theology than history. Clearly, the oracles against the first seven, the above-mentioned six plus Judah, are a foil, almost a straw man so that Amos can gain the attention of his audience, the Northern Kingdom Israelites, before blasting them. From those to whom more is given, more is expected, and Israel was given Torah. This is not to say that Scripture has not got real grievances against foreign nations.

Jeremiah's six chapters' worth of invective against foreign nations(46-52) may be at the root of the misanthropy charge of which we spoke. It's worth noting that he doesn't direct it at any Greek-speaking peoples. We expect that this is because by Jeremiah's time the early Greek elements had been so thoroughly worked into the Israelite population as to have lost their Greekness. He and Amos, the first creator of such a list, do curse the Philistines whom they knew only as having come from Crete.

Whether the prophets were aware of their places of origin is impossible to discern. There were, however, plenty of foes closer to home.

4. Edomites

"Remember, O Lord, against the Edomites, the day of Jerusalem's fall." – Ps 137:7 RSV

At this late date in our history we might suggest that Ps. 137, with its plea for the death of Edomite children, be honorably retired, but that idea would have been roundly rejected by the canonizers of the Bible's third part, *k'tuvim* ("Writings"), around 100 c.e. Memories of Edomite aggression might have faded, but Rome had been fully in control of the area for more than 150 years and its repressive measures, culminating in the destruction of the Second Temple in 73 c.e., were ongoing, raw wounds. It probably would have been suicidal to write pieces in which Rome was directly criticized, but the old pieces could be used with Edom, or whomever, being understood as a cover for the new enemy.

Erecting barriers between itself and the surrounding nations was still a necessity and this included, perhaps even as first among equals, those nations to whom Israel saw itself related by blood. As we saw in the chapter on Patriarchs and Their Significant Others, not all of those peoples related to Israel by blood had become true-blue Israelites. Edomites, neighbors to the southeast whom the Bible identifies as descendants of Esau, Jacob's twin brother, were already "written out" of the Israelite community, allegedly because of Esau's marriage to Hittite and other foreign women.

(One might ask why these women didn't assimilate to Esau's religion, as those marrying his brother presumably did. After all, they were living on his turf, not theirs, but the Bible gives us no direct help here.)

Between Israel/Judah and its blood kin, there was also a long history of enmity. Saul had Edomite allies—who were, ipso facto, enemies of David—notably one Doeg, the Edomite.[7] Doeg took an active part in the war with David; perhaps that is one operative factor here. Psalm 137, quoted above, gives another. Ps. 137 is now the only psalm that scholars agree is post-Exilic; just how long after the Exile is uncertain, but that doesn't matter much. It may refer to an Edomite attack circa 485 b.c.e. on a Jerusalem still digging out from the ruin of its catastrophic fall a century before. Some time between the fall of Jerusalem and Ezra's time, Edomites must have availed themselves of Judah's weakness and reclaimed parts of its erstwhile territory.

Was Doeg intermarried? According to the *Encyclopedia Judaica,* he had "taken the religion of his master," so the question of marriage would be academic. But the claim is specious. Based entirely on I Sam. 21:7, which only identifies Doeg as "the chief of Saul's herdsmen," it is evidence for tradition's desire to impute a religious unity to Israel from earliest times. But just as in the case of Ruth, the Moabite woman, whose story is set in roughly contemporary times, there would have been no known mechanism for conversion for the very good reason that there was no need for Doeg, or anyone else, to "convert." Like Ruth, he could have attached himself to Saul's people, in which case we would be interested in knowing whom Doeg's children married.

Perhaps the equation Esau = Edom indicates that Esau's people continued to live just over the border, if indeed there was one, to the southwest of Israel. In such proximity, one would expect continuing commerce of one sort or another between groups, no matter what Esau's mother thought of his marriages.

Alternatively, there is the intriguing story of the Judean King Amaziah (early 8th century). Both II Kings 14:7 and II Chron. 25:11-13 relate Amaziah's victory over Edomites. Chronicles, however, goes on to report that Amaziah brought back Edomite gods, which he then worshipped, earning a prophetic rebuke. The unnamed prophet angrily asks (v. 15) why Amaziah was worshipping gods who could not save their own people. It's a good question.

The *Encyclopedia Judaica* provides an answer, saying, "Apparently, there was an early connection between the religion of the men of Seir [Edom] and the early religion of Israel, a connection deduced from an Egyptian list from the time of Ramses II (13th. century)..."[8] According to some modern scholars,[9] the "connection" is nothing less than the identification of Seir as the original home of the god who became Israel's One God.

They suggest that Israel's God began his career modestly as a local Edomite god of weather. This contention has yet to be proved and, given traditional resistance to seeing God as having in any sense evolved, perhaps it never can be. But it certainly provides a cogent reason for Amaziah's action. What would be worth noting here is that such an Edomite-Judean religious connection was still felt five hundred years after Moses.

All of this is to say, again, that Ezra's gerrymandering of the lists of proscribed peoples is, at base, in service of an attempt to wrest control of Judah from "foreign" elements and return it to the Judeans whom he led.

Note that Ezra makes some changes[10] in the lists from Exod. 34:11 and Deut. 7:3—presuming that they are the lists he was consulting. Interestingly, neither of them lists Philistines and he omits two that are listed—Girgashites and Hivites—but adds Egyptians, Ammonites and Moabites, and Edomites from Deut. 23.

In regard to the last named, it seems that Ezra is playing fast and loose with a text that is designed not to prohibit intermarriage but to set time-limits after which Edomites (and Egyptians) are allowed to "enter the congregation," as opposed to Ammonites and Moabites, who are permanently excluded. It is easy to see why Ezra would have mined Deut. 23 and included Egyptians in his prohibitions. He knew that Israel had often gotten into trouble looking to Egypt for aid; Isaiah 36:6, written about 700 b.c.e., says, "Behold, you are relying on Egypt, that broken reed of a staff which will pierce the hand of any man who leans on it." (RSV)

Things hadn't gotten better a century later. In Jeremiah 2:18, the prophet asks: "And now what do you gain by going to Egypt to drink the waters of the Nile?" and answers (2:36), "You shall be put to shame by Egypt..."(RSV)

As a Persian employee/emissary, Ezra would have had a stake in discouraging his contemporaries from doing likewise. Adding Ammonites and Moabites had a similar rationale, but wanted a reason grounded in antiquity that would raise the prohibition ante out of the arena of political dispute.

5. B'nei 'Ammon and B'nei Moav

These two groups are often considered together, in part because they border each other and border Israel/Judah on the east, in part because we know so little of either, but mainly because Israel regards them as relatives, after a fashion. As the reader can discern from the title of this section, there is reason to differentiate between them. But before we do that, let's briefly examine the Bible's take on these two neighbors.

The story of Lot's unexpected[11] family in Genesis 19, despite outward appearances, has as its ultimate aim the exclusion of Ammonites and Moabites from civilized company even while acknowledging them as relatives. Relatives, yes; however, as children of incest they are *mamzerim*. The closest we can come to translating this word into English is "bastards," but our translation falls short.

Mamzerim are not simply children born out of wedlock, for such can be legitimized by the marriage of their parents; those born of unions that can never be legitimized, for example brother/sister or father/daughter are permanent outcasts. As such they could not marry Israelites (Deut. 23:3), but because they were relatives, they were apparently spared the rigors of conquest allegedly visited on those peoples living west of the Jordan.

Parenthetically, we might then ask why the marriage of Naomi's son to Ruth, the Moabitess, and Ruth's later marriage to Boaz, raised no eyebrows in the Israelite community. Later Judaism was forced to the conclusion that the prohibition didn't apply to foreign womenfolk, but it is more likely that at the time of Ruth's writing (mid-late 9th century), the prohibition was not in effect.

After all, even assuming that Torah had been given to Moses some centuries before, neither Deut. 7:3 nor Exod. 34:11

proscribes Moabites. It raises the question of just how original Deut. 23:3 is.

What happened between the acceptance of Torah and Ezra's time that might explain why these two related peoples are excluded from the community? The chronology here is like the Mississippi River: long, meandering and muddy. One thing that happened about seventy years before Ezra's visit was the return of Zerubbabel, a descendant of David, to Jerusalem to reestablish some measure of Judean autonomy. Another was the rebuilding of the Temple around 515 b.c.e., almost exactly on the "schedule" given in Jeremiah's letter to the exiles (Chapter 29). Hence, both politically and economically/religiously, Judeans had again become "players" in the contest to control their own land.

Since we have dealt with Israel's view of its genealogical relationship to Moab, all we wish to add here is a few words about their historical relations. II Kings 3:1 claims that Mesha of Moab paid a gigantic tribute to Israel every year. There is a famous Moabite inscription[12] of that very king, Mesha, which supports the idea that Israel exerted authority over Moab in the ninth century. When Moab revolted, both sides, in the best Near Eastern fashion, claimed victory. What this suggests, of course, is that the ironclad prohibition of relations with Moabites is due not to some fault in their putative genealogy, but to historical events that lay closer to Ezra's own time. This is certainly the case with Ammonites.

We know somewhat about Israel's relations with b'nei ammon, but before relating them we should say something about the terms "Moabite" and "Ammonite." These are our terms, not theirs. To put this in a contemporary context, the modern countries of Afghanistan and Iraq are not so much nations as they are geographical designations within which are contained multiple and often mutually antagonistic groups. There is no reason to suppose things were any different during biblical times with Ammon and Moab as, indeed, in Israel itself in the time of the Judges.

"Ammonites" is our term for the people who live in the area around what is now Amman, the present capital of Jordan. If the Bible has it right, their territory does not seem to have reached westward to the Jordan River, but borders the Transjordanian Israelite tribes of Gad and Manasseh.[13] Save for the fact that people have lived in that area for a long time, we know very little about the *b'nei 'ammon*, including what they called themselves. We do not know if they were one people or many, but the designation *b'nei 'ammon,* "children (sons) of Ammon," makes it probable that they, too, were a loose-knit group, looser-knit than Moabites.

Ammonites have left no written records of themselves, so we're thrown back on what the Bible tells us—not an altogether flattering picture.

To the biblical authors, the least attractive aspect of their culture—which is, paradoxically, the most interesting to us—is the accusation that Ammonites sacrificed children to their god, Milcom, and at various times inveigled Israelites into doing the same.

This reason, plus their allegedly incestuous ancestry, would seem to be sufficient cause for exclusion, but we think that there is more going on here than meets the eye. For one thing, Solomon's successor, Rehoboam, had an Ammonite mother, and it seems likely that a King Nahash of Ammon married David's mother after the death of his father. If so, then the Talmud's clever exclusion of foreign women from the prohibition on intermarriage has a fatal flaw.

There ought to be a better reason and one closer to the time of Ezra for his attitude toward Ammon, and there is. As we saw in Chapter II, an Ammonite king was involved in the plot that ended the last vestige of Judean autonomy in 582 b.c.e. This no doubt opened the way for other groups, for example, Edomites, to exercise independent authority over their own territories or to claim authority in Judah, as, indeed, we saw was the case when Ezra returned from Babylon. Among the latter we note Tobiah, whose tribe were perennial contenders.

In order to wrest control from them, he must have deemed it expedient to amend the list of peoples with whom relations were forbidden and to bid them divorce the foreign wives whom they had already taken.

This raises the fascinating question of what affiliation, what allegiance the children of these unions had, but the Bible is silent on this subject and so, therefore, must we be. The closest we can come to knowing the situation is found in Neh. 4:12 from which, unless it's simply a literary device, we gain the knowledge that Jews lived in such proximity to these others that they might be attacked on very short notice. The bottom line, though, is that Ezra's exclusion of Ammonites and Moabites must have been politically motivated.

The lists that we have from Egyptian, Hittite and classical sources don't mention another group of migrants because that group was coming into Israel from the opposite direction at about the same time the Philistines landed. That group were people whom the Bible calls Benjaminites.

6. *B'nei Yaminu:* Benjaminites

Ezra could conceivably have added the Benjaminites to his list of proscribed peoples. Despite their being officially one of the original twelve or thirteen tribes, and the one that tradition identifies as remaining with Judah after the departure of the other ten, relations between "all of Israel" and Benjamin were problematic from the period of Judges to the fall of the First Temple.

Some scholars think that Ehud ben Gera of Benjamin was the first judge, though he is not explicitly so-called. In any case, his assassination of the king of Moab, stabbing him in the king's own toilet, is one of the book's more believable stories. Halpern[14] reconstructs how this "locked cloaca mystery" can be solved, but that's not of interest here.

What is of interest is how the king allowed Ehud to get so close that he was able to kill him. The answer to that is the Benjaminites had, as it were, their own foreign policy. The ben Geras and others, especially Benjaminites who might have lived across the river, considered themselves autonomous, and Eglon was expecting to make common cause with Ehud.

The Bible does not know of any Benjaminite enclaves across the river, but in any case the territories of Benjamin, Ammon and Moab would have had a common border, if not also territory which all claimed. When David was at Mahanaim, which seems to be in Ammon, one Shimei ben Gera—a descendant or relative of Ehud?—cursed him with a fearful curse. On his deathbed, David reminded Solomon of this, and Solomon soon contrived to kill Shimei.

Why take the trouble to detain and then kill a bad-mouther?

Well, curses were seen as efficacious, hence worthy of reprisal, but another answer would be that Shimei represented a potentially

216

secessionist movement that Solomon needed to pre-empt. It was no accident that Saul, a Benjaminite, became Israel's first king; even when his line was not established, a strong and autonomous Benjaminite presence persisted. We may add to this the continuing agitation by Benjaminites after his death to have their own autonomous territory.

Paul Johnson[15] suggests that Benjaminite separatism remained so strong that during the time of Babylon's invasion of the South, the Benjaminites made a "separate peace."[16] If so, that would certainly incur the wrath of those resisting the Babylonians and would be more than adequate reason for forbidding Israelites from further intermarriage with Benjamin. And it speaks to the essential and continuing foreignness of the Benjaminites.

The most important text relating to this tribe is Judges 21:1. Coming at the end of a protracted account of war between Benjamin and "all Israel" that begins with Judges 19, 21:1, it forbids (further) marriage between "all Israel" and Benjaminites. Why was this form of response deemed necessary and appropriate? Whatever one's answer, the response indicates that marriage including Benjaminites had taken place until this point, but it strongly implies that this was really intermarriage consequent on the adherence of Benjamin to the emerging Israelite confederation.

It might be suggested that withholding Israelite daughters from Benjaminite unions was proper punishment for the abuse of the Levite's concubine, which allegedly precipitated the war. Supporting this reading, we could adduce the reaction of Simeon and Levi to the so-called rape of their sister Dinah. It is not at all certain, however, that this story was universally known—Judges doesn't mention it—and even so, on closer examination the case of Dinah is not analogous.

Dinah was a sister, not a concubine. What Hamor was proposing, by having relations with her, is that his people and

Jacob's should form a family alliance and thus pave the way for trade relations, what the Romans would later call *connubium et commerciam*. No one in Jacob's family is reported as opposing this in principle. Furthermore, the response of Simeon and Levi was so entirely uncalled for, so unjustified by Israelite law then or later, that they forfeited their leadership positions.

We might also mention the case of Adonijah, David's son, who had relations with one of father David's concubines. In both of these cases, the cohabitation was a symbolic act designed to show that the son had assumed leadership/kingship. The Levite's concubine could have no such symbolic significance; hence, reasons for the drastic reaction to her violation must be sought elsewhere. To do this we must examine more closely who the Benjaminites were.

It has become increasingly clear[17] that the Benjaminites were related in some way to the *b'nei yaminu* known to us from Mari texts of the 18th pre-Christian century. There is, admittedly, a wide waste of time between that period and that of the Twelve Tribes, but this works both for and against the theory. Against it is the fact that we have no hard evidence connecting the two, but it certainly gives time for Benjaminite groups to have made a slow migration westward. This they were inclined to do because they were a warrior tribe that resisted the authority of central government. When the central government of Assyria was strong, the *benei yaminu* were compelled to find territory outside that government's jurisdiction. Interestingly enough, the characterization of Benjamin in Jacob's blessing of his sons though vague enough, comports well with what we know of the *benei yaminu*. Here is the "blessing" in its entirety:

Benjamin is a ravenous wolf
In the morning he consumes the foe (or: booty)

And in the evening he divides the spoil (Gen. 49:27, NJPS)

It may not be too much to suggest that the story of the Levite's concubine and its aftermath in Judges is simply a fabrication designed to give antique authority to the intermarriage prohibition. But we need not go this far. From all the indications, Benjamin really was, initially, a foreign group.

In saying this, we discount the Bible's story of Benjamin's birth (Gen. 35)—as we do that of the other sons of Jacob—but since we have treated this question elsewhere[18] and it is not pertinent here, we will not repeat it.

To return to Judges 21, the victorious Israelite coalition agreed no longer to permit their daughters marry Benjaminites. Why this particular punishment and, anyway, wouldn't such a thing be superfluous after the coalition had just wiped out so many of the offending tribe's males? We have to conclude that the prohibition, necessary or not, implies a recognition of Benjamin's foreign origin.

The coalition then instructs the defeated tribe to carry off girls from Shiloh, and this the Benjaminites duly do. A question the Bible doesn't answer is: whose girls were these? Shiloh, after all, is in Ephraim: fully within Israel. Moreover, wouldn't such a mass abduction be far greater than the original Benjaminite crime that perpetrated the war in the first place? We cannot say.

We do think it's fair to say that choosing Saul and his Benjaminites to lead the emerging Israelite coalition was itself a marriage of convenience. Judges 20:16 reports that the Benjaminites had 700 picked men who were either left-handed or perhaps ambidextrous. This skill that would put them in the forefront in battle,[18] and with increased pressure from the Philistines, battle could not be avoided. It was logical to choose as leaders those with the best military skills.

Notes to Chapter VIII

1. Thorkild Jacobsen, *Treasures of Darkness: A History of Mesopotamian Religion* (Yale University Press,1976), Chapters 2-5.
2. See Harold Louis Ginsberg, *The Israelian Heritage of Judaism* (University of Michigan, 1982).
3. Victor (Avigdor) Tcherikover in *Hellenistic Civilization and the Jews* (Jewish Publication Society of America, 1959) 20-21.
4. Tcherikover, The Hellenistic Age: Political History of Jewish Palestine 332 B.C.E. – 67 B.C.E. (The World History of the Jewish People, Vol. 6, Jewish History Publications Ltd., 1973, Abraham Schalit, ed.) p. 89.
5. *Ibid.*, 45.
6. G. Johannes Botterweck, "Zur Authentizitat des Buches Amos" (*Zeitschrift fur Alttestamentliche Wissenshaft 70,* 1958), 176-189.
7. According to Yev. 76b-77a, Doeg questioned David's legitimacy.
8. *EJ* VI:377.
9. Notably Edelman and confederates in *Triumph*.
10. We assume that Ezra knew Exodus and Deuteronomy. If the Pentateuch was canonized ca. 550, there's no reason to assume he wouldn't know them.
11. Fleeing Sodom, Lot's wife dies and his two daughters, thinking all other men have perished, get their father drunk and on successive nights lie with him and so become impregnated.
12. Albright, W. F., "Palestinian Inscriptions" (*Ancient Near Eastern Texts*, edited by James B. Pritchard, 320-22. 3rd ed. Princeton: Princeton Univ. Press, 1969).
13. The tribe of Reuben was located wholly within territory also said to be that of Moab and possibly Ammon. It is too much to expect that all these entities kept strictly to themselves in respect to

marriage. Indeed, that would be one reason why Reuben seems to disappear from the biblical history. Scripture records that Machir, the son of Manasseh by an Aramean concubine, inhabited a region east of the Jordan, just north of but presumably overlapping with Ammon.

14. Baruch Halpern, "The Assassination of Eglon: The First Locked-Room Murder Mystery," (*Bible Review* December 1988) 32–41.

15. Paul Johnson, *A History of the Jews* (Harper & Row, 1987), p. 49.

16. As Jeremiah seems to imply in 6:1—not the customary reading, of course. John Bright in *Jeremiah* (Anchor Bible series V. 21, 1964) takes no notice of it.

17. As Jean-Robert Kupper posits in *Nomades en Mesopotamie au Temps Des Rois De Mari* (Les Belles Lettres, 1957), but the relationship is not clear.

17. Rosenbaum, *UBI*.

18. Walled city defenses were constructed to protect against assault by right-handed soldiers who carried shields on their left arms, leaving their right sides more exposed to the arrows or spears of defenders on the walls. Lefthanders carried their protection on the right side. See Halpern, "Assassination."

Chapter IX. Intermarriage in Early Monarchic Times

1. Israel: People or Nation? And If So, When?

As we noted in our first chapter, Sylvia Fishman quotes Shaye Cohen, who writes, "Biblical Israel was a nation living in its own land and had no need for a prohibition of intermarriage with all outsiders."[1] This seemingly innocuous statement misleads us in many directions at the same time! At best, Israel was a nation only under Saul, David and Solomon, a period of less than one century. And that was only because of Saul's military abilities, David's charisma and ruthlessness and Solomon's organizational skills—to put it much too simply.

Even during this period, ca. 1020 - 920 b.c.e., Israel was most like late, lamented Yugoslavia. It was an artificial creation held together by strong leadership, but doomed to fragment when the leadership failed. From Rehoboam's time onward it was two nations, sometimes more.[2]

We know from I Samuel 8:5 that Israel was late—and not at all united—in coming to the realization that it needed a monarchic form of government to trade or compete with or to protect itself from neighboring countries, some of which had had kings for 2,000 years. State-building in Israel likely followed much the same path as elsewhere; that is, it required small groups to amalgamate in service of the larger entity thus formed.

As to being in its "own land," such a claim would not have sat well with others living there whose tenure preceded and overlapped that of the Israelites. But just as peoples such as the Hurrians and Kassites, whose name the Bible scarcely knows, were absorbed into their Mesopotamian nation-states and have long since disappeared from history, pretty much the same thing happened in Israel, too. But not without a fight.

No less a personage than the prophet Samuel warned against going the route of kingship (I Sam. 9:9)—that is, the route of becoming a nation among other nations—but his cautions weren't heeded. As to being a nation at all, the Bible refers to Israel as *goi* (nation) only seven times and usually in a pejorative sense, for example Jer. 7:28: "This is the *nation* that did not obey the voice of the Lord their God." (RSV)

Scripture's preferred designation, used some 550 times to describe Israel, is *'am* ("people"), at once a vaguer and a more accurate term.[3] To be sure, there is some overlap between the two terms; Exod. 33:13 says, "Consider that this nation is thy people." (RSV)

Resistance to the formation of a national government was strong in the North and strongest among the Benjaminites (see above) who seem to have occupied a buffer territory between Israel and Judah. To be sure, Benjaminite resistance probably grew after Saul, the Benjaminite who was Israel's first king, died and his line produced no succession. But it didn't stop until after Jerusalem was destroyed in 586 b.c.e.

We can say with a great deal of certainty that the land inhabited by *'am yisra'el* continued to be occupied by many other peoples as well, people with whom the Israelites had complex relationships. Nevertheless, even this last statement is not entirely accurate. The people whom we now call Israelite were initially, in effect, their own mixed multitude, a phrase the Bible uses for those who came up from Egypt alongside the Israelites.

Finkelstein and Silberman put it more forcefully and, we think, correctly, when they say, "The early Israelites were—irony of ironies—themselves Canaanites!"[4] By this they don't mean only that early Israelites became geographical Canaanites by establishing residence in a land called Canaan. Rather, one-third to one-half of the Israelite core community were Canaanite to begin with.

If Israel came late to the table of nations, it did finally begin to emulate those previously established and better-organized neighbors. One way to do this once a kinship was established was to arrange for inter-dynastic marriages.

2. "What's Love Got to Do with It?" (Tina Turner)

Intermarriage among royal houses is a well-attested phenomenon even in antiquity; the oldest Near Eastern examples of this go back to the fifteenth pre-Christian century, when two marriages between Egyptian princes and Hittite or Mitannian women are mentioned.[5] The Egyptians did not usually give their women in marriage to those whom they considered inferior, namely, everyone else (though on the witness of Scripture this may have changed later).

Love had nothing to do with it;[6] the newlyweds would not have met until just before the wedding. The main purpose of these unions was to form diplomatic alliances between Egypt and one of the other major powers that would isolate the third. (A similar strategy was pursued by the United States in 1959 when then Vice President Nixon went to China, a move that was viewed with deep suspicion by China's erstwhile ally the Soviet Union.) Later in this chapter we will see that King David, too, played the game of international chess with gusto.

In addition to the reason stated above, inter-empire marriages were for the purposes of mutual trade and non-aggression between the empires solemnized by treaties that even included provision for the extradition of fugitives. Hence for a time the eastern Mediterranean was neatly divided into spheres of influence, lessening the strife caused by the overlapping commercial claims of Egypt and Hatti and facilitating their commerce.

Even in common circles in the Ancient Near East, marriage might be a business relationship, a contractual obligation; in traditional Judaism it still is.[7] As we have already observed, the women themselves might be seen as commodities.

Except, perhaps, for the reign of Solomon and the somewhat longer reign of Omri and his immediate successors in the Northern

Kingdom, Israel did not exercise much empire-level leverage except in its immediate region. Even so, marriage of Israelite and Judean kings to foreigners was not uncommon;[9] one thinks immediately of Solomon's Egyptian wife or of Ahab and the Phoenician Jezebel.

If we accept the premise that constituent parts of Israel were or had been foreign to each other—and that even in monarchic times some still were—marriages among different groups might also be considered intermarriages depending upon what deities were worshipped and by whom. But arching over these considerations is the realization that women, all women, had religious beliefs and practices peculiar to them which they did not automatically give up upon marrying, even upon marrying a king.

3. Saul

We first meet Saul, Israel's soon-to-be king, as a grown man. His father, Kish, is described as wealthy, which is neither here nor there. We do not meet his mother. Their tribe is Benjamin, which, as we saw in the preceding chapter, marks him as belonging to a distinct, foreign element within Israel. How foreign? Saul had children with both Baalist and Yahwistic names—that is to say, names that seem each to recognize a different god. Does this mean that his children had different mothers who came from differing religious groups? That would be a prima facie case for intermarriage. It might also indicate that children followed the religion of their mothers, but that is not attested at such an early period.

If we may extrapolate from the finds at Maqqedah, perhaps we can say that the idea of family religious "unity" is something that we've erroneously retrojected into earlier periods.

The reality of Saul's marital situation remains unclear. Scripture implies (below) that Saul had more than one wife, but the rabbinic literature praises him over David for having but one, in contrast to David's ten. More civilized states, for instance Hatti, limited their kings to one first-rank wife, probably to avoid the kinds of palace intrigues that inevitably dogged polygamous royalty—and would soon do so in Israel.

If we cannot answer the question wife or wives, there may be a way around it. It is possible that a theophoric (god-bearing) name construed with *Baal* might not have been indicative of another cult within Israel.[8] David himself had a son named Baaliada, "Baal knows." We know this from I Chron. 14:7, which, though it was written far after the fact, seems to have preserved the original name. In contrast, II Sam. 5:14 records it as Eliada, "God knows," indicating that its more contemporary author sought to suppress any connection between David and Baal.

Judean anathematizing of Baal worship was carried to such an extreme that the name of even Saul's son IshBaal is polemically vocalized in Samuel to read Ishbosheth, "man of shame" or "there is shame."

Whatever Saul's religion, the principle of dynastic succession had not been established (the kingship was earlier offered to Gideon, but he declined) and none of his sons succeeded him. This was an outcome that he no doubt feared (I Sam. 20:31). So as a sort of insurance policy to guarantee that children of Benjaminite blood would ultimately sit his throne, Saul first promised his daughter Merab to David and then, when she was given to another, his other daughter Michal to David. Saul reneged on this promise, too, and married her to someone else. David "repossessed" his promised bride and this, we submit, was an intermarriage—because, as we saw earlier and will revisit below, Saul's people, the Benjaminites, were "foreigners."

A close reading of the biblical text supports this. During the period of struggle between Saul and David, the king instructs his men to treat David as *'oyeb*, "an enemy" (I Sam. 18:29; 24:19; II Sam. 4:8). What is significant here is that Hebrew *'oyeb*, as opposed to *rasa'* (wicked), almost always[10] denotes an adversary of foreign origin. That street, however, runs in both directions.

The superscription to Psalm 18 reads in part, "Of David,... after the Lord saved him from the hands of all his enemies and from the clutches of Saul." (NJPS) None of the standard translations reads the *vav* ("and") as the explicative "namely." Reading it that way, however, indicates that David thought of Saul as foreign. And well he might.

For all the Bible's efforts to disguise the fact,[11] Benjamin was a tribe of distinctly foreign origin. This can be safely inferred from what we saw at the end of the Benjaminite-Israelite war (Judges 19-21), namely, that all Israel were thenceforth forbidden to intermarry with Benjamin. Note that this was a ruling that David apparently felt was not binding upon himself.[12]

4. David & Co.

Israel's founding dynast had ten wives, none of whom had identifiably Yahwistic names. They included, apparently, Saul's widow, her daughter Michal, and one Maacah, the daughter of Talmai king of Geshur—with whom we will deal shortly—plus an unknown number of concubines. And this despite the prohibition of multiple wives by Deut. 17:17.

And how many children? In Hebrew the word *ben* means both "son" and "child." The Bible usually omits mentioning daughters unless they are involved in something that is "worthy of saga," like Jacob's Dinah or David's Tamar.

Of all the wives named and unnamed, Bathsheba was easily the most famous, but was she Israelite, and did that matter? We'll deal with these questions below at greater length; it is better to begin the discussion with David's own family tree, because here you need a scorecard to tell the players and even then the line-up is incomplete.

Here's what it looks like in part:

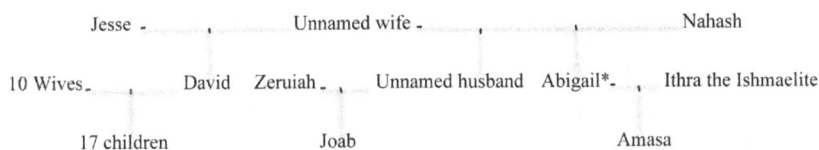

Jesse -		Unnamed wife -			Nahash
10 Wives.	David	Zeruiah.	Unnamed husband Abigail*.		Ithra the Ishmaelite
17 children		Joab		Amasa	

*Not David's wife of that name

The number of relatives by marriage would quickly become astronomical. Indeed, having a large extended family—assuming that they recognized each other—could be a source of strength as it still is, e.g., to the 2,000 or so princes of the ruling ibn Saud family

231

of Saudi Arabia. The half-brothers who were David's sons notably failed to achieve this sort of cohesiveness. That's scarcely a surprise when we note that II Sam. 3 already lists six David-sons by six different women.

We don't know much about most of these women. One, Maacah, was the daughter of the King of Geshur, a bordering kingdom to the north. Another was Saul's widow and another her daughter. All, we suspect, came from well-connected families who had or acquired political ambitions by virtue of their daughters marrying the king.

Also noteworthy were the two David nephews who vied for military power within his regime; one was the son of an Ishmaelite, grandson of King Nahash of Ammon. But it's more complicated than that. The most important player never to appear on the biblical stage—like Hickey's wife in O'Neill's *The Iceman Cometh*—is David's mother. Even her name is not recorded. Why not? Except for Saul (and Ahaz of Judah), the name of every king's mother is scrupulously recorded, even if little else is. Was Mrs. Jesse "foreign"—an Ammonite herself, perhaps—or was her subsequent marriage to a foreigner[13] reason for omitting her name? We think the latter was the case.

If she married King Nahash of Ammon, then Amasa, David's half-nephew, was her grandson. With the Bible's charming inability to hide all traces of what it wishes to conceal, we learn that Abiga(i)l, the daughter of King Nahash, was David's half-sister (or the sister of his sister Zeruiah; the texts are a bit ambiguous). How else could this happen, unless indeed Mrs. Jesse later married King Nahash?

Baruch Halpern audaciously suggests that David himself was foreign. At least David's enemies regarded him as a non-Israelite. Specifically, they thought of him as the Gibeonite agent of Philistine masters.[14]

The present work is not the place to engage in a detailed discussion of Halpern's astounding proposal, but it has a number of points in its favor. Like any hypothesis, it stands or falls by how well it answers certain questions, and in David's case the questions begin with his name.

We are so familiar with the name "David" and with the name of his father, Jesse, that most people do not know that "the evidence is not strong that David—*dwd*—is in [and?] of itself an Israelite personal name."[15] "Jesse" is a nickname or hypocoristicon from which the god element is absent, allowing us to ask why, and which god's name used to be there? Is this a case like Moses'[16] in which the god name is omitted because it is foreign?

The Bible knows that David served the Philistine King Achish, whose name means "Achaean", that is, Greek in origin.[17] According to Robert Graves,[18] Gibeon was an Achaean city, making Halpern's connection stronger than even he seems to know. Below we'll discuss the Philistine military contingent that served David, but putting these few things together, there is a strong possibility that David was not "mainstream" Israelite. Of course, such a conclusion would make almost any one of David's marriages a mixed marriage and his descendants even more a potpourri of peoples than the Bible admits to. However this may be, we begin with his marriage to Michal, Saul's daughter.

5. Michal and Her Mother

As we saw, Judges' prohibition against marrying Benjaminites did not prevent David from at least accepting the offer of Saul's daughter. Michal is the only woman in Scripture who is identified as having "loved" (I Sam. 18:20) her husband, at one point even helping save his life. Too bad she chose such a scoundrel....

True, he might now be seen as the George Washington of Israel for his military ability; he also exhibited the charm, musical ability and personal morals of Bill Clinton. Alongside these qualities, however, he displayed the political ruthlessness of Lyndon Johnson and Richard Nixon. Halpern goes so far as to characterize him as a "serial killer," claiming that he had a hand in the deaths of many who were close to him.[19]

Michal had no children, at least no sons, by him. If Halpern is correct, this probably saved her a certain amount of grief, since so many of David's children came to violent and untimely ends, including Amnon, the first-born son of Michal's mother by David! Michal's mother? How do we know this?

In II Samuel 12:8, Nathan's rebuke to David, the prophet/advisor reminds the king that God has given Saul's kingdom into David's hands and "possession of your master's wives" (NJPS)—some of whom must have had children, possibly older than David's. What can this mean? The plural "wives" is somewhat confusing. Saul's only named wife was Ahinoam daughter of Ahimaaz; the mother of David's son Amnon was Ahinoam of Jezreel, a northern valley. The two identifications are not exclusive; may we assume they are one and the same and that she was Saul's widow?

In the same vein, one might ask whether Leviticus 18:17, which prohibits marrying both a woman and her daughter, was in force in

David's time or a reaction to him? Admittedly, none of the sources we've consulted make this connection, but marrying King Saul's widow would have been a shrewd career move. In addition to Michal, he was already married to Abigail, the wife of Nabal, but possession is nine points of the law; marrying a queen goes a long way toward making one king.

Moreover, since Ahinoam was Northern, David's marriage to her might reassure both Northerners and Benjaminites disappointed by Michal's childlessness that "Benjaminite blood" would soon be flowing through the veins of an Israelite king—presuming that some principle of dynastic succession was in place and that a king's mother's ethnicity was seen as a benefit to her people. (Compare the rejoicing in the Kenyan village of President Barack Obama's father on the 2008 election of one they thought would inevitably show them special favor by reason of their blood connection.) The Benjaminites, still smarting over David's usurpation, might thus have consoled themselves.

In the event, Amnon, the son of David and of Saul's widow, did not succeed his father, but not for lack of trying. Amnon famously forced himself upon his half-sister, Tamar (II Sam. 13), but not in the way that is usually suggested and railed against by commentators. As we will discuss further below, cohabitation even without the consent of the woman is or can be a form of marriage. Amnon knew that.

Amnon also knew that, with so many rivals, succeeding David would be dicey; was not his mother Saul's widow? Would that work for him or against him? By marrying a daughter of David he hoped to strengthen his position. Interestingly, Tamar appeals to Amnon to desist long enough to get their father, David, to give them a dispensation from the law (Lev. 18:9) forbidding half-siblings to marry. Of course, if Lev. 18:9 were in force during David's time, then 18:17 must also have been.

Halpern audaciously suggests that David "set up" Amnon in order to prevent him from becoming king, favoring Absalom, Tamar's brother and the son of a Geshurite woman.[20] Geshur is that region slightly north and east of the Sea of Galilee that the Egyptians knew as *Ga<shu<ri* even before Moses's time.[21] The woman, therefore, was not Israelite and almost certainly foreign. David's marriage to her was another instance of establishing peaceful relations with a foreign country.[22] Or trying to. But why should he?

On the one hand, Geshur had earlier joined with Aram in wresting "sixty towns" from Hezron, the father of Caleb (I Chron 2:23)—this would have been about 1100 b.c.e.—and put them on the "wrong side" only a century before David became king. In his turn, David made war against the Geshurites (I Sam. 27:8). But a strategic peace with the Geshurites would give David leverage against the Northern tribes in the Israelite coalition, Benjaminites included, forestalling at least for a while any attempt on their part to break from his kingdom to set up their own.

It was from Geshur that Absalom drew his base of support, so it was predictable that he took refuge there when he fled from his father (II Sam. 13:37). Since his mother was Geshurite, he might well have expected some protection there.[22] However, it could be that Absalom agreed to return to Jerusalem because he might otherwise have been extradited by David's father-in-law despite or because of the family connection. This would be in keeping with the terms of inter-kingdom marriages that we noted earlier.

Returning in chains would hardly have strengthened Absalom's claim to the throne, but here we must leave off speculating about dynastic intrigues. For the purpose of this book, we have reached an important conclusion. In David's time, in male and especially royal circles, a mother's religion simply did not much matter. In other words, a woman's having a different religion from her husband was no bar to marriage. We suspect it was not even much noticed until the time of King Asa, David's great-grandson, who reigned about a century after his illustrious ancestor.

As we saw above, women spent most of their adult lives pregnant or nursing—that is, if they were lucky enough not to die in childbirth. Their worship revolved —in the case of the *'asherah* pole, perhaps literally—around those deities that provided for successful birth, nurture and the protection of their newborns from the myriad ills those fragile beings are prey to.

Everything else was in the hands of men.[23]

This worked well enough in polytheistic societies. However, as monotheism began to take hold (which it did only slowly in the first four centuries after Moses, faster after the rise of the prophetic movement), women's having their own deities became intolerable to the male-dominated establishment. Women had to convert or at least to suppress those practices that had sustained them for centuries, even millennia. That women resisted this change down to the fall of the First Temple can be seen in the jeremiads of Jeremiah.

All of this raises the important question of the matrilineal component in determining family or tribe, a question that must also have been raised in one way or another by David's many foreign marriages. Had Absalom ascended the throne, what then? Would his Israelite subjects thought of him as one of their own? Would they have been happier with him on the throne than they would have been with their own Benjaminite kinsman, Amnon? The books of Samuel do not say so, though there is in Deuteronomy 17:15 what looks like a later interpolation designed to discredit Benjaminites, at least; it says, "You shall not put a foreigner over you who is not your brother." (NJPS)

In all of this, the religion of David's wives seems to have played no part. Why should it? The notion that religion of the child followed that of the mother was still 800 years in the future. More important were the various tribal alliances such intermarriages signaled, the *Realpolitik*. A marriage alliance with Geshur gave David leverage over the North in much the same way that democratic France allied with autocratic Russia in the nineteenth century to exert leverage behind Imperial Germany.

A preference for Absalom gives us an indication either that the Geshurite alliance offered greater benefits or, perhaps, that the Benjaminites, Amnon's mother's people, were foreign in origin. Then again, who wasn't?

6. Was Bathsheba also Hittite?

Consider this: either she was a Hittite like her husband Uriah, so that her subsequent marriage to David would have been an intermarriage, or she was an Israelite woman married to a Hittite, hence intermarried. The Bible provides not one, but two somewhat conflicting accounts of her (Israelite) parentage, but even the *Encyclopedia Judaica* reports, "...there is reason to suppose that Bath-Sheba was of a family that existed in Jerusalem before its capture by David." (B-322) Another union in which politics trumped religion?

If the Bible's accounts of Bathsheba's parentage are fictitious, it is easy to see why this might be so. Later tradition would be more than a bit uncomfortable with the notion that Solomon's mother had begun life as a foreigner. Now it could be argued that—carrying the name "Uriah," a kosher Israelite name—her husband had converted and so had she. Even so, conversion was not a prerequisite for service; another of David's men (I Sam. 26:6) was Ahimelech the Hittite, whose name does not necessarily reflect the Israelite faith one would expect a convert's name unambiguously to proclaim. More likely retention of the cognomen indicates that he was only a *ger*,[24] a sojourner, but at this point we need to take some time to deal with the subject of proselytism.

It is instructive that the *Encyclopedia Judaica* begins its discussion of proselytism with the period of the Second Temple, that is, five hundred years after the period we're interested in here. The reason for this is that conversion as the changing of one's religion is a phenomenon that arises relatively late in Jewish history. As we saw in Chapter III, the one allegedly early counter-example, Ruth, is not so much a conversion as a throwing in of her lot with the people of her former mother-in-law. For all the nobility of

Ruth's gesture, it is not the same thing as conversion in our sense. People did not convert because it was not seen as necessary or, perhaps, even possible. Joseph, as was the custom for "Asiatic" slaves in Egypt, was given an Egyptian name, and Moses apparently carried one from birth, but this did not, nor was it expected to, make them Egyptian.[25] Similarly, had Abraham, say, adopted the gods and culture of Egypt, he would not thereby have become an Egyptian. (Even today, the only way one can become a citizen of Japan is... to have Japanese parents.)

Considering their history,[26] or perhaps because they employed thousands of them, Egyptians habitually referred to the peoples living to their East as "vile Asiatics." I mention this because Jewish tradition accounts for the enormous growth of Jacob's family from the seventy who "went down to Egypt" to the hundreds of thousands, even millions, who came out in a space of just four centuries (if that) by assuming Egyptians converted to Judaism in carload lots.

Leaving aside, for the moment, that before Moses was eighty years old there was no Torah, hence no Judaism per se to convert to, Egyptians would be about as likely to convert to some Asiatic religion as a Nazi official to sign up for bar mitzvah training. More to the point, Egypt quickly rejected the only native attempt to change its thoroughly polytheistic faith to something that we might call henotheism. That is, the famous "heresy" of Amenophis IV (ca. 1350 b.c.e.), who changed his name to Akhenaton to signal his elevation of the sun disk at morning, Aton, to the place of *primus inter pares*, first among the gods, lasted scarcely fifteen years and collapsed with his death.

It may be, as some have suggested,[27] that this Egyptian innovation influenced Hebrews/Asiatics in Egypt, but influence running the other way can scarcely be imagined.

Beginning with Abraham's sojourn in Egypt, the Bible shows no shortage of people who lived for long periods of time among foreigners. Our word "sojourner," in fact, is a translation of the Hebrew *ger*. Some of these people (*gerei tzaddikim*) did ultimately convert, but as late as the third Christian century most *gerim* (the plural) were people who had adopted Jewish customs without benefit of clergy, that is, without formal conversion.

We know this because the emerging Christian church prevailed upon the empire of Constantine to issue laws restricting Jews, Samaritans and "Heaven Worshippers," that is to say, those who had adopted Jewish customs without converting. ("Heaven" as a divine epithet is found in Daniel 4:23, itself a late book: outside of that only in Apocryphal literature.)

The reason this is possible, of course, is because being Jewish is defined not by what one believes, but by how one lives. In a sense, then, if you "live Jewish," you are Jewish.[28]

No one suggests that Bathsheba converted or had any reason to. The Bible gives her father two names, Eliam (II Sam. 11:3) and Ammiel (I Chron. 3:5), but these are close enough to make us think they may be variants of one name. And yet, her own name seems to mark her as a non-Israelite.[29]

Gail Streete[30] has another theory, namely, that some women engaged in adultery or even prostitution in order to acquire a measure of the power that their patriarchal societies routinely denied them. That is to suggest that Ms. Bathsheba slept her way to the top. And the top meant not just sharing David's bed and his attentions to his other wives, but lining up her son to succeed him. It's an attractive theory, but with real evidence for it so scanty we can't come to any firm conclusion. Such behavior would not mark her as foreign, in any case.

Following the biblical line, Bathsheba's grandfather was Ahithophel (II Sam 15-17), esteemed counselor of David, who, however, threw his support behind Absalom. (Why, one wonders, if his granddaughter had a shot at producing Israel's next king. Was he so fond of Bathsheba's late husband?) If so, she's upper crust, well-connected and knowledgeable. She's best known for her part in getting a dying David to bequeath the kingship to her son, Solomon, thus surviving the welter of plots and counter-plots among several of his sons and other relatives. How then did the disappointed Adonijah, Solomon's elder half-brother, think he could con her into getting Solomon to give him Abishag, the Shunamite woman who was the last to share David's bed?

Abishag was not exactly a mere party favor. Possessing a father's concubine was a way of establishing family headship, as both Adonijah and Bathsheba would have known if they read Genesis. Here they would find the story of Reuben, Jacob's first-born, whose failed attempt to do the same thing cost him family headship. It could be that, despite the Bible's providing an Israelite pedigree for her, she was foreign—and Adonijah's appeal was based on the assumption that she did not know how the politics of succession worked.

Then again, who did? Gideon had been offered dynastic succession in the period of Judges, but he refused. Until David's line became established, there was no dynastic succession and, as is well known, the choice of Solomon alienated more than half the kingdom, which promptly split off and went its own way, leaving us with the myth of the Ten Lost Tribes.[31]

We're left with the most likely possibility: namely, that Bathsheba was an Israelite woman married to David's Hittite military officer, Uriah. He was only one of a large number of foreigners who served David. Second Samuel reports *(passim)* that he also had a contingent of 600 Philistines on his side, a magnanimous gesture from the man who had killed their esteemed countryman, Goliath, it would seem. More remarkable, of course, would be their willingness to serve him.

That aside, David is said to have employed "Cherethites and Pelethites." Now, Cherethites means "Cretans," so these men might have been Cretans—or they might not have been. Even though Crete itself had long since ceased to be a major power, Aegean mercenaries of any ethnic persuasion benefitted from its legendary reputation long after Crete fell.[32] A sort of Swiss guard of their day, "Cherethites" were tough, skilled and loyal; armed with the double-bladed axe, they had long been the best fighters of their day. The standard explanation for the loyalty of these men was precisely that they were foreigners; that is, they had no local tribal allegiance, no pretender or usurper to promote[30]. Halpern has it that these Cherethites *were* Pelethites, that is to say Philistines.[33] That is of a piece with David's having been one, and more with his still being an ally of King Achish.[34]

The soldiers closest to David, his personal retinue of "mighty men," were a mixture of locals and foreigners (II Sam. 23). We can hardly see them living in quarters arranged along ethnic lines and hence maintaining complete separation from Israelites. The question then is: how many of them, or their children, married local folks? And if they did, was there any sort of conversion either way? Those who hold that Uriah converted point to his explicit refusal to have relations with his then-pregnant wife, contrary to what David hoped, before going into battle. But refraining from intercourse before battle is not an exclusively Israelite practice. So off he went and David had to arrange his death in battle to cover the fact that Bathsheba was pregnant with his child. And the rest is Scripture.

7. Solomon and the Religion of Women

Not including the Queen of Sheba, with whom he may or may not have had relations, Solomon is credited—if that's the right word—with 700 wives and 300 concubines. These numbers are symbolic, but their intent is to show that Solomon had many wives, as befits the king of an empire, even a small one.

How many of these were Israelite, how many foreign? One of Solomon's wives was an Egyptian princess. Apparently the earlier Egyptian practice of only accepting foreign women for marriage and not sending their own had changed. Or perhaps this was an exception. (There is another in I Kings 11:19.). In the same verse (I Kings 11:1) the Bible also mentions Moabite, Ammonite, Edomite, Sidonian and Hittite women.

Which one of these women might have written the phrase in Song of Solomon, quoted in Chapter V, "I am very dark, but comely..." (RSV1:5), which continues, "like the tents of Kedar...." we do not know. But Kedar is in the high desert of modern-day Jordan, Bedouin country; Bedouin tents are of goatskin dyed black. The woman was African.[35]

That Solomon had built for this wife, and perhaps for other foreign wives, places of worship merely underscores what we said above: in this period, having a wife with a "different religion" was of no consequence: that is, it did not require that she convert. As we have indicated, polytheistic societies are more tolerant of difference than the modern, militant monotheism we have so recently witnessed.

It is true that Solomon is criticized for this, but the criticism is *ex post facto*. That is, it comes from a later period in which this sort of gesture would have been unacceptable in Israelite religious circles.

In the secular sphere, according to Eric Heaton,[36] four of Solomon's district administrators, all Northern districts, were likely Canaanite, and he surmises that Zadok, the priest in Jerusalem who supported him, was similarly foreign. If that is so, it is hard to imagine that these officials lived in cantons separated from the people they administered. On the contrary, they probably intermarried with them, though it is not at all certain that the people involved would have seen what they did as intermarriage. Similarly, four of Solomon's district governors seem to have Canaanite names. II Chronicles 8:7 implies that he enslaved the remnants of native peoples, but does not include in its list Moabites, Ammonites or Edomites.

And Solomon himself? "[H]e [reading with the Greek] has forsaken me, and worshipped Ashtoreth the goddess of the Sidonians, Chemosh the god of Moab, and Milcom the god of the Ammonites." (I Kings 11:5 RSV) Earlier in the chapter Scripture blames this on the foreign wives who, it claims, exercised undue influence on the sick old king; NJPS follows the Hebrew text, reading "they" for "he" to spread the blame, but this attempt at whitewash won't do, as it doesn't reach the far wall. The end of the verse compares Solomon with "*his* father, David" (emphasis added), so here is a place where the editors' syntactic slip seems to be showing. Malachi 2:11, too often taken as a criticism of intermarriage, is more likely another reference to this apostasy.

Blaming his wives for taking advantage of a sick old man is an easy out; the truth it seeks to disguise has only recently become better known. But before we explore it we have to ask: why is it that Solomon's wives didn't convert? Why was not this, in fact, a condition for marrying the great king? Did not Asenath, sometimes identified as the daughter of an Egyptian priest, convert to the religion of her husband, the "vile Asiatic" Joseph, while still in her own country? How much more, then, a Pharaoh's daughter sent in marriage to a foreign country?

But, we learn from Scripture, not only did the Egyptian woman's conversion not take place, her new husband built a temple for her so she could comfortably worship whatever Egyptian deities she had brought along. Someone should have reminded him of Exodus 34:16:

When you take wives from among their daughters for your sons, their daughters will lust after their gods and cause your sons to lust after their gods. (ET)

Of course, this presumes the verse was written before Solomon's time; it was more likely a reaction to what tradition remembered of him. The clear implication is that Solomon was up to his nostrils in foreign worship. We say "nostrils" to remind the reader that some of the people who became Israelites had been burning incense to Nehustan, the snake-god of healing, since before Moses's time and would continue to do so for another 200 years after Solomon's.

(A relevant question here is this: just who or what was worshipped in Solomon's Temple? Put another way, is there serious evidence that the God of Israel was not so alone in First Temple times as later tradition would have us believe? The interested reader might wish to go on to our next chapter, The Contours of Israel's Religion.)

8. A Hard Act to Follow

Whether or not Solomon was as revered at his death as he has since become, he was a hard act to follow. While Solomon had more than his share of political sagacity, his son Rehoboam seems to have had less than a full measure. Or at least, that's the way the Bible tells it. Rehoboam gets more ink than many kings in Israel, but the news isn't good.

At his accession, he goes to Shechem for his coronation and there angers the locals, who were hoping for some tax relief after the heavy imposts of required by Solomon's empire. Unless he went to Shechem with the idea of shoving his kingship down Northern throats, that he went there at all is some measure of political astuteness. Shechem was the "Queen of biblical cities," the toll-keeper of the great north-south trade route and the seat of Northern disgruntlement with David's line. Getting any Northerners on board would smooth his path, and choosing the queen city of the North over Jerusalem as the place of coronation might be a way to do that.

But it didn't turn out that way. The Bible says (II Chron. 10:6ff) that the king's senior counselors, men who'd been with Solomon, counseled accommodation, but that Rehoboam chose to follow the council of younger men with whom he had grown up. Grown up where?

Chronicles reports that he was forty-one at his ascension. That is, he was born to Solomon at the very beginning of his reign and toward the end of Grandpa David's life. Did David and/or his inner circle have a hand in choosing son Solomon's wife? More than likely.

Rehoboam's mother was one Na'amah, an Ammonitess (I Kings 14:21). King Nahash of Ammon had been a friend to

David—and why not, if he was father to David's sister? While relations had cooled somewhat after Nahash's death, there must have been some groups in Ammon with whom the Davidites remained friendly. Ammonites are referred to in Scripture not as a nation among the other nations, but *b'nei ammon* =sons (children) of Ammon, a looser term. When we say king of Ammon, we are not saying king over all of Ammon; perhaps "a king in Ammon" would be a better description.

So where did young Rehoboam grow up? The Bible doesn't say. But the main city of Ammon, Rabbat Ammon, is where modern Amman in Jordan is today. Ammon and Jerusalem are about 35 miles from each other, an easy two-day trip by donkey, easily possible in one (by horse) if a person were in a hurry or fleeing enemies. From the time Rehoboam got preference for the succession, if not before, he might have been raised by his mother's people to keep him safe.

In any case, Rehoboam's younger companions, the ones who told him to disregard Northern grievances, were men whose power-base was Southern and/or Ammonite. They would favor strengthening ties between Jerusalem and Ammon even at the expense of the Northerners.

What does it say that Solomon willed the empire to a son whose mother came from across the river? The Bible remembers nothing of her besides her name, but we may be pretty sure that she was from a well-connected family. So the politics of empire and the politics of intermarriage went hand in hand, as they so often did in Israel. Her religion would have been immaterial.

9. Ahab and Jezebel

After the dissolution of Solomon's empire, the breakaway North was the stronger of the two successor states. It took a while for the Northerners to sort things out and they had a series of political assassinations, but ultimately a man named Omri became king (885-873 b.c.e.) and founded the North's first successful dynasty. In fact, the North was known as *bit humri*, "the House of Omri," long after his dynasty had perished.

Of Omri's successors, none was more successful than his son Ahab (ruled 873-853 b.c.e.). For most of us, Ahab is remembered only as the weak husband of a woman so evil that her name, Jezebel, has passed into the English language as a marker for "a shameless, wicked woman."[37] Is this what, and all of what, she was?

For one thing, we know that she was a Phoenician princess from the important port city of Tyre. The Bible makes no attempt to disguise Jezebel's foreign origin. In fact, that she is foreign provides a convenient excuse for loading her with sins that therefore need not be imputed to Israelites, even the much-maligned Ahab.[38] The two together provide foils for Israel's first national prophet, Elijah, in his fight to defend monotheism, but it is Jezebel the foreigner who is credited with or accused of introducing all manner of foreign worship into the kingdom. Part of this reflects the Southern bias of the collectors and writers of the biblical material, but there is no doubt Jezebel was a powerful woman.

The evil recounted of her reached a peak when she suborned perjury from witnesses in order to secure the death of a man whose field her husband wanted. Never mind that in refusing an offer to buy it, Naboth, the owner, is probably doing what in Jezebel's hometown they would have called treason. Alas, she didn't have the legal cover that we have here, the "right of eminent domain," by which our government can take property it says it needs, or she might have gotten the land more cleanly. The point here is that, again, a foreign woman exercised enormous power in Israel.

Why were this royal pair so greedy? By the ninth century, Israel had become part of the region's international trade. Their marriage itself is some proof of this. To support their royal life-style, Israel had to export oil and wine, and this, in turn, exerted pressure on the government to acquire lands on which these commodities could be produced. Naboth's vineyard was apparently such a piece of real estate.

Jezebel's story makes easy pickings for rabbis, priests or ministers who want to score moral points and, indeed, no one would have voted her Hollywood's Jean Hershholt Humanitarian Award even if she had played herself in the 1938 Bette Davis movie named for her. However, the critics overlook the fact that her marriage to Ahab had been one of those interdynastic affairs the point of which was to increase trade, and that it probably did.

She died the violent death of one who has caused violent death, but her influence didn't stop there.

10. Athaliah of Judah

Upon the death of her husband, Jehoram of Judah,[39] in 841 b.c.e., Athaliah became the first[40] woman to rule a Hebrew kingdom in her own right, albeit briefly. This singular occurrence gets far less space in Scripture than one would think it deserved. There is no coherent account of her six years on the throne (841-835). Kings gives her sixteen verses (II Kings 11:1-16); her story in II Chronicles 22:10 - 23:15 comprises eighteen verses, but only seven directly concern Athaliah. We shouldn't have even that much if she were not accused of murdering all of her own grandchildren—save one— justifying her subsequent violent overthrow and execution. (For Christians, her story is seen as a "prefiguration" of Herod's purported massacre of the male infants at Bethlehem some 800 years later.)

Lost in the horror that this story generates is what might be the reason for Athaliah's actions. It is well within the realm of possibility that she connived in the saving of the one grandchild, Joash, to avoid a struggle for the succession.[41] Such a struggle would have weakened Israel and invited a potential takeover by Israel, the Northern Kingdom.

Her preventive action would be the more astonishing because she seems to have been the daughter of Ahab and Jezebel. From what record remains we cannot be sure whether she was their daughter or Omri's, but the former seems to have been the case. If so, it is of major importance. Marrying her to Jehoram of Judah could then be seen as another example of trying to create alliances through marriage. Since she was both a Northerner and half-Phoenician, the architects of the policy—on both sides—apparently envisioned a unified country, or at least tight family alliances that would protect all of the constituent parts from neighborhood bullies like the Arameans or from Assyrian imperialists.

This can be more easily imagined if seen against the backdrop of the north Syrian coalition that Ahab was deep into, maybe the architect of, and that had withstood Assyrian arms four times in twelve years.

For us, however, the most important question is: was Athaliah's a "mixed marriage"? Her name is properly Yahwistic, but that tells us nothing about her practices. Safeguarding Joash—who was also the son of the high priest—as her successor would be strong evidence for a commitment to Judean monotheism. In that case, we have the paradox of a foreign queen protecting the Judean throne and the Yahwistic religious establishment upon which it stood.

The point of the above reconstruction is not a radical revisionism the point of which is to make Athaliah a heroine, but rather to point up that, in this early monarchic period, the religions that women brought to their marriages were not of great moment. Religion doesn't seem to have been much of a factor in marriage until the "prophetic revolution," sometime around 750 b.c.e.

Later, in the wake of the downfall of the Northern Kingdom (722 b.c.e.), Southern survivors suggested that intermarriage/apostasy was he reason for that kingdom's demise. They heaped abuse on foreign or Israelite women for introducing "foreign" practices into what they imagined had been pristine, pure Israel. However, as we saw in Chapter VII, women's religion was not foreign and Israel's religion was far from pure.

It is the Bible, in fact, that's radically revising the history its writers were heir to and, as we might expect, the tendency was exaggerated after the South itself fell victim to foreign armies. We can see this most clearly by examining how tolerant of other deities First Temple Israel was.

Notes to Chapter IX

1. Fishman, *Double or Nothing?* 134, quoting Shaye Cohen, *Beginning*, 170.
2. Two or more between 740 and 728 b.c.e. (Hosea 5:5). There seems to have been an independent kingdom of Israelites on the east side of the Jordan. Israel in the Maccabean period, 164 - 63 b.c.e., was much smaller than the united monarchy had been.
3. Ephraim A. Speiser, "Goi and Am" in J. J. Finkelstein and Moshe Greenberg, eds, *Collected Writings of E. A. Speiser* (Philadelphia: University of Pennsylvania Press, Oriental and Biblical Studies, 1967).
4. Silberman and Finkelstein, *Bible Unearthed*, 188.
5. See e.g. J. A. Wilson, "Egyptian Historical Texts" in *ANET* on Egyptian/Hittite and Egyptian/Mitanni marriages, 258. Herodotus reports (Selincourt, 74) that in 585 b.c.e. the Lydians and the Medes contracted a marriage to terminate a war.
6. For all that, there is a considerable body of regional love poetry, some of it fairly suggestive, that pre-dates Israel, so it is safe to assume that not all marriages were or remained of the cold, calculating type. Scripture's "Song of Songs," ascribed to much-married Solomon, is unabashed love poetry, though its inclusion in Scripture, in the third section, is due to the rabbis/collectors/editors reading it as allegory, the lovers being God and Israel. In this they were followed by the Church Fathers, who transposed it into the key of Jesus and the Church. How much ancient writing was lost because the authorities who controlled it could not fit it into their arrived-at theological or moral agendas? The question is especially important to Christians since the discovery of all the non-canonical gospels found at Nag Hammadi in Egypt in 1945. See Elaine

Pagels, *Beyond Belief: The Secret Gospel of Thomas* (NY: Random House, 2003).

7. Since rabbinic times, a *ketubah* ("document") has been drawn specifying what each party brought to the union and protecting the woman in case of divorce.

8. Orthodox Judaism maintains that kings were exempt from such minor prohibitions, but this stance merely indicates that they are aware that there's a problem here. Baron (Salo Baron, *Social and Religious History of the Jews*, 1951 VII: 1XX) thinks it uncommon.

9. Amos, after all, does not include Baal-worship in his catalog of sins being committed by the Northern Kingdom. See S. N. Rosenbaum, *Amos of Israel: A New Interpretation* (Macon, GA: Mercer University Press, 1990).

10. For *'oyeb* as denoting foreigner, see my dissertation and the work of Othmar Keel, e.g. Feinde und Gottesleugner, Stuttgart: Verlag Katholisches Bibelwerk (Stuttgarter Biblische Monographien # 7). The distinction continued to hold true later, for instance in Nehemiah 5:9. Lamentations 2:4f. is instructive. God could not possibly be Israel's enemy in this sense, but here he acts *like* an enemy.

11. Genesis 35, Benjamin birth narrative with bogus folk etymology; 37ff.

12. The lists in I Chron. 15:4-6 and II Sam. 5:14-16 each list about a dozen offspring and each lacks Amnon, Absalom and Adonijah, but they do not entirely match each other.

13. This would help explain why Nahash, an enemy of Saul, was David's friend. The Talmud, which goes to some lengths to "kosherize" David's Moabite ancestry through Ruth ("Yevamoth" in *Enc. Jud.*) says nothing about David's mother. On the other hand, the same Talmudic discussion doesn't even mention that David was part "Canaanite" on his father's side as well, Jesse being

descended from Tamar, the Canaanite woman whose father-in-law, none other than Judah himself, impregnated her. (Gen. 38)

14. Halpern, *David's Secret Demons* (Grand Rapids; Wm. Eerdmans, 2001), 479.

15. Halpern, 269.

16. The most likely explanation of Moses's name is that it is Egyptian, like Ahmose, Kamose, but with the divine element removed.

17. Brown-Driver-Briggs, *Hebrew and English Lexicon of the Old Testament* (Oxford: Clarendon Press, 1906).

18. Robert Graves, *The Greek Myths,* II (Pelican Books, 1955) 169:6

19. This is no offhand insult. Halpern (op. cit.) devotes 30 pages (73-103) to the exposition of this claim in his Pt II, ch. 4, "King David, Serial Killer."

20. Ibid. If that were the case, one has to ask why wait until the son was grown? Infanticides abounded in Israel.

21. Yohanon Aharoni, *The Land of the Bible: A Historical Geography* (Phila: Westminster, 1972 Rev. ed.), 143, cites El Amana Letter #256.

22. Halpern suggests David's marriages were made with the purpose of encircling the North with potential enemies.

23. Hayim Tadmor, in Haim-Hillel ben Sasson 100, does readers a disservice when he refers to Absalom merely as "a scion of a royal family on his mother's as well as his father's side." Geshur is not mentioned anywhere in ben Sasson's work. When David fled from Saul, he sent his father and still-unnamed mother to Moab for safety. Why Moab? Because Jesse was Ruth's grandson and probably had relatives there who would take them in.

24. Shaye Cohen, 266 in Dever, *What Did.*

25. "Whether marriage effected full assimilation into the community may be debated." Hayes, 226, n. 25. Africans brought to this

country before 1808 were forcibly Christianized, but this did not make them or their descendants free, American or even very welcome in the churches of their converters.

26. Through the course of history, Egypt was invaded from every direction except outer space. Their distrust of foreigners was to be expected.

27. This idea of Freud's (e.g. in *Moses and Monotheism)* continues to attract adherents.

28. Modern surveys of intermarriage still keep track of those married to Jews who practice some Jewish customs without conversion.

29. Baruch Halpern, *David's Secret Demons,* 88, fn 26.

30. Gail Corrington Streete, *The Strange Woman: Power and Sex in the Bible* (Knoxville: Westminster/John Knox, 1997).

31. One of the Bible's more enduring myths. We say "myth" because, to borrow a bit from Voltaire, the tribes in question numbered no more than seven, they weren't lost and they were not tribes in the sense that the Pawnee or Oglala Sioux were.

32. When American soldiers reached France in 1917 they were called "Yanks," much to the chagrin of the Southerners among the troops. And English-speaking Jewish students at the Hebrew University in Israel are commonly referred to in university notices as "Anglo Saxon," to their sardonic amusement.

33. Alter, *David Story,* 286 fn.

34. See Halpern, ibid., and Rosenbaum, *Understanding.* The word "pelethites"—a capital letter represents an attempt at interpretation—comes from a Hebrew root that means to "to flee," as from a natural disaster. They were, at best, descendants of people who had fled the Cretan homeland or been unable to return to it. So we can and perhaps should read the phrase as "Cretans, that is, those who were refugees."

35. Was she black? Very likely, if we interpret Jer. 13:23 as indicating that Ethiopians (Cushites) were noticeably different in appearance from Jeremiah's people. As we saw with Mrs. Moses, NJPS"s omission of "very" is a concession to what we can only call rabbinic racism, a view that did not exist in Solomon's time. Hebrew Scripture has no word for "race," and it is likely that the Hebrew language similarly lacked it.

36. Eric Heaton, *Solomon's New Men*, p. 54.

37. Thus the Random House Collegiate Dictionary, 1984.

38. Israel, with its closer proximity to the cosmopolitan city-states on the Mediterranean coast, was more open to polytheistic influences. The Talmud says that but for the incident of Naboth's vineyard, Ahab would have been accounted a righteous man.

39. There is some question concerning whether her husband was also briefly king of Israel, thus reuniting the kingdoms that had separated 70 years before, until the usurpation of Jehu.

40. Or so most scholars assume. The second, and last, did not come until almost 800 years later.

41. Radical as this suggestion may be, no less conservative a source than *Encyclopedia Judaica* mentions the possibility. See: "Athaliah," *ad loc.*

Chapter X. "...And His Name One:" The Changing Contours of Israel's Religion

1. Truth is Stranger than Tradition

There is a delightful *midrash*[1]—which we "update" here—that tells the story of young Abram being put in charge of his father's idol store while Papa Terah is out to lunch. The kid drops one and it breaks. Nothing happens. Emboldened, he breaks another.... By the time Terah comes back Abram has established himself as the world's first and foremost iconoclast; all the idols in the store are smashed. Terah thunders about the broken merchandise, but his son says, in effect, "Yeah, Dad, but look: nothing else happened; these things are not divine. They're bogus."

Thus does Jewish tradition propose a radical break between Israel's religion and all that went before. It's a nice story for teaching Judaism to children, but if DuBose Heyward's character Sportin' Life could say of the Bible in George Gershwin's rendering, "It ain't necessarily so," how much less so the Midrashim? Historically, Judaism itself has not tried seriously to maintain this posture, though what it has proposed may be equally off-base.

Maimonides (Rabbi Moses ben Maimon, twelfth century c.e., Spain/Egypt) thought that monotheism was mankind's original worldview and that polytheism represented a decay of our early, pristine religion. The same position was still held by some nineteenth century Christian anthropologists, and a lot of people in between. But all these folks were conditioned by a belief, already more than two thousand years old in Maimonides' time, in the single-family origin of mankind, which pretty much compelled such a conclusion.

In Chapter VIII, we suggested that monotheism is not humankind's original religious posture, but we don't think it came about through revelation, either. Instead, we accept the idea that monotheism arose as the result of a long, evolutionary process.

Our earliest religion seems to be animist. That is, the Stone Age ancestors of our Bronze Age parents inhabited a world in which whatever moved, lived—and, consequently, might require propitiation. Not only the sun, the moon, constellations and single stars were objects of worship; the sea and storms and much else besides were seen as living things with their own will and the source of power to implement it. Deities also inhabited holy mountains: that is, if the mountains themselves were not held to be holy, an even earlier form of worship.[2] (This is, we think, reflected in the Hebrew appellation for God in the phrase "my Rock and my Redeemer." More below.)

If this is a reasonable reconstruction, proposing that some early Israelites were still polytheistic should not come as a surprise. After all, when Israel came into being near the cusp between Bronze and Iron Ages, (ca. 1200 b.c.e.) so was everyone else.

Furthermore, Deut. 4:19 acknowledges that the moon, sun and stars were given by God to other peoples as objects of worship. But not only did polytheism have many more facets than that, polytheism itself seems to have been a result of evolutionary development, as we'll see later.

Polytheistic beliefs included powerful creator deities, craft deities, healing deities, a deity of good fortune and divine messengers, which we acknowledge as "angels." It's hard to establish a timeline for this religious evolution, but the most recent research (as reported on National Public Radio, 7/6/04) suggests that there was a dramatic rise in the percentage of older people in Upper Paleolithic populations about 30,000 years ago. Grandparents, of course, would be repositories of lore to pass on to their grandchildren; monotheism would not be part of their lore.

Through all the ages monotheism was and remained a counter-intuitive proposition.[3] The idea that there should be only one god and that this deity was necessarily in control over all these elements and everything else would have struck most Bronze Agers as absurd on its face, to say nothing of raising the deeper philosophical problem of how to account for evil in a monotheistic system.[4]

The Bible, however, and even more the later commentaries, have a set agenda, one that begs an important question. To use the phrase "Israel's religion" assumes there was only one, that what began with Abraham spread smoothly, effortlessly and without variation to one of his eight sons, one grandson and their many converts. (Gen. 12:5)

Better we should refer to "Israelite religions." That we propose there was more than one religion in early and even later Israel will not sit well with modern defenders of the faith, Jewish or Christian. From their vantage point atop a mountain of tradition, they have a vested interest in demonstrating the superiority of Israel's religion over what had gone before[5] and preserving the view that Israel was *ab initio*, from the beginning, separate from its neighbors. But in this they are as wrong as the above-referenced Midrash on young Abe. If Israel arose from the confluence of many ethnic streams, there will have been many variations on Abraham's theme competing with others within Israel.

Claims of Israelite difference from and superiority to its "neighbors" lose much of their punch when we acknowledge that "in the beginning" Israel was itself partly Canaanite. Tradition has forgotten, if it ever knew, how religiously diverse early Israel was.

This chapter will examine how Israelite religion may have coalesced or, dare we say, evolved from its constituent elements. It also examines how the slow growth of monotheism would have affected what we call intermarriage, not just between Israelites and others, but among Israelites of different ethnic/religious origins.

2. People, Ethnicity, Religion

Going out to dinner tonight? What'll it be? Chinese or Greek? Italian or Ethiopian? Thai or Mexican? We are so used to the idea of definite ethnic differences reflected in food, language, customs, religion and you name it that we have no trouble accepting the time-honored idea of Israelites as separate from Canaanites. Consequently, we think of Israelite religion as so separate, distinct from and even hostile to those of the Canaanites among whom they lived, that marriages among the two groups would have been rare and frowned upon if not totally forbidden.

However, this badly misconstrues or at least magnifies the initial differences between Israelites and Canaanites, between Israel's religions and those of their Canaanite neighbors. These peoples could not be so neatly separated, as we have seen. And if the people cannot be so neatly separated, marriages between them may have been far more common than tradition knows or admits.

First, however, we need to say a word about when and how Israelite religion(s) arose. It's easier to ask the question than to answer it because the answer depends upon whether one accepts the historicity of such figures as Abram/Abraham and Moses, where one puts them chronologically and, in any case, how swiftly the ideas associated with them took hold of the popular mind. This book assumes that both are, indeed, real figures even if somewhat exaggerated. Abraham, we think, lived about the turn of the fifteenth pre-Christian century,[6] Moses some two hundred years later, about midway between Abraham and David.

Tradition makes of Abraham the recipient of a direct revelation from God, which started his spiritual and physical journeys. However this may be, we think that there was a natural event, a cataclysm, nearly contemporary with the time of Abraham, that at

263

least aided in the development of the idea of monotheism as well as occasioning the journeys of many thousands of people; this was the explosion of Santorini.

We have mentioned that the eruption of this volcanic island caused a tidal wave that pulverized the north coast of Egypt. Asiatics living there as slaves would be just as interested as their "hosts" in explaining what it was that could defy and destroy the gods of Egypt and, what's more, do it for their apparent benefit. How likely is it that some of them might have concluded that there was One God above all the others, more powerful than all of them combined, and that He alone was responsible?

This idea is not inconsistent with the idea of revelation, it merely changes the means by which God makes Himself known. As Job says, "God speaks in one way and in two, but man perceives it not" (33:14). Here, however, is not the place to argue theology, so here we will leave it.

Whatever the case, new religions scarcely arise in a void and a large part of their success depends upon how well they accommodate what has gone before. Hence, according to Islam, Muhammad is "the last and greatest of the prophets" of whom Jesus is only one. For their part, Christians hold Jesus to be *the* Messiah and the fulfillment of Judaism. In its turn, the Israelite precursor of Judaism attempted to superimpose itself upon a preexisting religious foundation, but this was not the attempt of rank outsiders to mount a "hostile takeover." Elements of older religions were found among some of those peoples who allied with early Israel; other "foreign" practices and beliefs were doubtlessly those of original Israelites, if we may indeed use such a term.

Earlier beliefs did not vanish overnight in the wake of God's revelation to Abraham, or even six generations later, when "all Israel" stood at Sinai, or even forty years after that, when Joshua exhorted the people to give up the gods of their ancestors: "[P]ut away the gods that your forefathers served beyond the Euphrates and in Egypt, and serve the Lord. (24:14, NJPS) Three hundred years later, Amos (8:14) criticized people who swore by the god of Dan, something that was dramatically underlined when Prof. Avraham Biran's Dan excavation found a trilingual devotional plaque there that read, "To the God who is at Dan"; the object of the devotion was almost certainly not the God of Israel.

Other cities featured a *massebah*, the "sacred pillar" which symbolizes deity and an olive press just inside the city gate.[7] What was their purpose? One can imagine farmers coming from the surrounding area pressing some of their olives and anointing the stone as an offering. Later tradition might equate these stones with the one Jacob put under this head (Gen. 28:11) or even more that of I Sam. 7:12, but it's likely that people were erecting and anointing sacred pillars long before Jacob's time.

Erecting stones for various purposes can be found in a wide arc of civilization, from the island of Malta in the Mediterranean to the northern tip of Scotland and all over continental Europe.[8] The most famous stone array is, of course, Stonehenge, but there are more stones at nearby Avebury and across the channel in France.

When Joshua first led the Israelites across the Jordan, they paused to set up a circle of twelve standing stones (even though there were by then thirteen tribes). For what purpose? Four hundred years later, Jeremiah was still criticizing Israel's lack of adherence to the One God.

While trying to establish its superiority, early Israelite religion acknowledged both the presence and strength of older, competing belief systems. Indeed, like Muslims accepting Jesus in a reduced role or Christianity finally[9] accepting what it disparagingly labeled the "Old Testament," Judaism adopted, adapted and syncretized many foreign elements.[10]

Archaeologists working in Israel have uncovered all sorts of altars—some with stylized, attenuated bulls'[11] horns at their corners—and representations of people, some obviously fertility goddess figures, and animals that people used as devotional objects. They come from all periods of Israel's history, but tradition attempts to sweep them all under the rug, assigning them to Israel's Canaanite "hired help." This evasion won't do at all.

The bases for Israel's religious calendar with its three "pilgrimage" festivals of Passover, Shavuot and Sukkot are celebrated as historical events, but they "cover" earlier harvest festivals. In their turn, the Jewish festivals have been "covered" by the Christian holidays of Easter, Pentecost and Tabernacles. This is widely acknowledged by modern scholarship, including that sponsored by liberal denominations.

Following the millennia in which inhabitants of the Ancient Near East had been practicing polytheists, the new monotheism would not come to displace polytheism overnight, especially when polytheism was still seen to be efficacious. On the other hand, that the Egyptian gods had been unable to avert the destruction caused by Santorini's explosion might give fleeing Asiatics something to think about.

Forty years later, by the Bible's reckoning, on the eve of their entrance into Canaan, Israelites were invited to participate in the sacrifices of the Moabites through whose territory they were passing. (Num. 25) As the Bible later tells it, "the people profaned themselves by whoring with the Moabite women who invited the people to the sacrifices for their god." (v. 1, NJPS)

It is more than likely that the phrase "whoring with" was meant literally as well as figuratively. Beginning as early as the ninth century, prophetic Judaism, with its insistence on exclusive monotheism, back-read the worship of any other gods as being parallel to marital infidelity. Of the indigenous religions, some at

266

least had retained ritual sex acts in the service of their fertility deities, acts that had sustained their culture for thousands of years.

One of Judaism's "tasks," then, was to convince people who had had success with their ancestors' practices that here, too, Yahweh would be a better fertility god than Baal or whoever else the other religions might call upon. This is one of the lessons to be learned from Elijah's contest with the Baal prophets on Mt. Carmel.

Turning for a moment to modern Jewish worship, we see that during the Yom Kippur liturgy there is one and only one phrase that is repeated seven times running. That phrase is, *'adonai hu' ha-'elohim,* "God, he is the Lord." This seems like an unexceptionable statement, so why is it repeated like a mini-mantra? There is no other piece of liturgy so treated. Who are the worshippers trying to convince? And of what? And how long have they been doing so? The oldest *mahzor*, the New Year prayer book, is only 1100 years old, but this prayer is no doubt much older.

Obviously, the phrase is a complement to, perhaps even a *drash* (commentary) upon the Shema, Deut. 6:4's "Hearken, O Israel, Yahweh our God is God alone" or, if you will, "the only God you need." That there is only one God seems pretty apparent to us now, now that gods of Ammonites, Moabites and their like have crumbled into dust like Ozymandias. But it was not always so. In fact, there is some possibility that other gods were acknowledged in Solomon's Temple.

3. What We Can Learn from Services

Of Solomon's Temple not one stone remains. The famed Western (or "Wailing") Wall was never part of the building proper, but a retaining wall to prevent the platform of earth on which it stood from eroding. Archaeologists are not even sure where exactly on the present Temple Mount (the Muslim Haram es-Sharif) the Temple itself stood.

All is not lost, however. We do have the Israelite "hymnal," the Book of (150) Psalms, almost half of which are ascribed to David. This does not mean that they all come from his period or even from his son's Temple. In fact, it used to be thought that almost all were post-Exilic pieces, but that is no longer the case. Still, the book presents us with two interpretive hurdles.

First, Psalms was not finally included in Scripture until 1,000 years after David's time. So it was subject to the same editing process that we find in the rest of Scripture. This is evidenced by the doublets Pss. 70 = and 40:7-13, Pss. 14 =53, and II Sam. 22:1-51 = Ps. 18. At first glance, variants between members of a pair seem so minor as to make us wonder why both were included. But a closer inspection shows telltale adaptations. For example, it seems apparent that Ps. 53:4-5 has been reworked to mirror the then-recent (ca. 680 b.c.e.) defeat of Sennacherib's army.

More to the point, Lowell Handy[12] identifies nine Psalms that assume the existence of other gods. For example, there is the very old Ps. 29:1: "Ascribe to the Lord, heavenly beings" (RSV) or "sons of gods"; NJPS has "divine beings," which, we submit, is close enough for government work. Whatever they are, "divine beings" must occupy a place on the cosmic scale that is higher than humans, hence, they could be worshipped by us.

The Bible does not, perhaps cannot, disguise the belief that there are, indeed, other divine beings even if they are only the "messengers" (*mlakim*)[13] by whom God makes his will known to us. If Handy is correct, Judaism eventually gutted the four-tier pantheon that it shared with, among others, the people of Ugarit. It took out the intermediate levels, the "active gods" such as Baal and 'Anat and the gods of crafts and of healing—though not without a fight[14]—but retained the high God, married or un-, and the divine messengers.

Psalm 29 offers another interesting window into this aspect of Israel's religion, too. In v. 6 we read: "He makes Lebanon to skip like a calf, and Sirion like a young wild ox." Except for the spelling—some translations use Siryon—there seems nothing remarkable here in this staple of Jewish Sabbath service. But the variation in spelling here[15] is not trivial.

Deuteronomy 3:9 observes that Sidonians called Mt. Hermon "Sirion" but 4:48 spells the name "Sion." Now, this latter spelling is quite close to "Zion," and while we have identified Zion with Jerusalem since David's time, the word itself does not have that meaning. Rather, as H. Ringgren and J. Botterweck[16] tell us, it means "the place where God causes his name to dwell."

The Psalm is attributed to David. If he is indeed the author, he will have been grateful that copyright infringement laws were not in operation during his kingship.[17] Mitchell Dahood writes, "Virtually every word in the psalm can now be duplicated in older Canaanite texts."[18]

Dahood begins his translation of the piece: "Give Yahweh, O gods, give Yahweh glory and praise."

This psalm, then, contains evidence that God was not the only object of worship in Israel, or at least not the only god who could be recognized.

We already had evidence of syncretistic worship from the Temple at Elephantine, a Jewish colony's place of worship deep into southern Egypt and much later (end of the fifth pre-Christian century) than the period of David and Solomon. There is additional early evidence, especially from the Northern Kingdom, as the following verse from a Psalm of Asaph attests. Ps. 82:1 says, "God has taken his place in the divine council; in the midst of the gods he holds judgment." (RSV)

And what is God's judgment? That these gods will die like men (v.7). But to say this is to score another "own goal," to admit that there are still other gods even while consigning them to death.

NJPS, the New Jewish Publication Society translation (1985), however, prefers "divine beings" to RSV's "gods." This attempt to disguise the reality, while consonant with Jewish tradition, is not adequate, but is an improvement on the 1917 JPS version, which reads: "God standeth in the congregation of God; In the midst of the judges he judgeth."

The 1917 JPS translation represents no difference from the first English translation of Scripture in this country done by a Jew, the 1866 Isaac Leeser version. Clearly, there was a conscientious attempt to deny that Israel ever recognized the validity of other gods, let alone incorporated them in the context of its own worship.

This is not the worst of the tradition's mishandling of its texts, nor is Psalms the only place in which we can look for a "religious pluralism" that later Judaism would vehemently deny.

Handy suggests that the temple worship "...may well have included songs to the other deities,"[19] an idea modern monotheists would abhor, but he has a point. Psalm collectors would have discarded these songs, at least the more overt ones, and reworked others; there is well-known psalmic material, some of it very old, that two millennia of tradition have not completely disguised.

In this connection we might remind readers that our song "Our Country, 'Tis of Thee" and Britain's "God Save the Queen" share the same melody.

Except for the omission of the word *'eloheka* ("your God") in the original, the phrase "God, he is the Lord" (*'adonai, hu' ha'elohim*) goes back to Deut. 7:9. In this context—that of the prophetic/deuteronomist movement—we can see an attempt not simply to equate the two but to superimpose one upon all the others, the One for the Many.

One way of accomplishing this end was to incorporate or attach to God as aspects the names of earlier deities, e.g., *'El 'elyon* ("God Most High"), *"'El 'olam* ("Eternal God") and even *hakkodesh* ("the Holy One"). In chapter seven we discussed *shaddai* as possibly originating as a feminine(!) lactation deity. In all, Scripture contains about three dozen names that are presently used as appellatives for the One God. We are not suggesting that all of the names for God found in Scripture began as names of other gods that greater Israel gradually absorbed. It's pretty clear, however, that some were. As we'll see in section IV, Baal was not so fortunate.

A freer understanding of Deut. 6:4, traditionally rendered as "Hear, O Israel, the Lord your God, the Lord is One (or Alone) might be, "Hearken, O Israel, YHVH, your God, is all the gods you need." But the writers of Scripture, aided by centuries of time, did their job too well. Now we easily accept both the Tetragrammaton and Elohim as names for our deity and translate them "God" and "Lord" respectively.

4. A Golden What?

At Ugarit, both El and his son Baal are often referred to as "Bull" or "the Strong One," and for good reason. The ox was the strongest and most sexually potent of domestic animals, something that would not have been lost on Hebrew husbands and husbandmen. As we note elsewhere,[20] there are hints in Scripture that some Israelite elements, Northerners or people living across the river in Bashan, might have donned bull-costumes or headdress for annual copulation/fertility rituals as late as the time of Amos (mid-eighth century b.c.e.).

However this may be, use of bull skulls as altars are known from the Neolithic age,[21] that is to say, many millennia before anything resembling Israel appeared upon the scene. If, as we suggest, Israel was composed of many disparate elements, then it may be assumed that some will have brought their traditional ways of worship with them.

That bulls were religious objects for people across the river in the twelfth century we know from Amihai Mazar's excavations in the tribal territory of Manasseh.[22] The bronze bull he found there is remarkably similar to others found elsewhere, e.g., at Hazor in an even earlier stratum. This supports our contention that many of the elements that were or became Israelite brought bull worship with them: an innovation would hardly have persisted for so long.

Moreover, bull worship is more than a barnyard phenomenon or an excuse for orgiastic rites. Taurus,[23] the "Bull of Heaven," rises at the time of the summer barley harvest, now celebrated by Jews as Shavuot. Barley, because of its ability to grow in poor soil, was the most important grain crop of early Israelites, so knowing when to plant and harvest it is crucial. Taurus's role is so important that this constellation gives the word/letter *'aleph* (= "ox," but by extension all domestic cattle[24]) to the first letter of the Hebrew *'aleph-bet*. In earlier, more pictographic forms of the *'aleph*, the image of an ox's head is readily apparent.

The confluence of the "identification" of the constellation as a bull's head and the domestication of the ox produced one of the most powerful religious symbols ever seen. Too powerful. Even if, as some have suggested,[25] the Baal/Bull was merely the visible mount for the invisible God of Israel, confusion of the two was possible, even likely. Like Nehushtan the serpent-god of healing, Baal the Bull had to go.

Scripture excoriates Jeroboam I, (ruled ca. 930-910 b.c.e.) first king of the breakaway Northern Kingdom after Solomon's death, for introducing bull-worship from "Dan to Bethel," that is to say, throughout the length and breadth of the Northern Kingdom. But it was none other than Aaron, Moses's brother, who first makes a Golden Calf while waiting for Moses to descend from Sinai. For this transgression, Aaron is rewarded by becoming the founder of the priestly line.[26] What we have just presented answers the question: why a bull rather than some other animal?

5. Also in the Cast Were

Baal is prominent in Hebrew Scripture, but usually as an object of scorn, a thing—or, since the name was often pluralized, a generic name for all the other gods whom Israelites were, perforce, forbidden to worship and finally even to recognize. Hosea (mid-seventh century) plays upon the dual meaning of *baal* as both a god's name and the generic "husband." He is underscoring the message that God, not Baal, makes the better husband-provider-fertility god.

But if Israel is enjoined not to dally with baalim, the prohibition does not seem to include creative re-use of baalistic hymns. From a comparison of Ps. 92:10 with a text from Ugarit, we see that a change of god name can make a world of difference. The Ugaritic text reads:

Lo, thine enemies, O Baal,
Lo thine enemies wilt thou smite
Lo thou wilt vanquish thy foes.[27]

Ugarit was a powerful city-state on the coast of Syria that fell out of history sometime between the time of Abraham and Moses, and did it so completely that the Bible was not left even a name by which to remember it.[28] But some of it lived on, if anonymously. Ps. 92:10 (9 in RSV) has:

For, lo, thy enemies , O Lord,
for, lo, thy enemies shall perish;
all evil-doers shall be scattered.

We should recognize that even in the Iron Age people "borrowed" each other's poetry and, presumably, their music in service of their own religion—and thought nothing of it. Here, not only does Ps. 92 rework the Canaanite hymn, it borrows its 3 + 3 +

3 meter as well, leading us to wonder how much other borrowed material was, ultimately, rejected or lost along the way.

Albright[29] called the Israelite version "theologically superior," though he does not say why. Certainly the Judeans found it expedient to change the name of Baal to that of their God; what explains the other changes? We can hazard a guess. The superiority of the Bible's version is that it uses the term *po 'alei 'aven*, meaning something like "those who work to destroy the social fabric and therefore invite a return to chaos," an idea we haven't found in other Ancient Near Eastern cultures.[30]

We can identify the names of several of the other Psalms authors as Northern. This means that these pieces were probably used in Northern worship before being incorporated, with appropriate changes, in our psalter. And that brings up another issue.

6. The Convergence of the Twain?

Judeans, whose kingdom outlasted its Northern sister by some 138 years, heavily criticized the Northern Kingdom for persisting in the use of bull-bovine accessories—assuming the bull was not a direct object of worship—in their services. This means that marriage between a Southerner and a Northerner, say David's marriage to Saul's widow, would have been an intermarriage—not that they would have thought of it in those terms. We will shortly return to this subject.

On at least two occasions, Northern elements revolted from Southern overlordship; the Bible seems to report their rallying cry as "Back to your tents, O Israel."(II Sam. 20:1; II Kings 12:16) This sounds very romantic, after the manner of Lawrence of Arabia, but for one thing. The Israelites weren't nomads and, except for the Rechabites, hadn't lived in tents for centuries. Some modern scholars[31] see here an emendation to "tents" (*"'ohelim"*) from an original *'elohim* ("gods"), which makes much more sense. As we saw earlier, the North was home to Canaanite elements well before those who called themselves Israelites set foot there. Besides, the South was not exactly in a good position to cast that stone.

The Bible's collectors might not have understood the texts in question, but it is more likely that after so much time had passed—the North had been overrun more than three centuries before Samuel and Kings joined the canon—they did not want to accuse even the hated North of this most grievous of religious deviations. It would be too confusing and perhaps put ideas in people's heads.

7. Why Didn't I Learn This in Sunday School?

Obviously, the answer to this question is that Sunday or Hebrew school teachers don't and didn't know it. But they would have been reluctant to teach it even if they had. When Tevye in *Fiddler on the Roof* doesn't exactly know why his eastern European Jewish contemporaries do a certain thing he thunders, "Tradition." And this is no parody. Jewish tradition holds that people who fulfill those commandments for which no reasons are given and that are not open to commonsense explanation are more meritorious than those who choose only the ones they can see reasons for.

While this position has redeeming social value, the analogous position for scholars—that is, to repeat what they've been taught without doing the requisite homework, is intellectually dishonest.

In Ps. 86:8, however, NJPS does bite the bullet and translates: "There is none like you among the gods, O Lord,..." If we can extrapolate from these examples it seems clear that the Jewish translation tradition is only now getting over its embarrassment at having canonical psalms that recognize the existence of other gods even as they proclaim these deities inferior, subservient to God and doomed.

But consider: Deut. 4:19, cited above, recognizes that Israel's God made other deities for foreign nations. The name Adonai Zebaoth (God of the Hosts of Heaven) seems to indicate that, yes, God has taken over this function, too. So why there should be any reluctance to recognize this in Psalms, some of which are even older than Deuteronomy?

For their part, Jewish translators might object that Protestants go too far, for example, when RSV translates the famous Ps 8:6 as "thou hast made him (man) little less than God,..." Here NJPS falls back on the beautifully ambiguous "divine" and footnotes that others have translated it as "angels." The word in question is *'elohim,* used (by us, anyway) to indicate foreign deities when its meaning seems to be plural—in which form it always is—but our God when the appellation is understood as singular.

This is a fine bit of equivocation. It's also another example of how older divine names were appropriated by and to Israel's God. Note as well that while Ps. 53 also uses *'elohim,* its doublet, Ps. 14, uses the four-letter name. No one makes too much of this because both names came to be used almost interchangeably in Israel. But were they always?

We may draw two connected conclusions from this. The first is that Psalms confirms tolerance for, if not worship of, other gods at least in First Temple times. The second, following from this, is that if people married others whose gods were in some way different from theirs, it was not seen as a matter to be concerned about. In other words, "intermarriage," as a situation in which two people of separate and distinct faiths marry, simply was not a biblical category.

We have less information on the marriage practices of common people; no descriptions of their ceremonies remain. It's too bad, too, that Ezekiel 16:3's "Your origin and your birth are of the land of the Canaanites; your father was an Amorite and your mother a Hittite" (referring to the [people of] Jerusalem) doesn't go on to describe the ceremony describing the marriage of an Amorite and a Hittite. Of course, he is speaking metaphorically, not literally— unless he knows more about Abram and Sarai than we do, in which case it would be interesting that he still remembers those origins. But it is interesting to note that Solomon's commercial partner, Hiram of Tyre, sent Solomon a craftsman whose father was Tyrian and whose mother was Danite. This would seem to indicate that intermarriage was not just a two-way street, but also existed at the crossroads of cultures.

And why not? Biblical people were not concerned with maintaining "faith communities" as we are today. Tribal structures and alliances? Yes. Fertility in women, fecundity of crops and herds and protection of their respective produce/offspring? Yes, yes and yes. Intermarriage might not have been anyone's first choice, but in the time of David and Solomon it was simply no big deal.

As we saw in Chapter V, Mrs. Moses, NJPS's omission of "very" in the verse "I am very dark, but comely..." is a concession to what we can only call rabbinic racism, a prejudice that did not exist in Solomon's time. Jews knew color (Jer. 13:23), but the Hebrew Bible has no word for "race," and it is likely that the Hebrew language similarly lacks it.

8. "...And His name one."

The above phrase, which is still used in Jewish Sabbath liturgy, comes from Zechariah 14:9. Like Malachi, the prophet with whom we began, Zechariah is an exilic prophet. He is speaking eschatologically, that is, he looks forward to a time when, as NJPS translates it "...there shall be one Lord with one name." But is he, perhaps, not also looking backward to the many names of god or, as we think, names of gods that were incorporated into Israelite worship to bring on board the peoples who had for so long used them in their worship?

The process by which newer religions adopt and adapt facets of previously existing religions has evidently been going on for a very long time. We noted the ascription of Nehustan to Moses, above. The same goes for sacred places, as anyone who is aware of the history of Jerusalem's Temple Mount is aware.

For us, of course, that is now Jerusalem, but for pre-Israelite dwellers in the area, Mt. Hermon had been sacred for 15,000 years.[32] Obviously, our Israelite ancestors appropriated the designation "sion/siryon/zion" to identify the spot where, they proclaim, God had caused his name to dwell.

And we're not playing fast-and-loose with spelling here. E. A. Speiser[33] observes that spelling was never regularized in Israel, and shifts among sibilants are common. The Bible tells us this much in the famous "shibboleth" incident of Judges 12:6.

David's city, captured from Jebusites, was not the highest piece of real estate in the area even with Solomon's Temple on it. It is a testament to the increasing sophistication of emerging Judaism that its holiest site did not have to be physically higher even than its own immediate environs. Conversely, Jerusalem is accounted as earth's spiritually highest place, so that no matter where one lives, even on top of Mt. Everest, one speaks of "going up" to Jerusalem.

But if Israelite religions appropriated sacred sites, objects, and poetry of other religions, it would be logical to suggest that the theologies connected with these peoples interpenetrated religion in Israel for a time despite establishment efforts to sunder them. This is particularly noticeable when we come to consider marriages with women captured in war and with concubines.

Notes to Chapter X

1. Gen. *Rabbah* 38. A midrash is an ancient rabbinical commentary, first codified in the second century c.e.
2. For an explication of mountains as deities, see Rosenbaum, *Understanding.*
3. ibid.
4. This, we think, is the principal theme of Job. Whatever the book's age, it was not included in Scripture until well after Jesus's time.
5. W. F. Albright, *Yahweh and the Gods of Canaan* (Garden City: Doubleday, 1968). The Albright "school" dominated much of American biblical scholarship throughout the twentieth century.
6. This is a "low" chronology; tradition, by simply adding up the biblical numbers for lifespans, puts him ca. 1800 b.c.e.
7. *Masseba* in Dever, *What Did*, 181, 183.
8. Evan Hadingham, *Circles and Standing Stones* (London: Heinemann, 1977).
9. Not without some heated discussion, beginning with the Council of Jerusalem in 50 c.e. and continuing at least through Luther's rejection of Johannes Agricola's perceived antinomianism.
10. Rosenbaum, *Understanding.* Perhaps the outstanding modern example of syncretism is the Roman Catholic Church's morphing of the Great Goddess of antiquity into the Blessed Virgin Mary, mother of Jesus.
11. For the Bull as representing El, see Dever, *What Did,* 175.
12. Handy, p. 31n. Other Psalms passages that Handy lists which are not discussed here and which could be cited in support of this include: 89:7; 95:3; 97:7; 135:5; 138:1; and 148.
13. Franz Kafka had a lot of fun punning on the Hebrew words *ml'akim* ("couriers") and *mlakim* ("kings") in his parable

"Couriers," in *Parables and Paradoxes* (NY: Schocken, 1953, N. N. Glatzer, ed.), 175ff.

14. Nehushtan, the snake god of healing was apparently so entrenched among Israelites that it was "kosherized" by ascription to Moses (Num. 21:9ff.) and could not be extirpated until the reign of Hezekiah some 500 years later.

15. For cases in which spelling variants are trivial, see James Barr, *The Variable Spellings of the Hebrew Bible* (Oxford, 1989), 10.

16. Helmer Ringgren and Johannes Botterweck, *Theological Dictionary of the Old Testament* (Grand Rapids: Eerdmans, 1974), VII: X.

17. Asaph is one of the identifiably Northern psalm composers.

18. Dahood, *Psalms I*, Anchor Bible Series (Garden City: Doubleday).

19. Handy, "The Appearance of Pantheon in Judah," op cit. 31.

20. Rosenbaum in *Amos of Israel.* See also Hans M. Barstad, "The Religious Polemics of Amos" (*Vetus Testamentum,* Supplement 34. Leiden: E. J. Brill, 1984).

21. James Mellaart, *Earliest Civilizations of the Near East* (London: Thames and Hudson, 1965) 96-97. Many four-horned altars, lineal descendants of the bull-skull altars, have been found in Israel, the latest documented by Yoel Elitzur and Doron Nir-Zevi, "Four-Horned Altar Discovered in Judean Hills," in BAR 30:3, May/June, 2004, 35-39.

22. Amihai Mazar, "The 'Bull Site'—An Iron Age I Open Cult Place," *BASOR* 247 (1982) 27-42. Cited in William Dever, *What Did,* p. 173.

23. The present work has no room to discuss the origins and constituents of the zodiac, but we feel that it goes back a very long time.

24. Hebrew *sor*, "ox" or singular head of cattle, is cognate with Greek *taurus*. *'Aleph* is used for the plural of cattle. For a fuller discussion see Rosenbaum, *Understanding*, 21ff.

25. E.g. in *Eerdmans Dictionary of the Bible*, David Noel Freedman, Allen C. Myers, Astrid B. Beck, eds. (Grand Rapids MI: Eerdmans, 2000) 626.

26. Causing some interpreters to claim that he actually tried to stop "the rabble" from creating the idol, but gave way because he was afraid for his life. See James L. Kugel, *The Bible As It Was* (Harvard, 1997), 423-5.

27. Cyrus H. Gordon, *Ugaritic Textbook*, Rome: Pontifical Biblical Institute (Analecta Orientalia 38), 1965, 180.

28. Only by an accidental discovery in 1929 did the city and its treasures of information begin to re-emerge into the light of day.

29. In Yahweh and the Gods of Canaan, 6.

30. Rosenbaum, "The Concept 'Antagonist' in Hebrew Psalmography: A Semantic Field Study," doctoral dissertation, Brandeis University, 1974, and Keel, *Feinde und Gottesleugner* (Stuttgarter Biblische Monographien # 7. Stuttgart: Verlag Katholisches Bibelwerk, 1969).

Compare Enuma elish, the Babylonian creation epic in which Ti'amat, the unruly salt-water ocean/chaos goddess is destroyed and her body cut up in order to make the earth. Levenson, *Creation and the Persistence of Evil* (Princeton NJ: Princeton University Press, 1988).

31. E.g. Gottwald, Norman Karol, *A Light to the Nations: An Introduction to the Old Testament* (New York: Harper, 1959) 45, and Levin, *The Father of Joshua/Jesus* (Binghamton NY: State University of New York, 1978), 85.

32. Eynan, a well-known Natufian burial site from some 9,000 years ago excavated by James Mellaart contains the decorated skeleton of a man (a chief?) in a reclining position facing Mt.

Hermon, about 100 km. away. James *Mellaart, Earliest Civilizations of the Near East* (London: Thames and Hudson, 1965), 27.

33. Ephraim A. Speiser, *"Goi* and *'Am"* in J. J. Finkelstein and Moshe Greenberg, eds, *Biblical and Oriental Studies* (1967).

Chapter XI. Cohabitation, Concubines and Captives

"It is not good that the man should be alone" – Gen. 2:18 (RSV)

We tend to think of marriage as the ultimate, or at least the normative, state for women, but it is also the means to an end: actually, to two ends. In many ancient and even some modern societies, a woman, more usually a barely pubescent girl, leaves her father's house and acquires the protection of her husband's. In present-day rural Iraq, he may well be a cousin, reminding us very much of the marriages made by the biblical patriarchs.

The husband, in turn, gets children upon her[1]—preferably males—thus insuring his posterity, strengthening his household and his clan. *Quid pro quo.* Since barren women might be divorced[2] or obliged to provide a fertile surrogate, as Sarah and Rachel did for their husbands, it is not too much to say that a woman's place in biblical society depended largely upon her ability to produce (male) children. In common circles in ancient Israel, marriage was a business relationship, a contractual obligation; in traditional Judaism it still is.[3] To say this, however, is to narrow our focus unduly.

In the Bible, the acquisition of someone with whom to have children is a bit more complicated even than signing a contract implies. In this chapter we examine three forms of sexual union that we don't usually think of as marriage, but which have similar ends: simple cohabitation, concubinage and marriage with war captives.

1. "Now the man⁵ knew Eve, his wife..." (Gen. 4:1)

Adam and Eve were married without "benefit of clergy," by which is meant the authorization usually given by priests, ministers or rabbis. But they were the parents of us all, so later Jewish law was constrained to recognize simple cohabitation as a legitimate form of marriage.

So important was the fact of physical relations that, even if it was not looked upon with favor, a woman might be considered married by having been raped. As we saw previously, marriage was apparently the object of the prince of Shechem, who allegedly raped Jacob's daughter, Dinah.⁶ Later—we don't know how much later—Jewish law gave the raped woman the right to refuse marriage to her attacker, who would then be obliged to pay a fine to the victim's family for "damage" to the woman's marriage marketability. In this case, the prince had no idea that Dinah's family's response would be so drastic.

Before codification of the law, there seems to have been a lot of tolerance for what we presently perceive as sexual transgressions. Thus, when David's son Amnon raped his half-sister, Tamar, he was ultimately done in by her brother, Absalom—but only two years after the fact! The delay should apprise us that there were other factors operating in this case—as we saw in Chapter IX.

Some feminist writers delight in holding the incident up as a prime example of the mistreatment of women. But Amnon's act was more than an expression of lust; he was in fact trying to force marriage upon a half-sister in order to strengthen his position as the heir to David's throne. With as many as seventeen heirs, to say nothing of other relatives of David, in the running, Amnon may be excused for looking after his own interests.

288

Absalom, who stood to gain if Amnon were no longer in the running, did not kill his half-brother simply to avenge his sister, else he should scarcely have waited two whole years to do it. Israel may have opted for monarchy, but it was well behind the curve when it came to protecting its royal family from the threat of murder consequent on the death of a ruling king.[7]

In any event, the bottom line, so to speak, was that a raped woman, like one who was divorced, was no longer a virgin, hence her value in the marriage market was diminished—as it still is. She could not, for example, become the wife of a *cohen* (priest).

We said above that marriage was the normative state for women, but the same can be said of men, as well. The Hebrew word for bride, *callah,* derives from the verb /c-l-l to "be complete." In biblical thought, a man is not complete until and unless he is married. What this tells us about the Bible's attitudes toward exclusive homosexuality—that is, male homosexuality that excludes females[8]—or about Jesus's fellow-Jews' views of him as an unmarried man[9] are both interesting topics, but too far from the interests of our study to be discussed here.

2. Sleeping with... Goodness Knows Who: The Incident in Numbers 25

It is no surprise that tradition becomes positively apoplectic when it discusses sexual union in the service of religion, e.g., the incident at Baal Peor (Numbers 25). Here, apparently, Israelite men were invited to participate in Moabite sacrificial/sexual rites. And did. Tradition skewers the men as Phineas did Zimri, but also faults the foreign women who, knowing Israelite men's alleged appetites for sex, used it to entrap them.

Understandably, our religious schools do not teach children that, long after the advent of agriculture, many peoples used ritual intercourse of, say, their king and a chosen priestess as sympathetic magic. This widespread practice, called *hieros gamos* ("divine marriage") was an act of copulation done in the fields, not simply for sexual pleasure but to insure the growth of newly planted crops. It was not the sort of outdoor orgy the Bible treats it as.

With no real understanding of women's physiological contribution to procreation, the people who repeated copulation rituals did so because they probably understood birth on the analogy of planting seeds in passive, receptive soil. *Hieros gamos* was an annual "planting of seeds" that would insure the growth of that year's crops.

Since in most years crops did what was expected, the practice would be seen as efficacious. Connecting the two acts, copulation and crop growth, is a logical fallacy called *Post hoc ergo propter hoc*—"what comes after is caused by what came before"—but there would be no arguing with results.

As we saw earlier, ritual copulation was done in the spring when the planet Venus was at its apogee. Our adoption of Venus as the "Goddess of Love" may come to us from the Romans, but even this source represents the attenuated "covering" of her older function as a fertility deity.

Even in monotheism's early days, there will have been many who "hedged their bets" by continuing the ancient practice, even though this would not sit well with those who were becoming more and more exclusive. The Bible, however, adopted a very critical stance toward sex with strangers, however noble the motives for engaging in it. When Exodus 20:5 states, "I the Lord your God am a jealous God..."[10] what is meant is that Y is unwilling to share his adherents with any other deity. God is not merely first among equals.

In Numbers 25, Scripture paints a somewhat murky picture of orgiastic apostasy when the Israelites stop at Shittim, on the east side of Jordan about midway between Rabbat Ammon and Jerusalem on their way (back) to Canaan. There they participate in worship of the Baal of Mt. Peor and sleep with the local women (and not the converse, again; what were *their* wives doing?).

The Bible isn't sure whether these women are Moabite or Midianite, but that hardly matters. Way back in the introduction we mentioned the principle of *cuius regio euius religio*. This means not only that regional entities control that region's religion, but that all religion, like all politics, is local. What the Bible doesn't see in regard to this incident is that the notion of local religion makes eminent sense in the absence of a universal and universally acknowledged god.

Now, the Bible implicitly recognizes religious localism in the period after 722 b.c.e when foreign peoples imported into Israel by their Assyrian overlords request a Levitical priest, that is to say, a functionary of the region's religion, to alleviate a plague of lions. Similarly, the Bible credits Pinchas' murder of the Israelite man, one Zimri, and a woman identified as Cozbi, daughter of an important Midianite, with stopping a local plague that had killed

24,000 people. Whether the victims were Israelites, Midianites or both is not stated.

However, Psalm 106:28 adds a critical bit of information, namely, that these Israelites were eating "sacrifices offered to the dead." Was that to get the dead to stop claiming more lives from the living? If so, it is likely that the Israelite/Midianite sexual unions had the same end in mind, though what the connection is here we cannot be sure.[11] To make this claim necessarily involves us in questions such as whether or not Israelite religion was ever orgiastic or if virgins were required to volunteer themselves for sex with strangers at local shrines.

One hundred years ago there was considerable opinion saying "yes" on both points, though evidence in support of such notions is scanty at best. William Robertson Smith wrote in 1889, "From the earliest times, therefore, the religious gladness of the Semites tended to assume an orgiastic character...."[12] By inherently contrasting "licentious Semites" with his fellow Scottish Protestants, people who had accused him of being too liberal, he might have been hoping to regain some favor.

Robertson Smith's is probably intended as a defense of Western Christianity's puritanical side, but "the curse of Eve" was alive and well in his United Kingdom. Remember, as recently as the 1930s, parents of English girls who slept with their boyfriends could put the girls in mental institutions and have them kept there indefinitely. In Ireland, the last of the Catholic Church's infamous Magdalen laundries for "wayward girls," that, is young women who were even suspected of flirting, didn't close until 1996.

There may also be in Robertson Smith's assessment a hint of old-fashioned anti-Semitism. In this country a tide of anti-Semitism rose with large-scale immigration of Jews from Eastern European after 1881, and much of it concerned the so-called salacious behavior of the newcomers, especially Jewish women.

292

Still, we do need to consider whether some Israelite elements ever engaged in ritual copulation. We think the answer is yes. The collectors of Holy Writ might not censor information about a nephew marrying his aunt, as with Amram and Jochebed, Moses's parents, or a man marrying two sisters as Jacob did—acts that later law prohibited—but they would be reluctant to attribute wholesale sexual transgressions to any of them.

Had the collectors known that some of the peoples who became Israel began life as something else entirely, they could have shifted the blame to these elements and away from the mainstream, as they in fact do with Esau, Jacob's twin brother. But the issue is larger than a game of pin-the-blame-on... somebody.

Five hundred years after the incident at Baal Peor purportedly took place, in the mid-eighth pre-Christian century, Amos seems still to inveigh against the practice of ritual copulation (2:7; 4:3-4). Though the texts in question[13] are rather indirect, we get the picture of a man, or men, donning bulls' horns and copulating with women in that combination burial society and country club, the *marzeah*.[14] By Amos' time we think the practice might have trickled down— that is to say, become "democratized"[15]—and its original sacred purpose perhaps overshadowed by its sexual component.

Amos' further criticism (2:8) that his Northern brethren cohabit around all their altars upon garments taken in pledge is, at once, another complaint that the rich exploit the poor and a condemnation of licentiousness. This the Bible's writers could countenance no more than ritual sex for religious purposes. After all, cohabitation was a form of marriage.

Emphasis on the physical act of sex made even street-level prostitution a very serious crime. The *pshat*[16] of Proverbs has several warnings to young men to stay away from prostitutes, and if all its warnings were insufficient to stop the practice, Jewish law still could not recognize these casual unions as marriage. In extreme cases, as we saw (Judges), tradition comes to the rescue, e.g., of Joshua by determining that the prostitute at Jericho converted, married him and mothered an important line that included Jeremiah the prophet.[17]

The Bible has numerous passages that compare "harlotry" to religious apostasy, something that we should expect in a society that championed one God. Monotheism and monogamy are a logical pair, the more so when earlier nature religions used sacred prostitution as a sympathetic magical practice to stimulate crop growth. There are, however, two forms of marriage that, while foreign to us, were perfectly legitimate in biblical times: concubinage and the (forced) marriage of women taken in war.

3. Concubines, or: A Girl of One's Own

A concubine is a woman who has a recognized, ongoing sexual relationship with a man but is by definition of lower status than first-rank wives. Writing about Middle Kingdom Egypt, Geraldine Pinch says:

> Some men seem to have had sexual relationships with free women whose families did not have the social or financial status to negotiate a property settlement for them.[18]

The Middle Kingdom ended before Israelite ancestors made their way to Egypt, but there's no reason to think the practice didn't continue. It was probably fairly universal among societies that did not routinely murder unwanted female children. Concubines were infinitely better off than murdered babies, but were unprotected in case of widowhood or divorce, and their children did not usually receive property inheritances alongside those of first-rank wives. If the first rank wife were barren, a bearing concubine might be raised to wife status, but her prospects were not good.

In this regard it is interesting to note that Jacob's twelve sons were evenly split, six from wives and six from concubines, but that all fared equally in inheritance, whereas Abraham's six sons by Keturah did not. On the basis of I Chron. 1:32, tradition assigns her a place among the concubines of Gen. 25:6, but this is not entirely fair.

The reason for this is that, in the case of Jacob, the sons/tribes allegedly springing from concubines Bilhah and Zilpah apparently represent Canaanite groups that became part of Israel. Hence, they had to be given not only an Israelite paternity, but some semblance of parity with the others regarded as purer Israelite. What is odd about this is that Rachel was barren but Leah was not, and she had a seven-year head start on her sister in which to demonstrate her fertility. There was no need for her to provide Jacob with a concubine, but she did because, the Bible says, two were born to her maidservant after she had stopped bearing children. How one knows this short of menopause is beyond us, but she was evidently mistaken. She bore her last two sons, Issaschar and Zebulun, *after* she had seemingly stopped bearing.

This would seem to reflect a history similar to that of the United States, in which additional states attached themselves to the original thirteen colonies over a period of time. In Israel, however, we're not sure who the originals were.

One other facet of the concubinage system is provided by the stories of Reuben, son of Jacob and Adonijah, David's son by his wife Haggith. Both men tried to possess their fathers' concubines—Reuben while his father was still alive—as this act apparently carried with it a claim to family headship. For this, Reuben lost his place as first-born and Adonijah lost his life. One wonders if Adonijah knew the story of Reuben and what effect it had on his actions, but that is not germane here.

Since we no longer use this system, we have to ask why anyone ever did and, of course, what the institution of concubinage might say about intermarriage in Israel.

When a man had both bearing wives and concubines, the children of the concubines were ordinarily of lower status unless the first rank wife was barren. We might posit that a concubine was a kind of "insurance policy" against the barrenness or death of a first wife in (first) childbirth. In such a case, the children (sons) of the concubine would automatically become the man's heirs unless he remarried another first-rank wife and had sons by her.

More to the point is the question of who these women, the concubines, were and how they were chosen? As regard to the first question, kings might collect concubines as a symbol of wealth. Solomon is said to have had 300 of them, in addition to his 700 wives. Both numbers are probably exaggerations. If not, Solomon was lucky to live before Talmudic times, when the frequency of intercourse with one's wife was mandated according to her husband's occupation, and failure to comply was grounds for the wife seeking divorce!

Saul had a concubine and David had several, but even the anonymous Levite of Judges 19 had one. In regard to him as well as other, more common individuals, the question is: why?

First, however, let us note that concubinage was not an exclusively Israelite or even exclusively Near Eastern practice. Greeks and Romans had them, as well.[18] So, the answer can't have had anything to do with religion. That being so, it must have had something to do with economics.

A man might take a concubine with advantage to both. If the woman were the excess daughter of a poor family with little or no dowry, her marriage prospects would be none too good. And if the man were a small farmer, he would not have to look forward to subdividing a subsistence farm among the too many heirs (sons) that both a wife and a concubine might produce. The Levites were landless, so such an arrangement would have suited them, too.

As we said, such women were unprotected in case of widowhood, and if divorced must have faced a very uncertain future unless they could return to their fathers' houses. On at least one occasion, the son of a Canaanite concubine rose to brief prominence in Israel. Abimelech, the son of Gideon by an unnamed concubine, "judged" in Israel for three years, albeit his reign seems to have been little more than a local thugocracy.

Rizpah, daughter of one Aiah, Saul's concubine, was mother of IshBaal, who would have been king had Saul's line prevailed. If these two stories were broadly known, it might offer some hope to women compelled to accept second-class marriage.

If the first-rank wife produced no children, then the sons of concubines had a clear shot at the inheritance, as was the case with Hagar's Ishmael before the birth of half-brother Isaac. Here, however, we must be careful to distinguish concubine from "handmaid." Hebrew has different words for these two functions, but I think the real differences are only a) the manner in which the woman is acquired, and b) whether she is the property of the wife or the husband. A handmaid might be acquired from one's then-barren wife, a concubine from her father's house. The question is, were any of these women foreign and, if so, did it matter?

Since so little is known about any concubines—even their names are often omitted—we can tell nothing of their ethnicities. Abimelech had help from his Canaanite mother's people at Shechem, but we don't know who her people were because "Canaanite" is such a catch-all term. We might be on safe ground to assume that in this case the concubine-mother was absorbed into her husband's household, perhaps even submerging her beliefs in his, but we've no way of knowing for sure.

One thing we may understand from all this, at least, is that no taint automatically attached to children of concubines. That is, as we saw earlier, there was no requirement that such children be kept in an inferior position. We'll have more to say below, and in our concluding chapter, about the notion of race and just how absurd it is—or ever was—to attach the label to Israelites.

4. Captives: Sleeping with the Enemy

"The Asiatics, according to the Persians, took the seizure of women lightly enough,..." – Herodotus[19]

Herodotus' observation doesn't seem to have applied in the case of the unfortunate Dinah. As we saw in Chapter IV, her alleged rape led to the death of all the males in the city of her rapist, Shechem. But the treatment of women captured in war gives us another avenue for the understanding of how Israel saw itself.

Deut. 21:10-14 provides for the treatment of women captured in war whom their Israelite captors wished to marry. This text probably comes from a time no earlier than the mid-eighth century b.c.e. If so, it demonstrates that, without question, intermarriage is not against Jewish law. Rashi (v.10) extends this to include woman from the seven proscribed nations who might be captured outside of Canaan.

This is in marked contrast to Jewish and especially Christian exegetes who could not readily accept the notion that Moses should have given permission to marry foreign women under any circumstances.

True, the woman is at somewhat of a disadvantage, but even if she does not please her new husband, she may not be sold as if she had been nothing more than a slave. Further, the text says that such a woman was to be given "a month's time in your house lamenting her father and mother."[20] But this is no statutory period; if it were the word used would be *hodesh yamim*. What the text says is: *yareach yamim*, which we must understand as the time until the next new moon, when women would have their periods.[21]

For some reason, the biblical text shies away from saying that these war captives might be married women—though the commentaries in Siphre and Kiddushin are cited by Rashi as knowing that this might be the case—so that it would be necessary to wait and see if they were pregnant. Here we have to acknowledge that the incident in Numbers 31 includes a command to spare only virgins, but while this might be applied by later rabbis to amplify the text of Deuteronomy 21,[22] we do not think it was ever a universal principle among Israelites.

The purpose for waiting until the captive woman showed that she was not bearing must have been to avoid questions of paternity. But why would this have mattered? In the pre-Civil War American South, getting children on slaves was a way of increasing the slave population and "improving the breed." We might find this abhorrent and disgusting, but writing fourteen centuries before our conflict, St. Jerome opined that engendering children on these captives would be a good source of "domestics for Lord Sabaoth."[23]

That cannot be the case here. Israelites must have wanted to be sure that the first offspring of captive women were theirs, indicating a desire to integrate them into their families alongside their other children. If not, why wait until after the woman's next period?

Presumably, these captive-begotten children would not have suffered any impediment from marrying other Israelites. At least Scripture gives us no indication of their being second-class. Hence, here we see another avenue through which Israelites became "intermarried." In sum, there were a lot of folks running around out there like the children of Esau with "Israelite blood" in them (another anachronism, to be sure) who were not considered Israelites, while some indeterminate percentage of "Israelites" carried foreign blood. This inevitably leads to the question of race.

5. Theology and Race

"What then can we Christians do with this damned, rejected race of Jews?" - Martin Luther, Concerning the Jews and Their Lies[24]

Luther to the contrary notwithstanding, Jews are not and never have been a family, much less a race. Hebrew itself has no word for "race."

However, no matter how often we might say this or what proofs we can bring to demonstrate its truth, the notion that Jews are a race has proved attractive to people who wish, for one reason or another, to do them harm.[25] Gentile histories mostly written by theologians or influenced by Christian theology delighted in seeing Jews as a race, a collective Cain-figure, shunned and despised by all and deserving of any bad thing that happened to them. Matthew 5:34's "His [Jesus's] blood be upon us and upon our children" founded an ideology that made the Holocaust possible.

Of course, Luther was constrained to believe what the Bible said about the Israelites. However, as we have seen throughout this study, Scriptural stories of Israel's single-family origin are a pious fiction, designed to show how its various constituent elements are related by blood. Anthropology tells a different story.

Human remains found in Canaan from the Middle Bronze Age[26]—that is, well before there was an Israel—are not at all uniform, indicating that the inhabitants came from various places. This is no surprise. The land we call Israel lies at the crossroads of civilizations, a meeting place for many peoples. Canaan/Israel was a reasonably well-watered and forested area that connected Asia and Africa, making it attractive for land-based traders who operated between the two areas, but it is also a land bridge between the Mediterranean and the Indian Ocean.

Biblical Israel arose when various groups, including Canaan's inhabitants and migrants to it, rallied around the idea of monotheism—truly one of the world's great revolutionary ideas. (If the idea was revolutionary, the revolution it spawned took a long time to reach maturity and longer to capture a majority of the people who we now call Jews.)

The Bible tells us that all the Israelites, more or less, were descendants of one couple, Shem and Mrs. Shem. We may wish to call Jews "Semitic," after Shem, but even this term is not terribly helpful.[27] For one thing, it was coined only in the late eighteenth century to describe a language family that includes Akkadian, the oldest Semitic language, Hebrew, Aramaic, Arabic, Ugaritic and Ethiopic among dozens of others. The term is far too general and, of course, it's been negatively freighted ever since by being used in the phrase "anti-Semitic" meaning strictly anti-Jewish. No one with an unreasoning hatred of Arabs is called "anti-Semitic," regardless of their language group.

Ironically, no ancient Semitic language has a word for "race," because it's a concept completely foreign to the ancients. High-culture peoples like the Egyptians and Greeks might think everyone else inferior, but this was based upon their language and culture, not some bogus valuation of external physical characteristics.

Still, the biblical stories themselves retain the memory that some of the constituent groups were "second-class" tribes, actually foreigners not initially related by blood. So, even on its own say-so, the earliest Israelites were a mixed bag. One may add to this mixture an indeterminate number of children whose mothers were either foreign slaves or war captives. How many of either group entered Israel is impossible to say. The laws governing such things are not accompanied by statistics.

For stories such as the mass absorption of 32,000 captured virgins in Numbers 31:35, there is no corroborative evidence. But consider this: given Israel's own population at the time, subject perhaps to the same exaggeration, 32,000 would be a significant percentage. Whatever their number, these women's "blood," their genes, became intertwined with Israel's. And even if some of them converted to whatever Judaism existed then, this would not affect their DNA.

To be sure, the ancients weren't "color blind." Jeremiah famously asks (13:23) whether Ethiopians can change their skins. But he would, no doubt, be tickled to learn that some of their (or other Africans') descendants, the Lemba, seem to be Jewish![28]

It would be pleasant if the concept of "race" could be buried in an unmarked grave. The bottom line is that Bible is not at all concerned with race,[29] at least not before the time of Ezra. Even then Ezra's concern masks a strictly political objective. Some proof of this assertion lies in the fact that only marginal elements within Judaism continued to hold what we might call a racist line.

Notes to Chapter XI

1. In some societies a woman is not considered really married until she has a child.

2. Elkanah's more humane treatment of the barren wife, Hannah, in the years before she had Samuel is exceptional.

3. From rabbinic times, a *Ketubah* (= written thing, "document") has been drawn as a wedding contract, specifying what each party brought to the union and protecting the woman in case of divorce. This formal arrangement represented a considerable step forward in the establishment of women's rights, which, historically, were often notable by their absence.

5. Thus NJPS. RSV has "Adam," though clearly the presence of a definite article favors the Jewish version. Conversely, RSV retains the article in 2:18, whereas NJPS omits it. Still, here is another example of the use of capital letters (Eve) that subtly change a text's meaning.

6. We say "allegedly" because we think there's a lot more to this incident than modern commentators have chosen to comment upon.

7. The Telepinu Proclamation in Gary Beckman, "Royal Ideology and State Administration in Hittite Anatolia," in Sasson, CANE I:535, contains a plea that family murders not follow the death of a reigning king.

8. Even though it is fiction, we have to read the story of Lot's offering his daughters to the sodomites of Sodom as indicating that the men in question were not exclusively homosexual as we understand it in modern times. What sense would it make to offer women to men who abhorred sexual contact with them?

9. Some Essenes, apparently, were unmarried; others were married. Such selective/elective celibacy is the case today, for example, with priests in the Greek Orthodox Church.

10. Thus RSV and AV. NJPS has "impassioned," a translation at once clever and cowardly; it avoids "jealous" because since 1611 that word has entered a semantic overlap with "envious," something Israel's God could not be.

11. Desperate situations call forth desperate measures; thus, the Egyptians seem to have sacrificed their firstborn to halt the series of plagues visited on them by the eruption of Santorini (see Rosenbaum, *Understanding*.) During the Black Death in the fourteenth century, Europeans tried all manner of desperate measures to stop the plague, or at least escape it themselves.

12. In The Religion of the Semites: the Fundamental Institutions (NY: Schocken, 1972 [1889]), 261.

13. See S. N. Rosenbaum, *Amos*, 56-57 and A. J. Williams, "A Further Suggestion" in *VT*, 206-211.

14. Rosenbaum, *Understanding*, 292 re marzeach.

15. In like manner, the Egyptian practices designed to insure eternal life for deceased pharaohs became, ultimately, available to anyone who had enough money to pay for the process. One thinks of Ted Williams: *plus ca change...*

16. One *drash* is that the loose woman whom good Jewish boys are warned away from is none other than Sophia, the Greek word for wisdom that we still use in the word "philosophy." Ibid.

17. This is not a claim Jeremiah makes, but rather Scripture's bald-faced attempt at *ex post facto* justification. Like Ezra's claim of descent from Aaron, it's hard to credit that biblical types knew their family trees back 600 to 800 years.

18. Baron, *History*, II:224.

19. Herodotus, *Histories*, I:5.

20. NJPS, KJV, NIV, RSV et al. render this "a full month."

21. As we saw in Chapter VIII, Hannah and Women's religion.

22. On the principle of *binyan ab*, but Num. 31 is specifically aimed at Midianites.

23. Cohen, *Beginnings,* 260.

24. In *The Jew in the Medieval World,* ed. Jacob Rader Marcus, (NY: Atheneum, 1972) 165.

25. William Montgomery McGovern, *From Luther to Hitler* (Boston: Houghton Mifflin, 1941). McGovern's book, written during World War II, is a bit polemical, but other people since have made a strong case for connecting the two. Racialist anti-Semitism enabled Nazis to negate Jewish conversions and exterminate people, some of whose grandparents had converted to Christianity.

26. Thus *EJ,* 3:45.

27. Arthur Koestler, in *The Thirteenth Tribe* (New York: Random House, 1975), made an attempt to show that Europe's so-called Jews were all descended from people of the Crimea, hence not even Semitic. On his reading, the Holocaust was a tragic mistake.

28. *Judaising Movements: Studies in the Margins of Judaism,* Tudor Parfitt and Emanuela Trevisan Semi, eds. (London: RoutledgeCurzon, 2002), 39-51, details the phenomenon of the Lemba people of southern Africa, who seem to have genetic and cultural ties to Middle Eastern Jews and Muslims. The percentage of their "Jewish genes" is actually greater than that of many European Jews (49)!

29. The Bible only has 8,000 distinct words from an estimated 60,000 total words of text, but given the way Israelites saw the world, race would not be a concept for them.

Chapter XII. Rahab and the Rabbis, a Hooker's Legacy, or: Two Jews, Three Opinions

1. "A good wife who can find?" (Prov. 31:10, RSV)

The Book of Proverbs ends with a paean to an anonymous "woman of valor." It is presently read in Orthodox and some Conservative Jewish homes every Friday night as a tribute to Ms Everygoodwife, as the RSV cited above understands it. But both the Protestant translation and Jewish popular use represent another example of democratization, the process by which restricted texts, practices or objects become the property of the many.

The phrase *'eshet hayil* originally designated someone whom we might call "lady of the manor" or "nobleman's wife," not the ordinary housewife. She is someone who commands independent recognition for an active life both inside and outside the house, and Proverbs 31:10-31 is a twenty-two line alphabetic acrostic describing her activities.[1]

Accordingly, Midrash *Hagigah* to Gen. 23:1 has a list of twenty-two biblical "women of valor." Not to be outdone, Midrash *Tadshe* 21 lists twenty-three Israelite "good women" in the Bible, mostly the "usual suspects," but including ten whose actual names are not known—and follows that with nine more good women who at least began life as foreigners.

On the kosher list are: 1. Sarah; 2. Rebekah; 3. Rachel; 4. Leah (but not Jacob's concubines, Bilhah and Zilpah); 5. Jochebed, Moses's mother; 6. Miriam, Moses's sister; 7. Deborah (see Judges 5); 8. Samson's mother; 9. Hannah; 10. Abigail, a wife of David (but not any others, particularly Michal and Bathsheba); 11. an unnamed wise woman of Tekoah; 12. the widow whom Elijah helped; 13. Abishag, the woman who last shared David's bed; 14. Huldah the prophet; 15. Naomi, Ruth's mother-in-law; 16. Jehosheba, who hid an infant from murderous Queen Athaliah; 17. the wife of one of the prophets aided by Elisha; and (18-22) the five daughters of Zelophehad who successfully petitioned Moses to be treated as sons for purposes of inheritance. (Esther is missing, as is Judith. These omissions may reflect a recognition of the apocryphal nature of their stories.)

The acknowledged foreigners are: Hagar, Asenath, Shiphrah and Puah, midwives before the Exodus; one Bathia, otherwise unknown, who brought up Moses; Moses's wife Zipporah! (but not his two mentioned but unnamed wives); Ruth; Jael, who killed Sisera; and Rahab. Interestingly, two-thirds of this group are Egyptian. We may wonder why such foreign women as Keturah, Abraham's third wife and the mother of three-quarters of his children, isn't in the second group, but so it is.

At least half in the second group are regarded as converts, an arguable assumption. The reader will remember that earlier we questioned the ethnicity, or at least the prior religious affiliation, of many in this first list, too. But even taking the Midrash as it is, foreign-born women constitute a significant percentage of the whole. From what we've seen thus far, this is hardly to be wondered at.

After the fact, sometimes well after the fact, tradition could afford to kosherize these foreigners, as in the case of Asenath, lionize them, as it did with Ruth, or sanitize them, as it did with Rahab—even if it required making stuff up out of whole cloth.

Perhaps the most unusual honoree comes from the second list: Rahab, the prostitute. Her story is first found in chapter two of Joshua. Some authorities obfuscate the plain meaning of the text where the word usually translated "prostitute" is found, and identify her as an "innkeeper." This is a role that was not uncommon for women, but is hardly incompatible with her other profession.

Those who admit that she was a prostitute go on to claim that she practiced this profession for forty years, from age ten to age fifty, before meeting Joshua's Israelite spies, "going straight" (like Hosea's wife, Gomer), marrying Joshua himself and becoming the ancestor of Jeremiah, among other illustrious prophets. In either case, her story, however burnished by traditional embellishments, was used as proof that neither foreign nor humble origins were a bar to success in later Israel's view of its society.

Paradoxically, Proverbs is shot through with warnings to the young men of Israel not to heed the blandishments of harlots.

Modern literature boasts no rags-to-riches story better than Rahab's, even if it took more than ten centuries to play out. That intimate details of her story could have been kept alive for 1,000 years—Jeremiah's big book doesn't mention Rahab as an ancestress—before re-surfacing beggars our imagination. But obviously it didn't faze the imagination of the rabbis or of early Jewish Christians, either. Matthew's Gospel extends her line to include Jesus![2]

(Of course, Christianity had a vested interest in taking over anything Jewish that might serve its ends, canonical or not, and Matthew was an early Jewish follower of Jesus. One is reminded of the Soviet Union's often comical attempts to claim that all of the world's important inventions were actually invented there first.)

Returning to Rahab, are we dealing here merely with pious fiction, or could it be at least partly based in fact? We are inclined to say "fiction" because the evidence on which the genealogical claims is based is nothing more assertion. On the other hand, why have such a story at all, if not to explain the later presence in Israel of the ethnic element Rahab presumably represents?

As to her conversion, that might come as a surprise to those who think that Judaism has always accepted converts only reluctantly. It is true that even during times when conversionary activity has not been forbidden, Jews have regarded those who expressed a desire to convert as being just a bit *meshuggah* (= crazy). Who else would voluntarily join a people habitually subject to persecution?

On the other hand, Judith Baskin writes[3] that claiming converts in the patriarchal period was simply a later proselytizing ploy, a "testimonial" attempting to present Judaism as an attractive and accepting faith from earliest time. George Foote Moore asserted that Judaism was "the first great missionary religion of the Western world,"[4] which may be true. Of course, that will have happened much later.

Serious proselytism probably occurred no earlier than the Maccabean period (164 - 63 b.c.e.) and perhaps not for a century after that, possibly in response to early Christianity's being an avowedly missionary religion.

In the early periods we have to ask, as we did in Chapter III, concerning Rahab's near-contemporary, Ruth: to what did the purported converts convert? The idea that anyone would want to convert to whatever it was that Israelites were practicing so soon after Sinai is strange for two reasons. As we saw earlier, on a theoretical level, the idea of monotheism is counterintuitive. Second, on the practical level, to espouse this faith was to ally oneself with what Pharaonic Egypt called "vile Asiatics": a low-class, outsider, outcast, pariah people.

On the other hand, scholars such as George Mendenhall and Norman K. Gottwald have advanced the theory that Israel was largely formed from oppressed, lower-class Canaanites.[5] This would have included, but not have been limited to, *habiru,* and such riff-raff would have no difficulty accepting the notion of a prostitute's—or any oppressed person's—conversion.

Both scholars and laypeople often extol the Israelite vision of things as superior to that of polytheism and especially attractive to people on the lower end of the socioeconomic scale. For Rahab's part, then, what would be better than to join a religion that espoused the cause of submerged elements in society?[6] To quote the Peter Sellers's parody of *My Fair Lady*, "See, I make her very touchable."

They might also be comfortable with the alternative notion, proposed earlier, that Rahab and Joshua could have been from the same ethnic stock. How else do we explain the sparing of Rahab's whole family from the destruction of Jericho? As Tikvah Frymer-Kensky writes, "[T]he amalgamation and incorporation of local inhabitants is strikingly like the account of the settlement of Israel that is currently accepted by archaeologists and historians."[7]

Are we to assume that Rahab's whole family converted and that, having done so, they would be free to marry other Israelites? Tradition might wish to consign such people as Joshua's Gibeonites to separate and subservient status, but that's definitely not the case with Rahab's kin.

2. Jewish Conversion: Objective or Subjective Genitive?

Throughout most of modern history, the phrase "Jewish conversion," whether voluntary or coerced, usually meant conversion "of" Jews, not "by" Jews, an objective rather than a subjective genitive. Grammatical niceties aside, converting from Judaism was usually seen as a step up in class or at least as a way to escape persecution.

We note the phenomena of Jews in Spain converting to Catholicism to escape the rigors of the Inquisition and Jews in nineteenth-twentieth century Europe converting to various forms of Christianity in order to enjoy privileges (the poet Heinrich Heine, in order to live in Berlin; composer/conductor Gustav Mahler in order to accept a job leading the Vienna State Orchestra) they were legally denied as Jews.

But what happens if we accept the traditional view that Israel's numbers in Egypt grew through proselytism? If, in fact, a goodly number of those two million or so people who made their way to Canaan were born something else, we may be fairly confident that a whole lot of intermarriage took place in the forty years of their wandering. That is, the newly cohered Israelite-Egyptians and other "Asiatics" who had converted would be acceptable mates for one another, would they not?

The Bible in no way indicates that the fugitives from Pharaoh set up separate camps like so many Chicago neighborhoods. If they were afraid of pursuit by the Egyptian army, we can't imagine that they segregated themselves on the way up to Canaan. And when they got near their destination, we might (again) mention the 32,000 Midianite women forcibly integrated into Israelite society on the eve of the Conquest.

What percentage of the whole might these have represented? Would their offspring be regarded as "full Israelites" or relegated to some kind of second-class citizenship that compelled them to marry only within their own group? It might be tempting to see the children of converts as separable from the rest of Israel in much the same way that Hindu Untouchables are cordoned off, but of this there is no hint.

We trust such offspring were free to marry whomever because here we need to raise the issue of genetic diversity. As is well known in Jewish circles, Eastern European Jews who have married within a fairly tight genetic circle have a notable incidence of Tay-Sachs disease. This is a condition that causes mental deficiency and blindness in infancy. Other tight-knit groups, such as the Amish, also show the effects of marrying within a limited gene pool. The question is: how much of Jewish survival is due to the hybrid nature of its original core group and to the adherence of others throughout its long history?

3. Can the Leopard Change his Spots? (Derived from Jer. 13:23)

To this point our discussion, however, is probably no more than an academic exercise. In Chapter III we noted that formal conversion, despite what the Talmud imputes to Naomi, could hardly have been a feature of Judaism before Talmudic times and, indeed, the Mishnah has numerous references to laws regarding both proselytes and resident aliens. We continue with a more detailed look at the complex issue of proselytism.

Gen. 12:5 reports that Abraham "acquired many souls" before leaving Harran. Tradition, as noted above, accounts for the enormous growth of Jacob's family from the seventy who "went down to Egypt" to the hundreds of thousands, even millions, who came out in a space of just four centuries (if that) by assuming Egyptians converted to Judaism in carload lots, as we discussed earlier.

This leaves aside, for the moment, the consideration that before Moses was eighty years old there was no Torah, hence no Judaism per se to convert to. But again, conversion as we know it would have been a category the ancients could not understand. For all the nobility of Ruth's gesture, it is not the same thing as conversion in our sense. People did not convert because it simply was not seen as necessary or, perhaps, even possible.[8] As Jeremiah asked, "Can the leopard change his spots?"

Had Abraham, say, adopted the gods and culture of Egypt, he would not thereby have become an Egyptian. And what of his descendants who did spend considerable time there? Joseph, as was the custom for "Asiatic" slaves in Egypt, was given an Egyptian name, and Moses apparently carried one from birth, but this did not nor was it expected to make them Egyptian.

314

This is not really so different than in our own times. After sharing their "superior" culture with all manner of Asians, the British sneeringly referred to those who bought into it as "wogs," that is, "westernized Oriental gentlemen." The British Prime Minister Benjamin Disraeli was often thought of as Jewish, although not he, but his father before him, had converted! This is because being Jewish is thought of as a nationality as well as a religion.

If we transpose into the key of nationality, things get worse. For example, even Turks born in Germany cannot get German citizenship and, as we have noted, no one who isn't biologically Japanese can become a citizen of Japan.

More to the point, Egypt roundly rejected the only homegrown attempt to change its thoroughly polytheistic faith to something that even came close to monotheism, namely, the famous henotheistic "heresy" of Amenophis IV (ca. 1350 b.c.e.). He changed his name to Akhenaton to signal his elevation of the sun-disk at morning, Aton, to the place of *primus inter pares*, first among the gods, including the sun disk in its other aspects.

Akhenaton's new wrinkle lasted scarcely fifteen years and collapsed with his death. As we suggested previously, it may be that this Egyptian innovation somehow influenced Hebrews/Asiatics in Egypt; influence running the other way can scarcely be imagined.

It's hard to say exactly when Jews began successfully to spread their religious views. As Rabbi Rembaum has pointed out,[9] Ezra didn't suggest that those who had married foreign women convert them because it wasn't (yet) an option in his time.

Forcible "conversion" of Jews whom the ruling Hasmoneans (164 - 63 b.c.e.) thought had strayed too far from the path of righteousness was a feature of the Hanukah heroes' rule that isn't taught in Hebrew school. By Jesus's time, Jews were actively engaged in proselytism among foreigners—one hopes with subtler tactics.

4. Jesus's Witness

That Jews were actively involved in proselytizing can be inferred from Jesus's criticism of the Pharisees for their heroic efforts to make converts while not tending to their own spiritual purity. (Matt. 23:15) Be that as it may, the appeal of Judaism should not be denied. For one thing, it is an essentially democratic religion, mandating equality before the law for both rich and poor (the true significance of the much maligned *Lex Talionis* of Exodus 21:23-25, "an eye for an eye…"), protecting the rights of women to a degree remarkable at the time, and making God's grace dependent upon mending fences with those we have offended.

When Jesus prayed, "Forgive us our trespasses as we forgive those who trespass against us," (Matt. 6:9ff.) he was stating, succinctly, what Jews have to do between Rosh Hashanah and Yom Kippur in order to obtain God's forgiveness. During the Ten Days of Awe Jews are required to seek out and apologize to those whom they have wronged. Only after this are the petitioners fit to go before God and ask his pardon.

It reminds us of the line from Robert Frost's poem "The Death of the Hired Man": "Home is the place where, when you have to go there, /They have to take you in."

Our point is that to go "home" to the Jewish God, you have first to seek the pardon of those you have wronged. Fortunately, the wronged parties are obliged to grant forgiveness.

In Jesus's world, the "home" religion of most people would have been some form of paganism, which, for whatever reason, was not proving satisfactory. Consequently, it is estimated that of the seventy million people in the Roman Empire in Jesus's time, fully ten per cent were Jews. Now, this result will not have come exclusively through natural increase, but must also have included the adherence of former gentiles to Judaism.

Judaism is a religion that is open to all (men, anyway, for most of its history, but inclusion of women has increased in the past hundred years) who are able to study and to practice what study leads to.

Or not! Non-Israelites could bless Israel's god, could sacrifice to him, could be impressed by his power and miracles, could even acknowledge him as greatest of gods, but they would not thereby become Israelites. Our word "sojourner," in fact, is a translation of the Hebrew *ger*. These were people some of whom (*gerei tza'dikim*) did ultimately convert, but as late as the third Christian century most *gerim* (the plural) were people who had adopted Jewish customs without benefit of clergy, that is, without formal conversion.

In Chapter III, we quoted Hillel's famous directive to an impatient, would-be proselyte, "What is hateful to you, do not do to others; that is the law; go and learn." The story does not go on to relate what action the man took. It's hard to determine how many of these early "fellow travelers" married into the core group, but we may get some idea from the treatment accorded them by occupying authorities.

In the fourth century the emerging Christian church prevailed upon the empire of Constantine to issue laws restricting Jews, Samaritans and "Heaven Worshippers"—that is to say, those who had adopted Jewish customs without converting. ("Heaven" as a divine epithet is found in Daniel 4:23, itself a late book: outside of that only in Apocryphal literature.)

The reason this juxtaposition is possible, of course, is because being Jewish is defined not by what one believes, but by how one lives. In a sense, then, if you "live Jewish," you are Jewish.

5. Room for Women

"Remember the ladies..." - Abigail Adams

One paradox of biblical intermarriage is this: the Hebrews having been built up through the contributions of so many foreigners, one searches for a "true Israel" in their midst. Without the contributions of all these foreigners, mostly women, Judaism would have had a vastly different shape—or perhaps no shape at all. It's just as likely Judaism would have disappeared along with the other faiths of equal or even greater antiquity whose adherents populate the Bible.

The question is this: if marriage to a Jew did not necessitate conversion in the early period and wasn't even allowed by Ezra, how is it that so many foreign women seem voluntarily to have embraced the religion?

Although Hebrew Scripture is not short on miracle stories, Jewish identity is not predicated upon accepting these stories as true. Judaism does not require any profession of faith in things that confound human reason. It is, at base, a religion that appeals to reason even while hoping that we can transcend reason, as Abraham did, in his willingness to sacrifice Isaac.

Furthermore, the ethical core of Judaism is not dependent upon any one person whether god-in-human-form or anyone less exalted. Judaism does not depend upon David, Moses or Abraham. In fact, although it is a religion of History, not Mystery, Judaism does not ultimately depend upon whether any of them even existed!

Still, the idea that Jews would consciously and systematically go out and attempt to convert people, to proselytize, seems strange to us. This is because the absence of proselytizing activity these past sixteen centuries was not Judaism's own choice. Shortly after Christianity's becoming licit in the Roman Empire, early Church

318

authorities moved the emperor to declare conversion to Judaism illegal upon pain of death for both converter and converted.[10] (Conversely, the Empire also made it easy for slaves owned by Jews to escape slavery by converting to Christianity, thus hamstringing, so to speak, Jewish enterprises that depended upon slave labor in order to compete with their slave-employing gentile rivals.)

From that time until the nineteenth century, Jews didn't engage in proselytism and even discouraged those who wanted to convert for fear of reprisals against their Jewish community.

6. Making the Best of It: Erecting New Barriers?

Israel's successor people, calling themselves Jews after 586 b.c.e., were ultimately compelled by history and their own increasingly rigid standards to become " a people that dwells apart" and to discourage intermarriage—at least that intermarriage which didn't involve conversion of the non-Jew. A remark[11] in Midrash Hagigah says of Naomi's sons that they died because they had intermarried.

However, Jewish opinion came to matter less and less as first Christianity, then Islam prohibited Jews from engaging in conversionary activity or marrying their faithful. Emerging Christianity's first known prohibition dates to 300 c.e., the Council of Elvira in Spain, and was followed soon afterward by prohibitions of intermarriage throughout the empire of Constantine.

But even had this not happened, Jews might have had to eschew either practice. For such a small minority group as Jews were and are, intermarriage could be seen, as it is today, as a one-way ticket to oblivion.[12] Active conversion efforts could be a problem for those Jews who espouse a pseudo-mystical attachment to blood and biology.

7. Two Jews, Three Opinions

Prohibition presupposes previous practice. – RaGBaG

The subject of rabbinic opinions, attitudes and rules concerning intermarriage is so complex that it has generated its own literature. How not? The rabbinic period is as long (from about 200 b.c.e. to 425 c.e.) as that between David and Ezra. It may be that the old joke, "Wherever you have two Jews you have three opinions," dates from rabbinic times. The Talmud, that massive compendium of biblical interpretation, contains the names of 140 rabbis and offers many opinions whose authors are not named.

In this book we have tried to integrate selected rabbinic commentary at places where such commentary was appropriate, but the reader might also benefit from a brief discussion of the main lines of argument used in discussing the problem of intermarriage. We do not claim to be adding anything original to scholarly discussion at this point; rather, we see it as our part to interpret that discussion for lay readers.

When we say "the rabbis," it effectively masks the vastly differing circumstances in which these men worked. There were two major centers of rabbinic activity, one in Palestine and the other in Babylon, and each produced its own Talmud. (Two Talmuds, three opinions). The first part, the Mishnah, comments on Torah. The second part, the Gemara, comments on the Mishnah. Like untidy court records, these Talmuds record both majority and minority opinions, the latter sometimes being brought back by subsequent authorities—like previously discarded chess strategies—for use in their now-desired reinterpretations.

Note, though, that the situations of the various communities in which decisions were taken will have differed, from each other and even within the same community, over the period in question.

The mainstream of rabbinic opinion did not interpret Ezra to mean that gentiles were genealogically impure, though that opinion continued to be held, e.g., by the authors of Jubilees and the Dead Sea Scroll known as 4QMMT. It's doubtful that these writings enjoyed a very great circulation.

The majority divided over whether gentiles were ritually impure or morally impure and what the consequences of each state were. This is discussed at length in Hayes.

To summarize her position, which strikes us as correct, both moral and ritual impurity were conditions that gentiles could overcome; hence, they could convert, could marry Jews and their children would (or should) be unencumbered members of the community.[13]

As we have seen, Samaritans were ruled to be outside of the Jewish community because it was held their ancestors had converted from fear. This later rabbinic "finding" continued the policy of Ezra, but his reason for excluding Samaritans had had more to do with politics and the fight to control Jerusalem.

8. Whose Bible Is It, Anyway?

Despite—even perhaps because of—its destruction, Jerusalem looms large in the determination of Judaism's subsequent shape. The last part of Jewish Scripture was canonized—that is, made "official" and unchangeable—shortly after the Romans destroyed the Second Temple. The "Writings," as they are called, bulk larger than the Torah itself and contain such well-loved books as Psalms, Proverbs, Ruth, the enigmatic Job... and Ezra.[14]

Job ends with God speaking directly to its aggrieved protagonist. The Almighty doesn't really answer Job's questions, but his verbal bluster blisters Job, who consequently consents to accept that which he cannot understand. The rest, as they say, is history. Or is it?

In a sense, the answer to this question doesn't matter. Having God simply appear to you, tell you where to go, or give you rules to live by must be a powerful incentive to do just as you are commanded. If, however, the people we call Jews practically invented themselves or, we might say, wove for themselves a coat of many colors, then their accomplishment is far greater than the Bible's own story.

Think of it! The towering ethical system that, alone among its contemporaries, survives until this very day and serves as a basis for the religion of half the world's people: that, indeed, is a mighty accomplishment.

The purpose of our book is to show that credit for this cannot be given to Israelites alone, unless we understand by Israelites that mixed multitude which coalesced about 1200 b.c.e. and went on to live and to write, rewrite and in some cases invent a history that we can read about in the Hebrew Scriptures.

Notes to Chapter XII

1. In Roman Catholic circles, as reported to us by Mary Heléne Rosenbaum, it has been customary when using this passage at Mass to omit the verses dealing with the woman's successes outside the house.

2. It's true that the other Gospels don't include this tidbit, but that's not too surprising. Matthew is conceded to be a Christian-Jew whose mission was to propagandize his former-fellow Jews. See Jonathan D. Brumberg-Kraus, "Were the Pharisees a Conversionist Sect? Table Fellowship as a Strategy of Conversion" in *Approaches to Ancient Judaism: Jewish Proselytism*, A.-J. Levine and R. Pervo, eds. (Atlanta: Scholar's Press for the Society of Biblical Literature, 2002).

3. Judith Baskin, "The Rabbinic Transformations of Rahab the Harlot" in *Notre Dame English Journal*, Vol. 11, No. 2. Judaic Literature: Critical Perspectives (Apr., 1979), 141-157.

4. George Foote Moore, *Judaism in the First Centuries of the Christian Era* (Peabody MA: Hendrickson, 1997), 324.

5. Norman K. Gottwald, The Tribes of Yahweh, A Sociology of the Religion of Liberated Israel, 1250 – 1050 BCE, Biblical Seminar (Book 66) (London: Bloomsbury T&T Clark, 1999) and George E. Mendenhall, The Tenth Generation: The Origins of the Biblical Tradition (Baltimore: Johns Hopkins University Press, 1973).

6. Note the modern phenomenon of Hindu Untouchables converting to Islam, e.g. in Abdul Malik Mujahid, *Conversion to Islam: Untouchables' Strategy for Protest in India* (Shippensburg, PA: Anima Books, 1989).

7. In Reading the Women of the Bible: A New Interpretation (New York: Schocken, 2002), 43.

8. In America and Imperial Rome, unlike Egypt, there were attempts forcibly to suppress the culture and religion that slaves brought with them.

9. "Dealing with Strangers: Relations with Gentiles at Home and Abroad," in *Etz Hayim* (Jacob Blumenthal and Janet L. Liss, eds. New York: The Rabbinical Assembly, 2005) 1377-1382.

10. See, for example, Marcus, Jacob R., ed., *The Jew in the Medieval World* (New York: Atheneum, 1972) 3ff.

11. Yet Pesachim says one should not marry a proselyte: Rodkinson, *New Edition of the Babylonian Talmud* (Paperback, Charleston SC: BiblioLife, LLC, 2009 (231).

12. This in fact happened to the Jewish community of Kai Feng, China who came there in the thirteenth century in the wake of Marco Polo but who were swallowed up through intermarriage.

13. Christine E. Hayes, Gentile Impurities and Jewish Identities: Intermarriage and Conversion from the Bible to the Talmud (New York: Oxford University Press, 2002).

14. Unlike the Christian Bibles, where his book is smack dab in the middle because the attempt is to put the books in chronological order. This is not a good principle of organization, since most books were not written in—and some not even near—the time they purport to describe. For all that, RSV breaks its own "rule" by putting Daniel at the head of the minor prophets. This would not be justified even if we took Daniel's word for when the book was written (ca. 586 b.c.e., far later than Amos, Hosea and Micah). For a comparative chart of canonical order of Jewish, Christian Orthodox, Roman Catholic, and Protestant Bible books, see http://catholic-resources.org/Bible/Heb-Xn-Bibles.htm.

Chapter XIII. Was God Ever Intermarried?

1. Limitations of Language

"Our Parent who is in Heaven..." – Politically correct version of Jesus's prayer

Maimonides, arguably Judaism's most important philosopher, proposed as one of his thirteen principles that God has no body—Jews sing this in the "Yigdal" after Saturday morning services—making any marriage for our Deity a dubious prospect at best. We recognize, of course, that on its face, the question seems absurd, even insulting to most religious people. All Jews and most Christians[1] reject the idea that God was married at all or ever could be. Nonetheless, we think the answer to this question is a limited "yes," and we will shortly examine a tantalizing bit of evidence to support this claim.

Note first, however, that the rabbis who closed the canon managed to include Song of Songs only by interpreting its lovers not as a man and a woman—which on the surface they clearly are—but as God and Israel. That was a metaphorical interpretation.[2] Until recently, there was no reason to suppose that any Jews had ever shared the widespread Ancient Near Eastern idea of a married deity.

But we should remember that "in the beginning," religion was largely anthropomorphic—that is, it represented a cosmic projection of earthly conditions. Even if Jesus's "...on earth as it is in Heaven" is construed as a sign for a one-way street, it comes a long time after the image of Jacob's Ladder. Many millennia after humans first created gods in our own image, religions contemporary with Israel featured deities that shared our genders, felt the same emotions we feel, did the same things we do; only, since they were so powerful, the results were often disastrous, as, for example, among the Greek gods.

Among Greeks some gods married, others paired up with each other like the first four pairs of Mesopotamian gods. Or with us. Genesis 6:4's pairing of b'nei 'elohim with "the daughters of men" is, after all, Scripture.

Nonetheless, to ask the above question is to risk ridicule by those for whom it simply does not compute. God cannot be intermarried, cannot be married at all except metaphorically, can he? Well, according to some monotheists, God sent "his only begotten son," a flesh-and-blood human being, to ransom the world. That son, considered divine by Christians, is considered inferior to their prophet, Muhammad, by Muslims and until recently[3] barely acknowledged by Jews. Are we all really speaking of the same God? It is to be hoped.

Part of the problem, if we may borrow a phrase from J. R. R. Tolkien, is that we are "caught in a cleft stick of [our] own making." We—all of us, Jews, Christians and Muslims, men and women—might have been able to come together and worship a deity we could refer to in gender-neutral language, as some modern religious elements now do. Why didn't we arrive at this place long ago?

The underlying problem was bequeathed to us by the limitations of Semitic language, Hebrew included. These languages have no neuter gender and consequently no neuter pronoun with which to represent "it." Hebrew lacks a generic for "parent," and after so many millennia of "our Father," saying "our Parent" sounds strange and even a little silly.

At any rate, this God of ours seems to have a history,[4] seems to have developed through the ages, and that's after the advent of monotheism. However, at this point it might be well briefly to examine theories of religious evolution leading to monotheism.

2. Arriving at Monotheism

As we indicated in the last chapter, by the time Israel arose, most of the ancient world was polytheistic. But polytheism itself probably represents a fairly advanced state of religion: the middle of Edward Tylor's five-step progression from animism to monotheism.[5]

Tylor was a nineteenth-century anthropologist who developed an overly schematic view of religious "evolution" that, nonetheless, can still serve as a basis for discussion. Briefly, he thought that early religion was animist, realizing the life in any living thing and some that we would not consider to be alive, like mountains or the sea; that it progressed to animatism, the belief that classes of things, such as trees, had their own tutelary deities; thence to polytheism, henotheism, and finally monotheism.

Henotheism is a form of polytheism in which one god, Zeus, for example, is the head of a pantheon. In polytheistic systems various gods have separate functions, but overlapping jurisdictions, hence they are not without opportunities for divine interaction. Thus, the Babylonian gods meet in council and elect Marduk, city god of Babylon, to oppose Ti'amat,[6] the saltwater ocean, and her plan to drown all of mankind. As we saw above, the religious reform of Akhenaton IV seems to qualify as henotheism.

This begins to change with the advent of monotheism, but it doesn't change all of a sudden. Early Israelite monotheism acknowledges the presence and legitimacy of other gods for foreign peoples (Deut. 4:19) and may even have allowed for their worship in First Temple services. Over the centuries, however, monotheism became increasingly exclusive, hence intolerant of anything that smacked of religious pluralism. This is seen within Israel, for example, in Hezekiah's destruction of "the bronze serpent Moses made," or in great-grandson Josiah's (reigned 640 - 632 b.c.e.)

desecration of Northern Israelite shrines and the attempt to concentrate worship on the one true sanctuary of Jerusalem.

(But God cannot develop, can he? Wouldn't that indicate a previous lack of perfection? Rather than get into a philosophical discussion, let's say that it is our apprehension of God that has changed over many millennia, becoming more and more sophisticated as we gain wisdom. But all of this is in the realm of philosophical speculation and there we shall leave it.)

Then in 1967 came the astounding discovery of the graffiti at Kuntillet 'Ajrud.

3. The World's First Holiday Inn?

"Yeah, we got that." – Staples commercial

We said that Israel was not only a land bridge between Africa and Asia, but that it also sat astride a portage route from the Indian Ocean to the Mediterranean. 'Ajrud was a caravansary, not exactly a Holiday Inn, let alone the world's first, but a needed stop on that over one hundred mile route. Right after the Six Day War in 1967, archaeologists at the site discovered a couple of graffiti which seem to link Yahweh and a female consort, one with an Asherah of Teman (in northern Saudi Arabia) and one with an Asherah of Samaria.

Since the graffiti are so brief, interpreters have a certain amount of wiggle room. Also, the inscriptions come from around 800 b.c.e., a time when the area in question was under the control of Israel's (evil, to Judean eyes) Northern Kingdom, a time that includes the reign of the wicked, foreign Queen Jezebel. So we don't know whether this Asherah was the Tyrian Asherah that Jezebel would have known or a native Israelite/Canaanite one.[7] Nonetheless, the discovery of these graffiti sparked an explosion in religious circles; some did not want the information published because, on its face, it seemed to give a positive answer to the question with which we began.

The ninth century is also the period that includes the career of Elijah, Israel's first truly national prophet. Elijah is remembered for his successful contest against the prophets of Baal during the reign of Ahab and Jezebel, a victory that very nearly cost him his life. Lost or neglected in the story is this fact: Baal is the consort of Asherah, and her prophets numbered almost as many as his, but nothing seems to have happened to her or to them in the wake of Baal's defeat.

Furthermore, we know from Scripture that worship of Asherah continued despite intermittent attempts to put it down from the time of King Asa in the late tenth century b.c.e. II Kings 15:13 says:

He [Asa] also removed Maacah his mother from being queen mother because she had made an abominable image made for Asherah; and Asa cut down her image and burned it at the brook Kidron. (RSV)

Much of human religion is an ascription to the gods of what we do here. Did not David marry Saul's widow? And did not Reuben and Adonijah try to possess the woman with whom their respective fathers had last slept? Why should God not possess the consort of his vanquished rival?

Putting all these things together, one can easily imagine that to some folks Elijah's victory over the Baal prophets represented God's victory over Baal... and his succeeding to Baal's consort, the lovely Asherah. And why not? Karen Armstrong notes[8] that a hundred years later "Hosea... was trying to argue that he [God] was a better fertility god than Baal." In a monotheistic system, as in a good office supply store, you have to have everything that people might want.

Crop growth and with human fecundity are the two most important elements in early agricultural religions and, using an anthropomorphic model, our ancestors recognized the necessary interplay of male and female elements, though, as we have noted, they little understood the part played by women in human reproduction. Still, the marriage motif is prominent in their myths and epics. In Ugaritic mythology, 'Anat, sister and wife (!) of Baal, annually retrieves his dismembered corpse in the fall, the time of autumn rains and a return to fertility.

Using an anthropomorphic model, it is at least possible to suggest that there was a time when some Northern Israelite elements considered God to be the successor of Baal as husband of Asherah. But attempting to confine this "apostasy" to the North would be a mistake.

On the basis of solid archaeological evidence, William Dever confidently asserts that "Asherah, the 'Lion Lady,' was worshipped alongside Yahweh at Arad, and for perhaps a century or more before this became a problem for religious reformers."[9]

Arad is in the South.

Conversely, there were other Northern elements, perhaps those responsible for the creation of Deuteronomy,[10] who were quick to combat any such idea; indeed, the ringing declaration of Deut. 6:4 that "God alone" is the God of Israel may have been coined precisely to combat this kind of syncretism.

There may also be an echo of intermarriage in Malachi in the mid-fifth century, that is, about the time of Ezra and Nehemiah. In a somewhat enigmatic passage (2:10 -16) the prophet says, "For Judah has profaned what is holy to the Lord—what He desires—and espoused daughters of alien gods." (v. 11, NJPS)

Commentators, both Jewish and Christian, think malachi (= "my messenger") may be one of Ezra's pen-names and, since Malachi is almost contemporary with Ezra, read this as another criticism of intermarriages in Judah. But a closer look at the text shows the Hebrew uses the singular, and RSV translates it "and has married the daughter of a foreign god."

This more correct translation fits with the notion that Yahweh succeeded to Asherah after vanquishing Baal on Mt. Carmel. The interesting thing here is that it would extend the notion of belief in a divine intermarriage into Judah as a continuing element in Judean worship.

And now, as we saw at the beginning of this book, we find an ostracon from 5th-4th century Maqqedah (Khirbet el-Kom) that indicates a man might have a son who followed a different religion than he.[11] This, of course, is reminiscent of the differing theophoric names we find in Saul's family. It goes without saying that the kosher line of Jewish tradition would forget all this as soon as it safely could and then deny that it ever was the case, even in renegade Israel. No sense putting ideas in people's heads.

All that will have happened long before the discovery at 'Ajrud, but long after those responsible for tradition had left their farms for cities. And afterwards? Would a nation of merchants and shopkeepers scattered throughout the world remember the uncertainties of farming and the measures their Israelite ancestors had taken to insure the gods favored crop growth?[12] It's doubtful.

In sum, it is probable that Israel produced some people who shared the ancient and widespread notion that god was not only married, but married to a foreign goddess who'd been the wife of a foreign god: in other words, intermarried. Now, this would emphatically not have been the word they used to describe this situation, and those who believed it were, in effect, shouted down by the canonical prophets.

Notes to Chapter XIII

1. Excepting the Church of Jesus Christ of Latter-day Saints—which, by the way, as of this writing is the fastest growing denomination in North America. Muslims don't exactly share this belief, but in the Koran Muhammad reports that Joseph, Mary and the Holy Spirit were a kind of menage à trois.

2. Taken over by Christians, who made it an allegory of Jesus's love for the Church.

3. The first Jewish-authored study seriously to consider Jesus was Joseph Klausner's 1925 *Jesus of Nazareth* (London: Allen & Unwin, 1925).

4. See: Karen Armstrong, *A History of God* (NY: Ballantine Books, 1993).

5. Edward Burnett Tylor, *Primitive Culture: Researches into the Development of Mythology, Philosophy, Religion, Art, and Custom* (London: John Murray, 1871).

6. An echo of Ti'amat occurs in the cognate Hebrew word *tehom,* "the deep," in Genesis 1:2.

7. Frymer-Kensky, *Wake,* 156ff.

8. Armstrong, *History,* 49.

9. Dever, *What Did,* 183; emphasis in original.

10. H. L. Ginsberg, *The Israelian Heritage of Judaism* (Ann Arbor: University of Michigan, 1982), 19-24, posits that Deut. arises in Northern prophetic circles ca. 740 b.c.e. Chs. 12-26 seem to be the core. How much of the rest is original, how much added? And by whom?

11. Andre Lemaire, "Another Temple to the Israelite God" in BAR 30:4, (July/August, 2004), 38-44, 60.

12. Fagan, *Summer,* 99.

Chapter XIV. A Provisional Conclusion

1. What Happened in History

Chicken Little was Jewish; when they moved here from Europe, they changed the name from Klein. – RaGBaG

We posited in our introduction that "something happened," probably near the cusp between the Bronze and Iron ages a little more than 3,000 years ago. In reality, what happened was a number of things coming together that facilitated the creation and rise of the people we know from history as biblical Israel. By our reckoning, one of the most important of the things that formed biblical Israel was "intermarriage" on a grand scale.

We don't know, of course, how much intermarriage took place on the popular level at any given period in Jewish history. Anterior, even, to determining that, we would have to know what the Israelites/Jews themselves considered to be intermarriage in our sense. However that may be, intermarriage in our sense seems only to have been objected to in the prophetic period and after: only five centuries after Israel had begun to take shape. Before then, no one would have taken the presence of more than one religion in a given household amiss, especially if the second religion had the production and nurture of children as its aim.

Consequently, the more outstanding examples of biblical intermarriage before the eighth pre-Christian century were coöpted by later tradition, especially if or because they involved the adherence, real or imaginary, of non-Jewish females such as Ruth to the Israelite community. The "honor roll" includes such well-known figures as Zipporah and Tamar, but also, we argue, the traditionally "kosher" Leah, Rachel and Rebekah and those whom Jewish tradition subsequently "kosherized," such as Joseph's wife Asenath and Rahab of Jericho.

By rabbinic times, the fact that so many of Israel's key early marriages had actually been in some sense intermarriages was conveniently forgotten. On purpose—if we have, like a *CSI* team, read the remaining clues correctly. The rabbis rallied 'round Ezra, who lived close to the time when tradition holds the rabbinate had its beginnings, but a thousand years after Israel's founding, as the figure who set the standard for their time, for all time, even if he hadn't been successful in enforcing it in his own. His idea of national purity was retrojected into the past, and examples of what we would call intermarriage at any level, up to and including those of kings, were subject to criticism.

Perhaps the paradox of biblical intermarriage is this: Israel could not have emerged in anything like its biblical shape had it not been for extensive intermarriage, not just of stray individuals but by the wholesale adherence to Israel's biblical ideals of many people we think of as "gentile." However, in order to maintain the integrity thus achieved, the community thus formed finally felt it had to erect barriers to keep out "foreign elements" or at least make it difficult for them to enter.

This should not be surprising. From 586 b.c.e. on—really, from the little-known Babylonian incursion of 597 b.c.e—Judah was under the gun. Judeans didn't know it then, but in the next twenty-five centuries, only one would witness an autonomous Jewish state on the soil of Israel. If the Judean survivors of the destruction of their Temple in 586 b.c.e. (and even more, the worse disasters of 66-73 c.e. and 132-135 c.e.) and the exile to Babylon wanted to avoid being completely submerged in history, they needed to maintain community cohesion.[1] It was not an easy task.

In Babylon, as in Israel itself, the community developed an elaborate series of commentaries on Scripture, the Mishnah ("seconding," written between 200 b.c.e and 200 c.e.) and, in Babylon, additional commentaries: the Gemara—"what is said," that is, commentary—were added, finally resulting in the creation of the Talmud ("what is learned").

By the time the Roman occupation of Israel began in 63 b.c.e., the last native Jewish government (until 1948!) was history and the community's leaders were already well into the process of formulating guidelines to keep their people from being absorbed by the Greco-Roman high culture. If the community's task seemed difficult before, it was more so now. By Jesus's time, the majority of Jews no longer lived in Israel. Other, major communities were located in Alexandria, Egypt and Baghdad—where they had been for five centuries—and anywhere else that Rome was in control.

To erect barriers between Jews and others meant finding the requisite authority to command respect for the barriers thus created. In rabbinic Judaism rather than in the Bible itself was the foundation for the prohibition of intermarriage laid. Even so, except for the minority voices of the apocryphal Book of Jubilees and the Dead Sea Scroll called 4QMMT, they did not accept the genealogical—we might say "racist"—idea that gentiles were impure because of being gentiles.

Tradition could call upon the "bad examples" of men who married out and consequently were "lost"—such as Esau of Scripture—or invent their own stories, such as the claim that Naomi's sons died childless because they had intermarried. Such intermarriage horror stories were no doubt effective, especially during the long, dark centuries in which gentiles kept Jews at such a distance that social interaction between the two wasn't possible anyway. In some parts of the Old World, enforced separation remained the norm until the beginning of the twentieth century.

However, after Jews came to American, beginning in 1654, and especially after 1881, when the trickle of immigration became a flood, mutually agreed-upon separation became increasingly impossible. Not surprisingly, intermarriage rates finally rose, though this happened only after, and partly because of, the Second World War.

2. What Happens Now? (Or Ought to)

"We have met the enemy and he is us." – Walt Kelly's *Pogo*

By retrojecting deep into history the notion of Israel's separation from the rest of the world, we have set up a false dichotomy. It is the case that this small but indomitable nation coalesced out of many disparate elements, elements that necessarily married amongst themselves.

Building on Ezra, rabbinic and modern misuses of the well-known intermarriage prohibitions in Exodus and Deuteronomy, to say nothing of the painful lessons of history during the past 2,000 years, have distorted the Bible's long-running engagement with our subject. Put it this way: it is one thing for America's political conservatives to claim support for a position on the grounds that theirs is what the Founding Fathers intended; it would be quite another if they claimed the aforementioned parents actually said what they wish them to have said. Transposing into the key of Scripture, however, the keepers of Jewish and Christian tradition have had no such hesitations. The Bible, they say, says what we say it says.

We understand that Judaism, Christianity or Islam, religion is in part an instrument of social control. Communities, after all, cannot stay together without staying together. Consequently, how each religion interprets Holy Scripture, its own or others', will serve ends other than the discovery of impartial historical truth.

What is the truth about intermarriage in Hebrew Scripture? It is too much to suggest that the Bible makes any case in favor of intermarriage. It doesn't, and neither do we. The present authors (one intermarried, one in-married), both of whom have

We feel strongly that the very positive role so many intermarriages played in Israel's formative centuries—and it really did take centuries for biblical Israel to achieve anything that we can recognize as resembling a cohesive community— ought not be neglected or, worse, misrepresented for partisan purposes.

In today's Jewish community, some have seized upon a putative statistic: that more than half of all marriages involving Jews these days are intermarriages, thus evoking a sense of panic. They blame intermarriage for the relative lack of cohesion among modern American Jews. However, when one factors out second and later marriages, the rate is considerably lower than the fear-mongers have it—less, in fact, than the intermarriage rate of other ethnic groups.[2] Moreover, sounder minds in the community point out that intermarriage is not the cause of any dissolution, but a symptom of it.

Jewish people who intermarry these days may do so because science has so constricted the area once ruled by faith that religious affiliation doesn't seem that important any more, or because they think we all might somehow become one or because the Judaism presented to them as children simply wasn't attractive enough to hold them.

Ezra, who came to Israel from Babylon well before the Talmudic period began, is credited with playing a major role in keeping the Jerusalem community together by insisting that men divorce their foreign wives. As we have seen, the paradox of biblical intermarriage is that, from earliest times, the role often played by foreign women was crucial to Israel's survival— certainly its survival in the form that we now know it. And this says nothing of the possible genetic benefits accruing to people who marry across ethnic or tribal lines.

We may safely say that never in history has a people succeeded in maintaining its identity after so many centuries of being either submerged upon or uprooted from its ancestral land.[3] But the face of that people has changed, literally as well as figuratively, and will continue to do so with the adherence of people with various genetic backgrounds.

The present situation is not terribly different than it was in Ezra's time, except... today's Jews have no Ezra. In modern Israel, "intermarriage" is a term applied to a union between Ashkenazi and Sephardi Jews, a phenomenon that has been on the rise. In the U.S., the community is so evenly divided amongst Orthodox, Conservative and Reform Jews (with a scattering of Reconstructionist and other demographically minor denominations) and between communities in the United States and Israel that there is not and cannot be a single policy toward intermarriage, at least in this country. Consequently, policies concerning intermarriage and what to do with or for intermarried couples differ from rank to rank and even within the ranks.

If intermarriage of a sort is on the rise in Israel, the growth of Christian/Jewish marriage here has been phenomenal. After forty years of growth, there are now upwards of one million such marriages in this country.[4] The past decade has seen the birth and growth not only of denomination "outreach" programs but also of organizations of, for and by the intermarried themselves.

The authors of this book were both founding directors of one such organization, the Dovetail Institute for Interfaith Family Resources, that served interfaith couples across the country until its dissolution in 2010. Some still active include the Interfaith Family Project (IFFP) in Washington, DC; the Chicago Jewish-Catholic Couples Group; the Interfaith Community, Inc. in New York and other cities; and the web-based interfaithfamily.com, which has a more explicitly Jewish agenda than the others named here. It is not our purpose to promote any of these organizations but rather to present what we hope is an informed and balanced examination of the phenomenon of intermarriage in biblical times. What readers make of this information is entirely up to them.

Notes to Chapter XIV

1. Little wonder, then, that it is Jews the exiled Tibetan religious leader the Dalai Lama consults for advice in keeping a community together in diaspora. See Rodger Kamenetz, *The Jew in the Lotus* (New York: HarperOne, 1995).

2. The National Jewish Population Survey 2000-01: Strength, Challenge and Diversity in the American Jewish Population, explicated by Egon Mayer at the Harrisburg (PA) Jewish Community Center forum on interfaith marriage, 1992.

3. In 1813, to be exact. In "second place" is Poland, overrun from 1795 to 1918, but the comparison is hardly apt; most Christian Poles remained on the land they had previously been on, while only a few Polish Jews did.

Bibliography

Aharoni, Yohanon. *The Land of the Bible: A Historical Geography.* Phila: Westminster Press, 1979.

Ahlström, Gösta Werner. *History of Ancient Palestine.* Sheffield, UK: Sheffield Academic Press, 1993.

___. *Who Were the Israelites?* Winona Lake, IN: Eisenbrauns, 1986.

Albright, W. F. "Palestinian Inscriptions." In *Ancient Near Eastern Texts*, edited by James B. Pritchard. 3rd ed., Princeton: Princeton Univ. Press, 1969.

___. *Yahweh and the Gods of Canaan*, Garden City: Doubleday, 1968.

Alter, Robert. *The David Story.* NY: W.W. Norton, 1999.

Alter, Robert, and Frank Kermode, eds. *The Literary Guide to the Bible.* Cambridge MA: Belknap Press of Harvard University Press, 1990.

Aptowitzer, Victor. "Asenath, the Wife of Joseph: A Haggadic Literary-historical Study." In *Hebrew Union College Annual* I (1924) I 239-406.

Armstrong, Karen. *A History of God.* NY: Ballantine Books, 1993.

Astour, Michael. *Hellenosemitica.* Leiden: E. J. Brill, 1965.

___. "Two Ugaritic *Snake* Charms." In *Journal of Near Eastern Studies* 27. Chicago: University of Chicago Press, 1968.

___. In *Genesis.* Anchor Bible, Vol. 1, edited by E. A. Speiser. Garden City, NY: Doubleday, 1964.

Baron, Salo Wittmayer. *Social and Religious History of the Jews.* NY: Columbia University Press, 1951.

Barr, James. *The Variable Spellings of the Hebrew Bible.* Oxford: Oxford University Press, 1989.

Barstad, Hans M. "The Religious Polemics of Amos." In *Vetus Testamentum,* Supplement 34. Leiden: E. J. Brill, 1984.

Baskin, Judith Reesa. "The Rabbinic Transformations of Rahab the Harlot." In *Notre Dame English Journal,* Vol. 11, No. 2. Judaic Literature: Critical Perspectives (Apr., 1979), pp. 141-157.

Beckman, Gary. "Royal Ideology and State Administration in Hittite Anatolia." In *Civilizations of the Ancient Near East,* edited by Jack M. Sasson et al., 529-43. NY: Scribner, 1995.

Ben Sasson, Haim Hillel. ed. *A History of the Jewish People.* Cambridge, MA: Harvard University Press, 1976.

___. *Social Life and Social Values of the Jewish People.* Journal of World History, 1968.

___. *See also* Abraham Malamat et al.

Bettelheim, Bruno. *Symbolic Wounds: Puberty Rites and the Envious Male.* New York: Collier Books, Rev. Ed. 1968.

Biblical Archeology Review (BAR)

Biran, Avraham. *Biblical Dan.* Jerusalem: Israel Exploration Society, 1994.

Bird, Phyllis. "The Place of Women in the Israelite Cultus." In *Ancient Israelite Religion: Essays in Honor of Frank Moore Cross.* Edited by Patrick Miller et al. Philadelphia: Fortress, 1987.

Botterweck, G. Johannes. "Zur Authentizitat des Buches Amos." In *Zeitschrift fur Alttestamentliche Wissenshaft 70,* (1958): 176-189.

Braudel, Fernand. "Histoire et science sociales: la longue duré." In *Annales. Economies, Société, Civilisations* 13 (1958).

Bright, John. In *Jeremiah,* Anchor Bible series V. 21, Garden City NY: Doubleday, 1965.

Bronner, Leilah Leah. From Eve to Esther: Rabbinic Reconstruction of Biblical Women. Louisville KY: Westminster, 1994.

Brown, Francis, Samuel R. Driver, and Charles A. Briggs, *A Hebrew and English Lexicon of the Old Testament,* Oxford: Clarendon Press, 1907; corr. repr. 1962.

Brumberg-Kraus, Jonathan D. "Were the Pharisees a Conversionist Sect? Table Fellowship as a Strategy of Conversion." In *Approaches to Ancient Judaism: Jewish Proselytism.* Edited by A.-J. Levine and R. Pervo. Atlanta: Scholar's Press for the Society of Biblical Literature, 2002.

Bulletin of the American Schools of Oriental Research (*BASOR*)

Cohen, Shaye J. D. *The Beginnings of Jewishness: Boundaries, Varieties, Uncertainties.* Berkeley: University of California Press, 1999.

Craigie, Peter C. "The Role and Relevance of Biblical Research." *JSOT 18* (1980), 19-31.

Cross, Frank Moore, and Helmut Koester. *Hermeneia—a Critical and Historical Commentary on the Bible.* Minneapolis: Fortress Press, 1971)..

Cryer, Frederick H. *Divination in Ancient Israel and Its Near Eastern Environment: A Socio-historical Investigation.* Journal for the Study of the Old Testament Supplement 142. Sheffield: JSOT Press, 2000, 272.

Curtis, Adrian H. W. "Some Observations on the 'Bull' Terminology in the Ugaritic Texts and the Old Testament," in *In Quest of the Past* (ed. A. S. van der Woude; *OTS* 26; Leiden, 1 990), 1 7-3 1 (17-18).

Dahood, Mitchell. In *Psalms I: 1-50*. Anchor Bible series V. 21, Garden City NY: Doubleday, 1966.

Day, John. *Yahweh and the Gods and Goddesses of Canaan*. Journal for the Study of the Old Testament Sup. 265. Sheffield: JSOT Press, 2000.

Deutsch, Robert. "Seal of *Baalis* Surfaces: Ammonite King Plotted Murder of Judahite Governor." In *BAR* 25 (Mar-Apr 1999)

DeVaux, Roland. *Early History of Israel*. Translated by David Smith. London: Darton, Longman & Todd, 1978.

Dever, William G. What Did the Biblical Writers Know & When Did They Know It? Grand Rapids MI: Wm. Eerdmans, 2001.

___. Who Were the Early Israelites and Where Did They Come From? Grand Rapids MI: Wm. Eerdmans, 2003.

Edelman, Diana V., ed. *The Triumph of Elohim: From Yahwisms to Judaisms*. Grand Rapids, MI: Wm. Eerdmans, 1996.

Eisenstein, Judah David, ed. *Midrash Tadshe, Ozar ha-Midrashim*. New York: Reznick, Menshel & Co., 2d ed., 1928.

Elitzur, Yoel, and Doron Nir-Zevi. "Four-Horned Altar Discovered in Judean Hills." In *Biblical Archeology Review* 30:3 (2004).

Encyclopedia Judaica. Cecil Roth and Geoffrey Sigoder, eds. Jerusalem: Keter; New York: Macmillan, 1972.

Epstein, Louis. *Marriage Laws in the Bible and the Talmud*. Cambridge MA: Harvard UP, 1942.

Fagan, Brian. The Long Summer: How Climate Changed Civilization. NY: Basic Books, 2004.

Feldman, Ephraim. *Intermarriage Historically Considered*. Cincinnati: s.n., 1905.

Finkelstein, Israel. "State Formation in Israel and Judah: A Contrast in Context, a Contrast in Trajectory." In *Near Eastern Archeology* 62, 35-52 (1995).

Finkelstein, Israel, and Neil Asher Silberman. The Bible Unearthed: Archeology's New Vision of Ancient Israel and Its Sacred Texts. New York: Simon & Schuster, 2001.

Finkelstein, Jacob J. and Moshe Greenberg, eds, *Collected Writings of E. A. Speiser* (Philadelphia: University of Pennsylvania Press, Oriental and Biblical Studies, 1967)

Firestone, Tirzah. *The Receiving: Reclaiming Jewish Women's Wisdom.* San Francisco: HarperOne, 2002.

Fishbane, Michael. *Biblical Interpretation in Ancient Israel.* Oxford: Oxford University Press,1985.

___. *Biblical Myth and Rabbinic Mythmaking.* Oxford: Oxford University Press, 2003.

Fishman, Sylvia Barack. *Double or Nothing? Jewish Families and Mixed Marriage,* Brandeis Series in American Jewish History, Culture, and Life & HBI Series on Jewish Women. Waltham MA: Brandeis University Press; Hanover NH: University Press of New England, 2004.

Fowler, Alisdair. *Silent Poetry: Essays in Numerological Analysis.* London: Routledge and Kegan Paul, 1970.

Frazer, James George. Folk-lore in the Old Testament: Studies in Comparative Religion, Legend, and Law. London: Macmillan and Co., 1919.

___. *Totemism and Exogamy.* London: Macmillan and Co., 1910.

Freedman, David Noel. "Kingly Chronologies, Then and Later." In *Eretz Israel* 24. Edited by S. Ahituv and B. A. Levine. Jerusalem: Israel Exploration Society, 1993.

___. Allen C. Myers and Astrid B. Beck, editors. *Eerdmans Dictionary of the Bible.* Grand Rapids MI: Wm. Eerdmans, 2000.

Freedman, Harry, and Maurice Simon, translators and editors. *Midrash Rabbah: Avodah Zarah.* Brooklyn: Soncino, 1951.

Freud, Sigmund. *Moses and Montheism.* Translated by Katherine Jones. New York: Vintage Books, 1967.

Friedman, Richard Elliott. *Commentary on the Torah.* New York: Harper and Row, 2001.

Frymer-Kensky,Tikvah. In the Wake of the Goddesses: Women, Culture, and the Biblical Transformation of Pagan Myth. New York: MacMillan, 1992.

___. Reading the Women of the Bible: A New Interpretation. New York: Schocken, 2002.

Gadd, Cyril John. "The Harran Inscriptions of Nabonidus." *Anatolian Studies* VIII (1958), The British institute of Archeology at Ankara.

Gimbutas, Marija, and Joseph Campbell. *Language of the Goddess.* London: Thames & Hudson, 1989.

Ginsberg, Harold Louis. *The Israelian Heritage of Judaism.* Ann Arbor: University of Michigan, 1982.

Ginzberg, Louis. *Legends of the Jews.* Henrietta Szold, trans. Philadelphia; Jewish Publication Society, 1954.

Glatzer, Nahum N. *The Judaic Tradition.* Springfield NJ: Behrman House, 1961, 1969.

___, editor. *Parables and Paradoxes,* by Franz Kafka. New York: Shocken, 1953.

Gordon, Cyrus Herzl. *Ugaritic Texts,* Acta Orientalia 38. Rome: Pontifical Biblical Institute, 1958.

Gottwald, Norman Karol. A Light to the Nations: *An Introduction to the Old Testament*. New York: Harper, 1959.

___ .The Tribes of Yahweh, A Sociology of the Religion of Liberated Israel, 1250 – 1050 BCE, Biblical Seminar (Book 66). London: Bloomsbury T&T Clark, 1999.

Grahn, Judy. Blood, Bread, and Roses: How Menstruation Created the World. Boston: Beacon Press, 1993.

Graves, Robert. *The Greek Myths,* II. Baltimore: Penguin Books, 1955.

Greenberg, Moshe. "Hab/piru and Hebrews." In *World History of the Jewish People,* edited by B. Mazar, pp. 188-200 Vol. II (on Patriarchs). Rutgers NJ: Rutgers University Press, 1961.

Gruber, Mayer I. "Private Life in Ancient Israel." In *Civilizations of the Ancient Near East.* Edited by Jack M. Sasson et al., Vol. I, 633-48. NY: Scribner, 1995.

Guthrie, Stewart Elliott. *Faces in the Clouds: A New Theory of Religion.* NY: Oxford University Press, 1993.

Hadingham, Evan. *Circles and Standing Stones.* London: Heinemann, 1977.

Halpern, Baruch. "The Assassination **of** Eglon: The First Locked-Room Murder Mystery." In *Bible Review,* (December 1988): 33–41, 44. 13.

____. David's Secret Demons: Messiah, Murderer, Traitor, King. Grand Rapids MI: Wm. B. Eerdmans, 2001.

___. *The First Historians: The Hebrew Bible and History.* New York: Harper & Row, 1988/Pennsylvania State University Press, 1996.

Handy, Lowell K. "The Appearance of Pantheon in Judah." In *The Triumph of Elohim: From Yahwisms to Judaisms.* Edited by Diana Vikander Edelman. Grand Rapids MI: Wm. B. Eerdmans, 1996.

___. "Sounds, Words and Meaning in Psalm 82," *Journal for the Study of the Old Testament* 47 (1990).

Hayes, Christine E. Gentile Impurities and Jewish Identities: Intermarriage and Conversion from the Bible to the Talmud. New York: Oxford University Press, 2002.

Heaton, Eric William. *Solomon's New Men: The Emergence of Ancient Israel As a National State,* Currents in the History of Culture and Ideas. London: Thames and Hudson, 1974.

Herodotus. *The Histories,* Revised. John M. Marincola, ed.; Aubery de Selincourt, trans. New York: Penguin Classics, 2003.

Hertz, Joseph Herman. *The Pentateuch and Haftorahs: Hebrew Text English Translation and Commentary* (English and Hebrew Edition). Brooklyn: The Soncino Press, 1960.

Jacobsen, Thorkild. *Treasures of Darkness: A History of Mesopotamian Religion.* New Haven: Yale University Press, 1976.

Johnson, Paul. *A History of the Jews.* New York: Harper & Row, 1987.

Kamenetz, Rodger. *The Jew in the Lotus*: A Poet's Re-Discovery of Jewish Identity in Buddhist India. New York: HarperOne, 1995.

Kaufmann, Yehezkel. *Religion of Israel,* abridged and translated by Moshe Greenberg. Chicago: University of Chicago Press, 1960.

Keel, Othmar. *Feinde und Gottesleugner: Studien zum Image der Widersacher in den Individuelen Psalmen,* Stuttgarter Biblische Monographien # 7. Stuttgart: Verlag Katholisches Bibelwerk, 1969.

Kermode, Frank. *See* Alter, Robert.

354

King, Philip J., and Lawrence E. Stager. *Life in Biblical Israel.* Louisville, KY: Westminster John Knox Press, 2001.

Klausner, Joseph. *Jesus of Nazareth: His Life, Times, and Teaching.* Herbert Danby, trans. London: Allen & Unwin, 1925.

Koestler, Arthur. *The Thirteenth Tribe.* New York: Random House, 1975.

Kugel, James L. *The Bible As it Was.* Cambridge, MA: Harvard, 1997.

Kupper, Jean-Robert. *Les nomades en Mesopotamie au Temps Des Rois De Mari.* Paris: Société d'Edition "Les Belles Lettres," 1957.

Lemaire, Andre. "Another Temple to the Israelite God: Aramaic Hoard Documents Life in Fourth Century B.C." In *Biblical Archeology Review* 30:4, July/August, 2004, 38-44, 60.

Lemche, Niels Peter. *Ancient Israel: A New History of Israelite Society.* Sheffield: Sheffield University Press, 1988.

___. *The Canaanites and Their Land: The Tradition of the Canaanites.* The Library of Hebrew Bible/Old Testament Studies (Book 110). New York: Bloomsbury Books, T&T Clark, 1991.

Levenson, Jon Douglas. Creation and the Persistence of Evil: The Jewish Drama of Divine Omnipotence. Princeton NJ: Princeton University Press, 1988.

___. Sinai and Zion: An Entry into the Jewish Bible. New York: HarperCollins, 1985. 60.

Levin, Saul. *The Father of Joshua/Jesus.* Binghamton NY: State University of New York, 1978.

Lieber, David L. ed. *Etz Hayim, Torah and Commentary.* Phila: Jewish Publication Society, 2001.

Malamat, Abraham. *Mari and the Early Israelite Experience.* New York: Oxford University Press, 1992, 1989.

Malamat, Abraham, et al. *A History of the Jewish People*. Edited by Haim Hillel Ben Sasson. Cambridge MA: Harvard University Press; London: Weidefeld and Nicolson, 1976.

Marcus, Jacob Rader, ed. *The Jew in the Medieval World*. New York: Atheneum, 1972.

Mazar, Amihai. "The 'Bull Site'—An iron Age I Open Cult Place." In *Bulletin of the American Schools of Oriental Research*, 247 (1982).

McGinity, Keren R. Still Jewish: A History of Women and Intermarriage in America. New York: New York University Press, 2009.

McGovern, William Montgomery. *From Luther to Hitler*. Boston: Houghton Mifflin, 1941.

Meiri, Menachem, *Beit HaBechirah*. On BT, Sanhedrin 17B, Soncino translation.

Mellaart, James. *Earliest Civilizations of the Near East*. London: Thames and Hudson, 1965.

Mendenhall, George E. *The Tenth Generation: The Origins of the Biblical Tradition*. Baltimore: Johns Hopkins University Press, 1973.

Midrash Rabbah: Avodah Zarah. Translated and edited by Harry Freedman and Maurice Simon. Brooklyn: Soncino, 1951.

Midrash Tadshe, Ozar ha-Midrashim. Edited by Judah David Eisenstein. New York: Reznick, Menshel & Co., 2d ed., 1928.

Miller, Patrick, et al., editor. Ancient Israelite Religion: Essays in Honor of Frank Moore Cross. Philadelphia: Fortress, 1987.

Milgrom, Jacob. Leviticus, a Book of Ritual and Ethics: A Continental Commentary. Minneapolis: Fortress Press, 2004.

Moore, George Foote. *Judaism in the First Centuries of the Christian Era.* Peabody MA: Hendrickson, 1997.

Morgenstern, Julian. *Rites of Birth, Marriage, Death, and Kindred Occasions among the Semites.* Cincinnati: Hebrew Union College and Chicago: Quadrangle Books, 1966.

Mujahid, Abdul Malik. Conversion to Islam: Untouchables' Strategy for Protest in India. Shippensburg, PA: Anima Books, 1989.

Naveh, Joseph. "Graffiti and Dedications." In BASOR 235 [1979] 27-30.

Newman, Harold, and Jon O. Newman. A Genealogical Chart of Greek Mythology: Comprising 3,673 Named Figures of Greek Mythology, All related to Each Other Within a Single Family of Twenty Generations. Chapel Hill NC: University of North Carolina Press, 2007.

Noldeke, Theodor. In Brown-Driver-Briggs, *Hebrew and English Lexicon of the Old Testament.* Oxford: Clarendon Press, 1906.

Pagels, Elaine. *Beyond Belief: The Secret Gospel of Thomas.* New York: Random House, 2003.

Pardes, Ilana. *Countertraditions in the Bible: A Feminist Approach.* Cambridge: Harvard University Press, 1992.

Parfitt, Tudor and Emanuela Trevisan Semi, editors. *Judaising Movements: Studies in the Margins of Judaism.* London: RoutledgeCurzon, 2002.

Pedersen, Johannes. *Israel: Its Life and Culture.* London: Oxford University Press, 1926.

Pike, James A. If You Marry outside Your Faith: Counsel on Mixed Marriages. New York: Harper & Row, 1954.

Pinch, Geraldine. In *Civilizations of the Ancient Near East.* Edited by Jack M. Sasson et al., Vol. I, 373. NY: Scribner, 1995.

Random House Collegiate Dictionary. New York: Random House Reference, 1984.

Redford, Donald B. *Egypt, Canaan and Israel in Ancient Times.* Princeton: Princeton University Press, 1992.

Rembaum, Joel. "Dealing with Strangers: Relations with Gentiles at Home and Abroad." In *Etz Hayim,* Jacob Blumenthal and Janet L. Liss, eds. New York: The Rabbinical Assembly, 2005, pp. 1377-1382.

Renfrew, Colin. Archeology and Language: The Puzzle of Indo-European Origins. London: Penguin, 1987.

Ringgren, Helmer, and Johannes Botterweck. *Theological Dictionary of the Old Testament.* Translated by John T. Willis. Grand Rapids MI: Eerdmans, 1974-.

Rodkinson, Michael L. *New Edition of the Babylonian Talmud.* Paperback –Charleston SC: BiblioLife, LLC, 2009.

Rosenbaum, Mary Heléne & Stanley N. Rosenbaum. *Celebrating Our Differences: Living Two Faiths in One Marriage.* Shippensburg, PA: Ragged Edge Press, 1994.

Rosenbaum, Stanley N. *Amos of Israel; A New Interpretation.* Macon GA: Mercer University Press, 1990.

___. "A Letter from Rabbi Gamaliel ben Gamaliel," in Beatrice Bruteau, ed., *Jesus Through Jewish Eyes*, Maryknoll, NY: Orbis, 2002

____. Understanding Biblical Israel: A Reexamination of the Origins of Monotheism. Macon GA: Mercer University Press, 2002.

Ryan, William, and Walter Pittman. *Noah's Flood*. New York: Simon and Schuster, 1998.

Sarna, Nahum M. "Paganism and Biblical Judaism." In *Studies in Biblical Interpretation*. Phila: Jewish Publication Society, 2000.

___. *Exploring Exodus*. New York: Schocken, 1986.

Sasson, Jack M. "Circumcision in the Ancient Near East." In *Journal of Biblical Literature* 85 (1966).

___. "Ruth." In *The Literary Guide to the Bible*. Edited by Robert Alter and Frank Kermode. Cambridge MA: Harvard University Press, 1987.

Selincourt, Aubery de. *See* Herodotus.

Silberman, Neil Asher, and Israel Finkelstein. The Bible Unearthed: Archeology's New Vision of Ancient Israel and Its Sacred Texts. New York: Simon & Schuster, 2001.

Silver, Daniel Jeremy. *A History of Judaism, I: From Abraham to Maimonides*. New York: Basic Books, 1974.

Smith, W. Robertson. The Religion of the Semites: the Fundamental Institutions. New York: Shocken, 1972 (1889).

Soggin, J. Alberto. Old Testament and Oriental Studies. Rome: Biblical Institute Press, 1975.

"Souad" (pseud.). *Burned Alive: A Victim of the Law of Men* (Warner Books, 2004), cited in *World Jewish Digest,* Calumet City, June, 2004.

Speiser, Ephraim A. "Goi and Am." In J. J. Finkelstein and Moshe Greenberg, eds, *Collected Writings of E. A. Speiser.* Philadelphia: University of Pennsylvania Press, Oriental and Biblical Studies, 1967.

Spycket, Agnes. "Le Culte du Dieu-Lune á Tell Keisan." *Revue Biblique 80* (1973): 384- 95.

Stager, Lawrence E. "The Song of Deborah: Why Some Tribes Answered the Call and Others did Not." In *Biblical Archeology Review* 15:1 (1989), 50-64.

___. See also King, Philip J.

Streete, Gail Corrington. *The Strange Woman: Power and Sex in the Bible.* Knoxville: Westminster/John Knox, 1997.

Tadmor, Hayim. In *Jewish Society Through the Ages,* Haim-Hillel Ben-Sasson and Shmuel Ettinger, eds. London: Valentine, Mitchell, 1971.

Talmon, Shemaryahu. In *Jewish Society Through the Ages,* Haim-Hillel Ben-Sasson and Shmuel Ettinger, eds. London: Valentine, Mitchell, 1971.

____. *King, Cult and Calendar in Ancient Israel: Collected Studies* (Ancient Near East). Lieden: Brill Academic Publishers, 1997.

___ ."Daniel," in Alter, Robert, and Frank Kermode, eds. *The Literary Guide to the Bible.* Cambridge MA: Belknap Press of Harvard University Press, 1990.

Tcherikover, Victor (Avigdor). "Social Conditions." In *The World History of the Jewish people: The Hellenistic Age: Political History of Jewish Palestine 332 B.C.E. – 67 B.C.E.* Edited by Abraham Schalit. New Brunswick: Rutgers University Press, 1972.

___. *Hellenistic Civilization and the Jews.* Philadelphia: Jewish Publication Society of America, 1959.

Transactions of the Parisian Sanhedrin, May 30, 1806. London: C. Taylor, 1807.

Tubb, Jonathan N. *Canaanites (People of the Past).* Norman: Univ. of Oklahoma Press, 1998.

Tylor, Edward Burnett. Primitive Culture: Researches into the Development of Mythology, Philosophy, Religion, Art, and Custom. London: John Murray, 1871.

Von Dechend, Hertha, and Giorgio de Santillana. *Hamlet's Mill.* Boston: David Godine, 1977.

Weber, Max. *The Sociology of Religion.* Boston: Beacon Press, 1964.

Williams, A.J. "A Further Suggestion About Amos IV 1-3." In *Vetus Testamentum* 29 (1979): 206-11.

Wilson, J. A., "Egyptian Historical Texts" in *Ancient Near Eastern Texts.* 246.

Winchester, Simon. Krakatoa The Day the World Exploded: August 27, 1883. New York: HarperCollins, 2003.

Wright, George Ernest. *God Who Acts: Biblical Theology as Recital.* Studies in Biblical Theology 8. London: SCM, 1952.

Yadin, Yigael. *Hazor.* New York: Random House, 1975.

About the Authors

Rabbi Secher (left) and Dr. Rosenbaum at a Dovetail conference (right)

Stanley Ned Rosenbaum obtained his doctorate in Near Eastern and Judaic Studies from Brandeis University. He also studied at Tulane University, the University of Chicago, the Sorbonne (Paris) and Hebrew University (Jerusalem). He served as Professor of Religion and Classics (Judaic Studies) of Dickinson College in Carlisle, PA for 27 years and Adjunct Professor of Hebrew and Jewish History at the University of Kentucky (Lexington).

Dr. Rosenbaum, for almost 30 years a lay leader of Congregation Beth Tikvah, frequently conducted Jewish religious services and led Torah study; he also lectured on biblical and related topics for Catholic and Protestant groups. For ten years, he was a director of the Dovetail Institute for Interfaith Family Resources, the only independent national organization for interfaith couples.

His other publications include, in addition to numerous scholarly and popular articles, the books *Amos of Israel: A New Interpretation* (Mercer UP, 1989) and *Understanding Biblical Israel: A Re-examination of the Origins of Monotheism* (Mercer

UP, 2002); with Mary Heléne Pottker Rosenbaum, he co-authored *Celebrating Our Differences: Living Two Faiths in One Marriage* (Ragged Edge Press, 1994). For more than ten years, he contributed the "Third Opinion" column in *Shalom*, the newspaper of the Central Kentucky Jewish Federation.

Stanley Ned Rosenbaum was killed in a road accident on November 29, 2011. At one of the three memorial services organized by people outside his family, a speaker who had been his student some 40 years before said, "Not a week goes by that I don't think about something he taught me."

Rabbi Allen Secher graduated Brandeis University with a Bachelor's degree in Philosophy. He was ordained by Hebrew Union College, New York in 1962; he subsequently earned his Doctor of Divinity degree. He has served pulpits in Chicago, Los Angeles, Mexico City, New York, Bozeman, and Whitefish, Montana. He co-founded Makom Shalom, a Chicago Jewish Renewal congregation that explored both traditional and holistic paths toward building spiritual intimacy.

He has also been a radio broadcaster, a winner of seven Emmy awards, played semi-pro soccer, marched with Freedom Riders, and acted in television and films. The first rabbi installed in Flathead County, Montana, he was appointed Commissioner on the Montana State Human Rights Commission by Governor Brian Schweitzer. He stepped down recently to take a position on the Montana Council for the Arts. Rabbi Allen also serves on the Ethics Committee of North Valley Hospital in Whitefish, Montana, and is a founding member of the Multi-Faith Coalition of the Flathead Valley.

About the Editor

Photo by Hannah N. Rosenbaum

Mary Heléne Pottker Rosenbaum, a writer and freelance editor, was founding president of the Dovetail Institute for Interfaith Family Resources and editor of *Dovetail: A Journal by and for Jewish/Christian Families* and of *Shalom,* the newspaper of the Central Kentucky Jewish Federation. Her books include *Jezebel's Daughter* [Blue Grape Press, 2007], a biblical novel on Queen Athaliah of Judah, and *A Seal Upon the Heart* [Blue Grape Press, 2006], a biblical novel on the prophet Jeremiah. With her husband of 48 years, Stanley Ned Rosenbaum, she co-authored *Celebrating Our Differences: Living Two Faith in One Marriage.* She has appeared frequently on television, radio, and in the print media, and conducts lectures and workshops for both Jewish and Christian groups.

www.ingramcontent.com/pod-product-compliance
Lightning Source LLC
Chambersburg PA
CBHW060325100426
42812CB00003B/886